JBuilder® 8.0 JFC and Swing Programming

Chuck Easttom

Wordware Publishing, Inc.

Library of Congress Cataloging-in-Publication Data

Easttom, Chuck.
JBuilder 8.0 JFC and Swing programming / by Chuck Easttom.
p. cm.
ISBN 1-55622-900-3 (pbk.)
1. Java (Computer program language) 2. JBuilder. 3. Java foundation classes. 4. Swing (Computer file). 5. Graphical user interfaces (Computer systems). I. Title.
QA76.73.J38E233 2003
005.13'3--dc21

2003005388
CIP

2320 Los Rios Boulevard
Plano, Texas 75074

Printed in the United States of America

ISBN 1-55622-900-3

10 9 8 7 6 5 4 3 2 1
0403

All inquiries for volume purchases of this book should be addressed to Wordware Publishing, Inc., at the above address. Telephone inquiries may be made by calling:

(972) 423-0090

Contents

Acknowledgments

This book has been a lot of work but a lot of fun as well. It covers a topic that I am really excited about. However, this could not have been done without the help of a lot of people. Although only one name appears on the cover of the book as the author, there were many people who were involved and helped make this project happen. I would like to take a moment to acknowledge a few of them here.

First of all I need to thank my wife, Misty, and my son, A.J. They are always so patient with me when I am working on a book. Their patience and understanding is what allows me to write.

Next I want to thank the incredible staff at Wordware Publishing. The editorial staff does a fantastic job of making sure I don't embarrass myself. And they are always patient with me if I am a bit behind schedule!

Finally I have to thank the fine people at JBuilder. They have consistently provided me with full access to their JBuilder product line, including beta versions, allowing me to get a first look at their products so that I can more thoroughly cover them in my books.

Without all of these people helping, this book would simply not happen. I think this is true for all books; one name may appear on the cover, but a team was involved in producing the work.

Introduction

Sun Microsystems' Java™ programming language has quickly become one of the most popular programming languages in use today. Its platform independence is only one reason for this success. Other reasons include its powerful object-oriented approach to programming and its built-in memory management. The fact that it is freely available from Sun Microsystems' web site does not hurt its popularity either! However, as many of you have undoubtedly discovered, programming from a text editor and a command-line compiler is not always the most efficient way to develop professional applications. This is where the Borland® JBuilder® product comes in. JBuilder gives you 100 percent pure Java but in an easy-to-use environment. The JBuilder development environment is as easy to use as any of the popular RAD (rapid application development) tools available.

Java offers a powerful set of classes you can use to create graphical user interfaces (GUI) for your users. The first set of classes that Java offered was the Abstract Windowing Toolkit (AWT). However, with the advent of Java 2, you have access to a newer and richer set of classes for constructing GUIs. This new set of classes is found in the Java Foundation Classes (JFC) and Swing classes. In this book I show you how to use the various JFC and Swing classes. Each technique is shown with JBuilder, but the complete source code is also given so that readers who do not have JBuilder can still use this book. The examples were all done with either JBuilder version 7.0 or 8.0.

Previous Knowledge

It is imperative that you have a basic working knowledge of Java. This book assumes that you basically know how to program in Java and proceeds on that assumption. It is not required, however, that you have extensive experience. Basically, it is assumed that you can write some basic console applications using Java. This book will go quicker for you if you have used JBuilder before, but it is possible to work through it without having that background. If you don't have a basic knowledge of Java or JBuilder, then I strongly recommend *Charlie Calvert's Learn JBuilder*, also available from Wordware Publishing. It is truly an outstanding introduction to JBuilder, and I give that book my unequivocal recommendation.

Book Format

This book has some specific characteristics of which you should be aware. Even though it is not a textbook per se, I still use some techniques you would expect to find in a textbook. The end of each chapter has a chapter summary and a set of review questions. These are provided to help ensure that you have mastered the essential concepts of that chapter.

The appendices in this book are designed to give you a quick reference to additional materials that can be used to supplement the book. Appendix A lists other resources, such as web sites and books. Appendix B contains a glossary of terms and definitions. Appendix C has the answers to the review questions. Appendices D and E are brief tutorials that are provided solely for those readers who might have a deficiency in some required knowledge area. Appendix D is a primer on database essentials. This knowledge is required in order to work with the material in Chapter 11. Appendix E is a brief HTML primer so that you can work with the applet material covered in Chapter 12.

Writing Style

I try to write in a conversational tone, much the same way I speak to students in classes. I certainly hope that you find this to be acceptable. I also like to place the entire code for an example in the text. I personally hate reading a computer book and seeing a small isolated code snippet. Therefore, I give you the entire code for any example right there in the text. This way you can see the portion that I am illustrating in context. I also like to put in lots of images. That way it's pretty easy for you to see exactly what I am describing. I tend to follow the old saying that a picture is worth a thousand words... only I like to give you the picture *and* the thousand words! Some readers may feel that this is just too much space devoted to code samples. If you feel that way, feel free to skip reading those code samples.

About the Companion Files

The companion files can be downloaded from the following web site:

www.wordware.com/files/jbuilder

These files contain all the examples discussed in the book, and are organized into folders named for each chapter. Simply copy the files to your hard drive to work with them.

Chapter 1

Introduction to JFC and Swing

This chapter covers the following:

- Java 2D API
- Pluggable look and feel
- Accessibility
- Swing
- Key JFC classes
- Writing a JFC application

Introduction

Java is a very powerful and flexible development tool. One of its many strengths is its platform independence. *Platform independence* simply means that the code you write is not tied to the operating system you write it on. This means that once you have developed an application on one particular operating system, you can take that executable to any operating system you wish and run it as is. You do not even need to recompile your program. Platform independence is a tremendous advantage to you, the software developer. However, as with any technology, this independence has a few issues of its own. One of the problems that can occur with any multiplatform tool is ensuring that graphical interfaces display the same way on different operating systems. In the past, Java programmers used the AWT (Abstract Windowing

Toolkit) to develop graphical components. This tool was, and still is, a very solid tool for developing graphical user interfaces. It is remarkably easy to use and has all the basic elements you might need to develop your interface. Despite its many strengths, the Abstract Windowing Toolkit does have a few problems. One problem is that the set of classes it offers is incomplete. Since AWT was first introduced, users have grown accustomed to a number of newer graphical components that AWT does not provide. Perhaps the most significant problem is that the graphics did not always display the same way on different operating systems. This was one factor that led to the development of Swing. The Java Foundation Classes (JFC) and Swing expand upon the original Abstract Windowing Toolkit and provide a comprehensive set of graphical user interface class libraries. Many of these classes are simply upgraded and improved versions of AWT classes, but several are entirely new.

JFC/Swing Features

The Java Development Kit (JDK) is a freely available download from Sun Microsystems' Java web site. If you have a later version of JBuilder (5.0 or later), you already have the latest version of the JDK, complete with the new JFC classes. You can get that URL in Appendix A of this book. The latest version of the JDK, as of the publication of this book, is version 1.3. Version 1.4 is currently in beta. When you download the latest version of the Java Development Kit, you have access to JFC and Swing (earlier versions of the JDK, of course, did not have this). JFC features a number of new items. The list you see here summarizes the most important features:

- JFC/Swing components
- Java 2D API
- Pluggable look and feel
- Accessibility API
- Drag and drop (Java 2 only)

The entire point of the JFC/Swing GUI classes is to provide a set of classes that will allow you to create windowing components that are platform independent. Basically, their purpose is to allow the programmer to create a variety of visual components that will have the same look and feel on any platform. JFC is a set of classes used to assist the programmer in creating Java programs. Swing is a part of the Java Foundation Classes that is devoted solely to creating a graphical interface. You can think of Swing as the GUI component kit within the JFC.

Swing allows you to create graphical interfaces that are consistent, regardless of the operating system they are on. Swing components permit a customizable look and feel without relying on any specific operating system. If you build your application with Swing on an MS Windows platform, it will look exactly the same on a Linux machine, Macintosh, etc. Swing is an integral part of the Java 2 platform. If you have the Sun JDK version 1.3.0 or greater or JBuilder version 5.0 or later, then you have access to JFC and Swing. If you do not have access to one of those products, you should consider acquiring one before you continue in this book.

If your system has JDK 1.1 installed, you can download and install the Java Foundation Classes separately. However, this is really unnecessary as the Sun JDK is free; you might as well simply download and install the latest version of the JDK.

Recall the list that I provided at the beginning of this section. That list gave all the major features of JFC/Swing but no explanations. Following are brief descriptions of each of those features.

Java 2D API

Let's be honest: You probably want some cool graphics in your application or applet. In fact, you may even need certain shapes and figures. The Java 2D application programming interface (API) is designed for just that purpose. This API facilitates the creation of a wide range of two-dimensional images and figures. You are exposed to the fundamentals of this API later in this book.

What Is a Pluggable Look and Feel?

Undoubtedly, you know what the term "look and feel" means. It is simply the general layout and impression that your graphical user interface provides. However, the term "pluggable" might seem a little unclear. In this context, *pluggable* simply refers to the fact that you can update the look and feel of an application "on the fly." To put that another way, you can adjust the graphical user interface at run time, without restarting your applet or application. This is a real improvement for graphical user interfaces. Now you don't need to reload the applet or application; you can simply alter specific components at run time.

Accessibility

The term *accessibility* simply refers to making your application accessible to people with disabilities. If your application is not made accessible, you are eliminating a significant market share, and that's usually a bad idea. Fortunately, there is an entire API that helps you make your application or applet more accessible. The Accessibility API provides you with an interface that facilitates assistive technologies communicating with JFC or AWT components. Notice that this API does support AWT components. That means that it is backward compatible. So far, Sun Microsystems has done a very good job with this. Any new Java technology they have produced has been backward compatible. Assistive technologies that are used by people would include items such as screen readers, screen magnifiers, speech recognition, text-to-speech engines, and more.

The Accessibility API built into the Java Foundation Classes is fairly extensive and makes it possible for software vendors to provide accessibility for disabled users. This means that your programs can now be more widely used. An entire segment of the population that might have heretofore been prevented from utilizing your software can now have access. While I don't claim to be a business process expert, I think you will agree that having more customers for your software is always a good thing.

Drag and Drop

This part is actually very interesting. In JFC and Swing you have significantly improved support for drag and drop. *Drag and drop* is simply the process of clicking on one graphical component and dragging it to another and then dropping it there. Drag-and-drop capabilities are significantly improved over AWT.

The Java Foundation Classes (JFC)

I already mentioned that the Java Foundation Classes are a set of classes that were added to Java 2. The JFC is an extensive set of classes that a programmer can use to build applications. Java Foundation Classes are simply the next logical step in Java, and that is providing you classes to handle a variety of tasks. In short, JFC allows you to focus more on your specific application issues, since many common programming problems are dealt with by various JFC classes. Each of these classes has a clearly defined purpose. Java Foundation Classes can be categorized into four major groups:

- User interface components
- Java 2D
- Accessibility features
- Drag-and-drop support

Throughout this book we look at all four groups of classes. Each of these provides a different type of functionality to the Java programmer. However, our main concern at this point (and for the next several chapters) is the user interface components. It should also be noted that the Swing components comprise the bulk of the JFC and also encompass the bulk of the chapters in this book. These components are significant improvements over the AWT components. Reasons for this include:

- Lightweight: The JFC components use less resources than AWT components. They are generally smaller classes and utilize less memory.
- Increased functionality: There are a number of components and functions that were not available with AWT that are now available with Swing.
- Consistent look: AWT components often did not have a consistent look across platforms. Swing components do have the same look, regardless of the operating system on which they are being run.

As with all things in Java, the Java Foundation Classes exist within an object hierarchy. All Java classes ultimately inherit from java.lang.object and therefore inherit all the methods from that class. All graphical components (both JFC and AWT) inherit from java.awt.component, which in turn inherits directly from java.lang.object. It is important to be aware of any Java class inheritance hierarchy because you have access to all the public methods and properties that you inherit from objects higher up in the hierarchy. Figure 1.1 summarizes the inheritance hierarchy for Swing components.

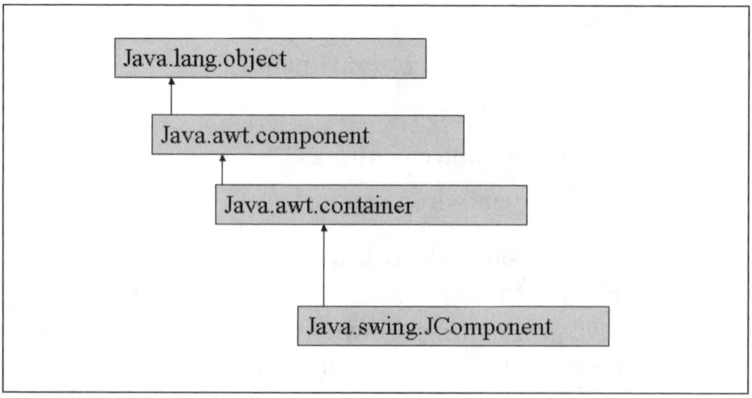

Figure 1.1 Swing component hierarchy

Swing

As I mentioned previously, the bulk of the Java Foundation Classes are concerned with the Swing visual components. These lightweight components have significantly expanded the possibilities available to Java programmers. The first question I need to address is: What is meant by "lightweight"? The lightweight user interface classes are an extensive set of user interface components written in 100 percent pure Java. They provide a wide range of simple and complex user interface components, from simple text labels and buttons all the way up to tabbed notebooks, color pickers, and spreadsheet-style tables. They also provide a level of function that was not previously available from the basic AWT controls. Because they are written 100 percent in Java, the lightweight user interface controls behave the same way no matter what the operating system. The term "lightweight" is used because the JFC classes do all of their own rendering and do not rely on the operating system's built-in components beyond basic windows.

An important feature about the Swing components is that their appearance is programmable. The JFC classes are shipped with a number of different look-and-feel sets that can be switched programmatically. You can choose a "Windows" look and feel or other schemes.

Some Key JFC Classes

JFC has a large number of classes. I attempt to cover the most commonly used first and then move on to other classes. The following table lists the names of some of the key JFC user interface classes and the functions that they offer. You will probably notice that many of these classes are simply upgrades from older AWT classes.

Table 1.1 Key Swing classes

Class Name	Purpose
JBorderFactory	This class is used to create borders to place around components.
JCheckBox	This component places a check box on the screen. Check boxes are for multiple selections.
JCheckBoxMenuItem	This component creates menu items with check marks.
JColorChooser	This component allows you to display a color wheel that the user can click on to select a given color.
JComboBox	This component creates an editable drop-down list.
JComponent	This class is the parent class of many other JFC components.
JFileChooser	File selection dialog.
JFrame	This class allows you to create frame windows.
JImageIcon	This class allows images to be loaded from storage and used in components.
JLabel	This class allows you to create labels.
JList	This class allows you to create lists.
JMenu	This class allows you to create menus.
JMenuBar	This class allows you to create menu bars that can be added to frames.
JMenuItem	This class allows you to create menu items that can be added to menus.
JOptionPane	Allows displaying of several standard dialog boxes.
JPanel	This class allows you to create and manipulate panels.
JPasswordField	This class allows you to create an entry field that is ideal for entering passwords.
JPopupMenu	This class allows you to create pop-up menus.
JProgressBar	This class allows you to create a progress indicator bar.
JRadioButton	This class allows you to create radio buttons.
JRadioButtonMenuItem	This class allows you to create radio buttons in menus.
JScrollBar	This class allows you to create scroll bars.

Class Name	Purpose
JScrollPane	This class allows you to create scroll panes.
JSeparator	This class allows you to create menu separators.
JSlider	This class allows you to create sliders.
JSplitPane	This class allows you to create window panes that can be split vertically or horizontally.
JTabbedPane	This class allows you to create tabbed notebook-style panels.
JTable	This class allows data to be displayed and manipulated in a two-dimensional (spreadsheet-style) table.
JTextArea	This class allows you to create multiple-line, editable text areas.
JTextField	This class allows you to create single-line text entry fields.
JToggleButton	This class allows you to create a button that has two states.
JToolBar	This class allows you to create a toolbar that can be made up of images as well as regular buttons and can be "torn off" and dragged to the desktop as a separate window.
JToolTip	This class allows you to create a pop-up tip window that displays as the mouse moves over a component.
JTree	This class allows you to create a tree view of data.

Once you have JDK on your system (again, either by downloading the latest version of the JDK or by installing JBuilder), your first step will be to get comfortable with the JFC classes. There are several demo programs that you can run to see what JFC can do and to verify that you have everything installed properly and the CLASSPATH variable is set correctly.

The SwingSet Demo

The Java SDK ships with a SwingSet demo program. This program is quite useful when getting acclimated to Swing, and it can also be used to verify that you have successfully installed the JFC classes and updated the CLASSPATH and other environment variables. The SwingSet program is located in the \examples\swingset directory. For those of you using JBuilder (and I hope that is most of you, given the book title!), you will find your JDK under the folder where you installed JBuilder. It will be located in a directory called \\jdk1.3.1\demo\jfc\SwingSet2\. To run the SwingSet demonstration program on any Windows system, execute the runnit command from the SwingSet directory. This executes the file runnit.bat and starts the program. There is also a runnit script file for Unix/Linux users. If you are using JBuilder, there is an HTML file that will demo the Swing classes for you, as seen in Figure 1.2.

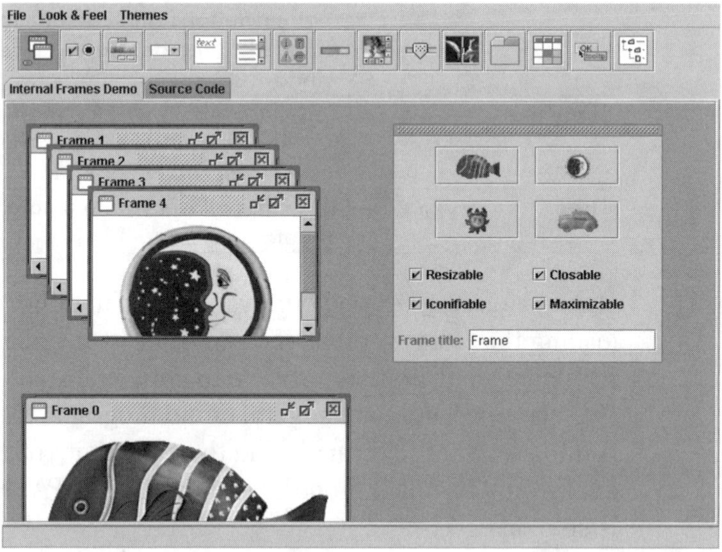

Figure 1.2 SwingSet demo

The SwingSet program gives a good demonstration of all the major JFC user interface classes and lets you play with them. It also lets you experiment with the different look and feel options.

Writing a JFC Application

Obviously, you will want to do more than look at the SwingSet demo and see items that others have written. You will want to write your own JFC applications. This chapter does not begin with writing programs, but all subsequent chapters do have you writing your own programs. Let me tell you that writing a JFC/Swing application is no different than writing any other Java application or applet. In the next chapter we step back and take a look at the Abstract Windowing Toolkit (the precursor to Swing) and work through several examples. All of the chapters after that have several complete examples that you work through. So don't worry, you will get plenty of practice working with Swing!

Summary

This chapter has given you a basic introduction to JFC and Swing. The purpose was to explain to you exactly what the Java Foundation Classes are and why they are a significant improvement over Java 1.1 technologies such as the Abstract Windowing Toolkit. After reading this chapter, you should have a basic familiarity with JFC/Swing, the classes involved, and their purpose.

Review Questions

1. What is AWT?
2. What is Swing?
3. What is JFC?
4. What are the four major groups of JFC classes?
5. What is the purpose of the JFC accessibility features?
6. List any four key JFC classes.
7. What is the purpose of using Swing instead of AWT?
8. What is the purpose of the BorderFactory class?
9. What version of the Sun JDK first shipped with JFC/Swing?
10. What is a pluggable look and feel?

Chapter 2

The Abstract Windowing Toolkit

This chapter covers the following:

- What is AWT?
- Components and containers in AWT
- Types of containers
- Creating a container
- Managing component layout
- Event handling
- A significant JBuilder example

Introduction

You might be wondering why a book on Java Foundation Classes and Swing has a chapter on the Abstract Windowing Toolkit. There is a very good reason for this; well, there are actually two reasons for this. The first is that there are many situations in which you will still need at least a basic knowledge of AWT. You might, for example, be required to convert an application or applet from AWT to Swing. It is also possible to use both AWT and Swing in the same application. In fact, it is not at all uncommon to see both technologies used in conjunction. Another reason to devote some time to the study of AWT is that Swing is, to an extent, an expansion of AWT. Your understanding of Swing might be facilitated by first getting a firm grasp of AWT. If you already have experience working with the Abstract Windowing Toolkit, you may wish to simply skim through this chapter or even skip it altogether.

What Is AWT?

AWT stands for *Abstract Windowing Toolkit*. The AWT is, in fact, part of the Java Foundation Classes, but it is an older part, first introduced in earlier versions of Java. Essentially, AWT is a set of classes that you can use to create graphical components in your applications and applets. The AWT is primarily used to create graphical user interfaces. The user interface is the part of an application or applet with which the user can interact directly. A user interface can come in any number of different variations. Some user interfaces are simple command-line interfaces, whereas others are very appealing graphical interfaces. AWT is primarily used to create such graphical interfaces.

At some point, the user's interactions must be processed by the computer hardware and the operating system. The operating system transmits information from the mouse, keyboard, or other device to the program as input. The operating system must also take output from the program and send it in an intelligible format to the printer or monitor. Having to deal with all of this directly would be a daunting task even for the most seasoned programmer. AWT was designed so that programmers don't need to be concerned with the details of these activities. The programmer need only know what class in the AWT is needed and what method(s) to invoke. AWT handles the low-level details for you.

Remember that one of the hallmarks of Java is its platform independence. The Java motto is "write once, run anywhere." Because the Java programming language is platform independent, the AWT also has to be platform independent. Of course, this brings us to the question of how exactly AWT manages this. It can be a daunting task to properly render graphical elements on a single operating system. It's a much more difficult task to have a single component render properly on several different operating systems. AWT handles this by letting the operating system do some of the work. The user interface elements provided by the AWT are implemented using each platform's native graphics toolkit, thereby preserving the look and feel of each platform. This means that an AWT button on a Windows machine will look like a Windows button. The same button, when displayed on a Macintosh, will look like a Mac button. The disadvantage of such an approach is the fact that a graphical user interface designed on one platform may look very different when viewed on another platform.

Components and Containers in AWT

I have already mentioned that the primary purpose of AWT is to enable the programmer to implement a graphical user interface and to interact with the user, without having to concern himself with the low-level details. I have also mentioned that this is done via classes that create components. Therefore, it is probably time to give you a formal definition of what exactly a component is. A *component*, in this context, is simply a graphical element used to create user interfaces. Typical components include such items as buttons, text fields, check boxes, etc. Components allow the user to interact with the program and can also be used to provide the user with visual feedback. In AWT, all user interface components are instances of the Component class or one of its subtypes. Actually, most are instances of a subtype, but they do inherit from the Component class.

That explains what a component is. The next concept to address is the container. A *container* is exactly what its name implies; it is a specialized component that can contain other components. Containers contain components and control their layout. You use containers because you need to organize your components in logical areas. Since containers are themselves components, containers can even contain other containers. In AWT, all containers are instances of class Container or one of its subtypes. Like the aforementioned components, most of these are instances of a subtype that simply inherits from the Container class.

Proper layout can be a significant problem for all programmers. This problem is even more significant when your application or applet might be run on any number of completely different operating systems. Components must fit in some spatial orientation within the container that contains them. This nesting of components into containers creates a hierarchy of graphical elements. AWT provides nine basic noncontainer component classes from which a user interface may be constructed. These nine classes are TextField, TextArea, Label, Button, Canvas, Choice, Checkbox, List, and Scrollbar.

Types of Containers

In addition to the nine noncontainer controls that the AWT provides, it also provides four container classes: Window, Frame, Dialog, and Panel. Note that the Frame and Dialog classes are subclasses of the Window class. In addition to the containers provided by the AWT, the Applet class is a container; in fact, it is a subtype of the Panel class and can therefore hold components. Brief descriptions of each container class are given in the following table.

Table 2.1 Container classes

Class Name	Purpose
Window	This class provides a top-level display. An instance of the Window class is not attached to or embedded within another container and has no border and no title.
Dialog	The dialog is a top-level display with a border and title. You cannot have an instance of the Dialog class without an associated instance of the Frame class.
Frame	The frame is a top-level display with a border and title. An instance of the Frame class can have one or more menu bars.

Class Name	Purpose
Panel	The Panel class is just a generic container for holding components.

A few clarifying notes are in order concerning this table, the first being an explanation of exactly what a top-level display is. Simply put, a *top-level display* is not contained within another component. You can certainly have a number of nested components. A top-level display would be at the top of any such nested hierarchy. Another clarifying point that needs to be made is what is meant by an instance of a Dialog class having an associated instance of the Frame class. What this means is that the Dialog class is not meant to be used alone. It is used in conjunction with the Frame class. It is important to note that the Frame class can be used without the Dialog class but not vice versa.

Creating a Container

Now that you have seen that components can be, and often are, contained within other components (namely container components), it seems like an appropriate time to show you how to create these container components. When building an application that has a graphical user interface (GUI), the programmer must first create an instance of the Window class or the Frame class. Recall that both of those are top-level displays that can stand alone or operate independently. The Dialog class is not used for the initial container component because it does not operate independently; it requires an associated frame. Whether you use the Window class or the Frame class, you must instantiate some top-level container class before you can add any components to the application. This is because you don't add components directly to the application; you add them to the container.

Building an applet is similar to building an application with a GUI with just a few minor differences. When building an applet, a frame already exists. That frame is the browser itself. Since the Applet class is a subtype of the Panel class, the programmer can add the components directly to the instance of the Applet class itself. You do not need to create a Container class in order to add components to an applet.

Now that I have discussed the basics of adding AWT components to an application in order to give it a graphical user interface, it seems like a good idea to show you an example.

Example 2.1

The purpose of this example is simply to show you the basics of using the Abstract Windowing Toolkit within an application. This example demonstrates the use of a top-level container and adding other containers to it. The example uses the Sun Microsystems JDK. Later, I give a few examples using Borland JBuilder.

Step 1: Open your favorite text editor and enter the following code:

```
import java.awt.*;
public class example1
{
   public static void main(String [] args)
   {
      Frame f = new Frame("Hey Java is Cool");
      Button b = new Button ("Click me");
      f.add(b);
      f.show();
   }
}
```

Step 2: Save the file as **Example2.java.**

Step 3: From a command line (DOS prompt in Windows 98, Command prompt in Windows NT/2000, Shell in Linux), compile the program using the standard JDK compilation:

```
Javac Example.java
```

Step 4: Run the application by simply typing in **Java Example.java.** When you run this application, you should see something like what is depicted in Figure 2.1.

Figure 2.1 Illustration of Example 2.1

You should pay particular attention to the add method that is used in this application. All containers have an add method that you can call to add components to the container. This is very simple, but you will see it in virtually every example in this book or any other book that discusses Java components.

I readily admit that this example is not particularly exciting; however, it does demonstrate the basics of how to create an application that uses a container component and then adds other components to that. Now let's see how this works with an applet rather than an application.

Example 2.2

Step 1: Open your favorite text editor and enter the code you see here:

```
import java.awt.*;
import java.awt.event.*;
import java.applet.*;
public class example2 extends Applet
{
  public void init()
    {
       Button b = new Button("Click Me");
       add(b);
    }
 }
```

Step 2: Save the file as **example2.java.**

Step 3: From a command line (DOS prompt in Windows 98, Command prompt in Windows NT/2000, Shell in Linux), compile the program using the standard JDK compilation:

```
Javac Example.java
```

Step 4: Create a simple HTML page to display the applet, as you see here:

```
<HTML>
<HEAD>
  <TITLE>Applets Are Awesome  </TITLE>
</HEAD>
<BODY BGCOLOR = white>
<CENTER>
  <APPLET>
     CODE="example2"
     WIDTH=600
     HEIGHT=300
  </APPLET>
</CENTER>
</BODY>
</HTML>
```

Now if you view this HTML document in a browser, you should see something like what is shown in this image:

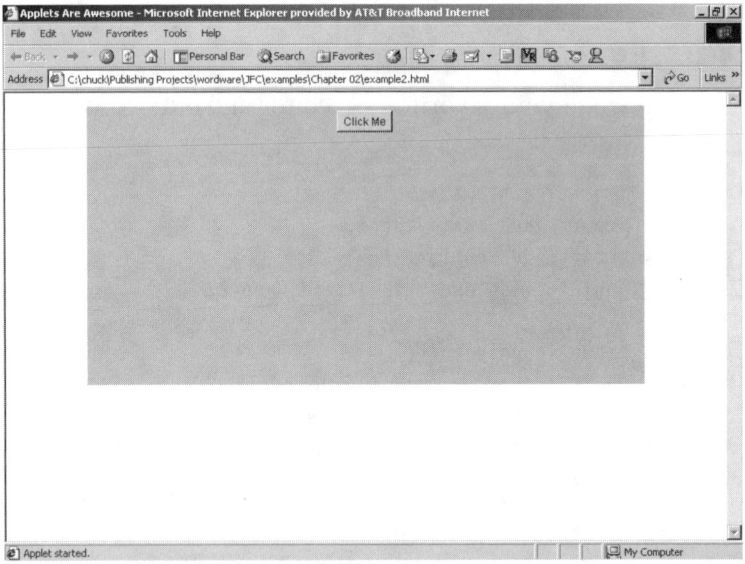

Figure 2.2 Illustration of Example 2.2

There are several things about this example that should stand out to you, the first being that there was no container component used to hold the button. Remember that with applets, the applet itself can act as a container component. Another thing you should notice is that the add command was issued not to a container but directly to the applet. You can do this with applets but not with applications. With applications, the add command can only be called as a method of a container component.

We discuss applets in relation to Swing components later in this book. We spend an entire chapter on them. So if you are not totally clear on applets at this point, don't worry: It will all be made clear later on.

Managing Component Layout

If you simply add components, either to a container or to the browser, you will have a rather unappealing display. The components will be placed one after the other on the container. Most programmers prefer to have some control over the layout of their components. The Abstract Windowing Toolkit provides layout managers to handle the layout of your components. Layout is controlled not by the container but by a layout manager associated with the container. In the AWT, all layout manager classes implement the LayoutManager interface.

The Abstract Windowing Toolkit provides programmers with five layout managers that can be used to organize components in a logical and visually appealing manner. Of course, some are simpler than others. The five different layout managers are listed and briefly described in Table 2.2.

Table 2.2 Layout managers

Manager	Format
GridLayout	The GridLayout manager places components in an evenly spaced grid. Each row in a grid must have the same number of cells.
GridbagLayout	The GridbagLayout manager also places components in a grid; however, each row can have a different number of cells.
CardLayout	A CardLayout manager displays one component at a time, like going through a deck of cards.

Manager	Format
FlowLayout	The FlowLayout manager simply places the components one after the other from left to right and from top to bottom.
BorderLayout	This layout manager allows you to place components around the border of the container or in the center.

As described in the table, the BorderLayout class has five zones in which to place components. The zones are named North, South, East, West, and Center. A single component can be placed in each of these five zones. When the enclosing container is resized, each border zone is resized just enough to hold the component placed within. It is, in fact, commonplace to put other container components into each of these zones. The zones and their layout are depicted in Figure 2.3.

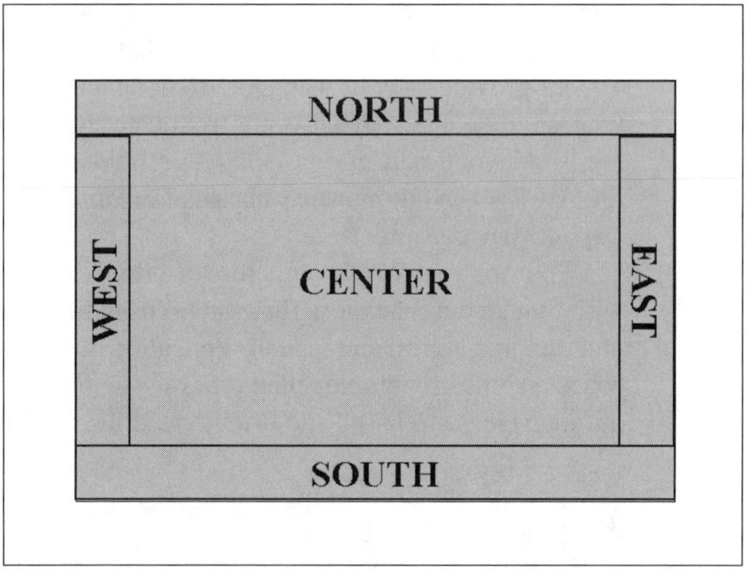

Figure 2.3 BorderLayout zones

Container managers are an important part of the Abstract Windowing Toolkit. You can choose any layout manager for any container; however, each container class has its own default layout manager. The default layout manager for the

Panel class and the Applet class is the FlowLayout manager. The default layout manager for the Frame class and Dialog class is the BorderLayout manager.

Let's take a look at an example that uses two layouts. One is for a panel that has a button on it. The second layout is used to place that panel in a specific location on the applet.

Example 2.3

Step 1: Use your favorite text editor to enter the following code:

```
import java.awt.*;
import java.awt.event.*;
import java.applet.*;
public class example3 extends Applet
{
  public void init()
    {
         setLayout(new GridLayout(2,2));
         Panel p = new Panel();
         p.setLayout(new BorderLayout());
         Button b = new Button("Click Me");
         p.add("Center",b);
         add(p);
    }
 }
```

Step 2: From a command line (DOS prompt in Windows 98, Command prompt in Windows NT/2000, Shell in Linux), compile the program using the standard JDK compilation:

```
Javac Example.java
```

Step 3: Create a simple HTML page to display the applet.

In this example I used two different layouts. The first, a grid layout, simply displays items in a grid. The numbers passed to the grid layout class constructor tell it how many rows and how many columns to make the grid. The second layout, a border layout, is applied to the panel itself and allows the programmer to place code in various locations around the border and in the center. Also note that the button expands to fill the space it's in. If you entered the code properly and compiled it, you should be able to use a browser to display this applet and see something much like what is depicted in Figure 2.4.

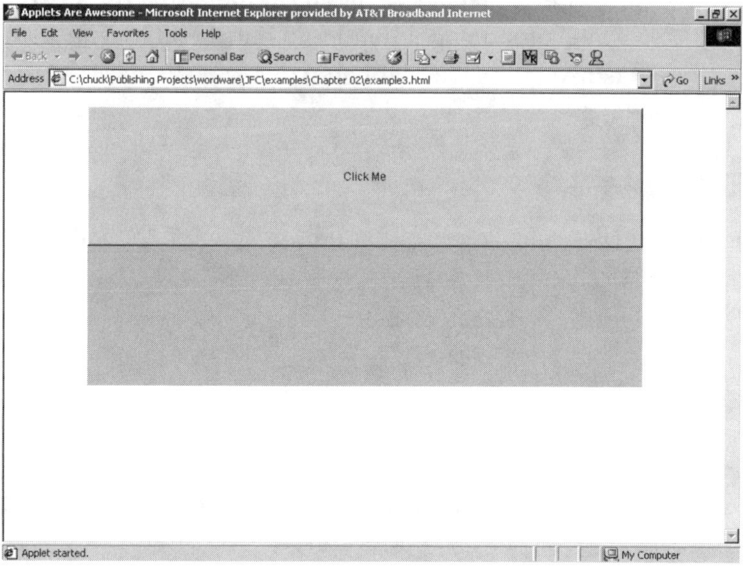

Figure 2.4 Illustration of Example 2.3

Event Handling

The preceding examples simply display certain components — specifically a button on a panel. None of them reacted when the user pressed a button or did any action at all. Building a graphical user interface is only part of the story. The other part is interacting with and responding to the user. Java provides an excellent mechanism for doing this. That mechanism is the event model. Each action by a user generates some events. You merely need to add some code to your class to allow that class to respond to those events. There are a number of AWT events, one for each separate type of action. The action event is used to respond to the user clicking a button, whereas the mousemove event is used to respond to the mouse moving into a specific area. Let's take a look at an example that uses an event to respond to a user clicking a button.

Example 2.4

Step 1: Open your favorite text editor and enter the following code:

```
import java.awt.*;
import java.applet.*;
// The purpose of this little applet is to demonstrate //how
java //applets
// create controls on the screen and respond to //events on
those //controls.
// This class inherits the java Applet class. All //applets
must do //this.
public class example4 extends Applet
{
  Button hiButton;
  // applets use an init instead of a main function.
  public void init()
{
// create a button component with a caption
hiButton = new Button("Click Me!");
// Add that button to the browser window
add(hiButton);
}// close init
// The action function handles the various events the //applet
// can potentially respond to.
public boolean action(Event evt, Object objme)
{
// see if the event was on our hi button
if(evt.target == hiButton)
{
// change that button's caption
hiButton.setLabel("Ahhhh!");
return true;
}// close if statement
else
return false;
}// close action
}// close class button
```

Step 2: From a command line (DOS prompt in Windows 98, Command prompt in Windows NT/2000, Shell in Linux), compile the program using the standard JDK compilation:

```
Javac Example.java
```

Step 3: Create a simple HTML page to display the applet.

After compiling the applet and viewing it in a browser, it should look like what you see in Figure 2.5.

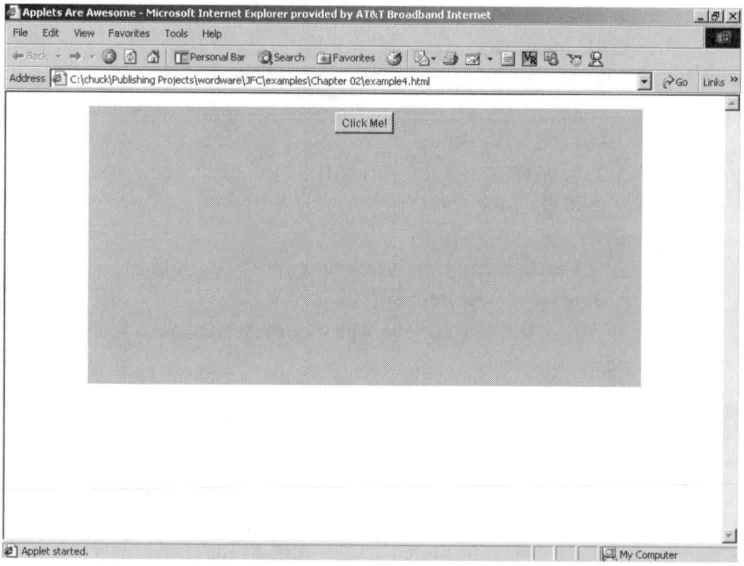

Figure 2.5 Illustration of Example 2.4

When you actually click on the button, as its caption bids you to do, you will see something like Figure 2.6.

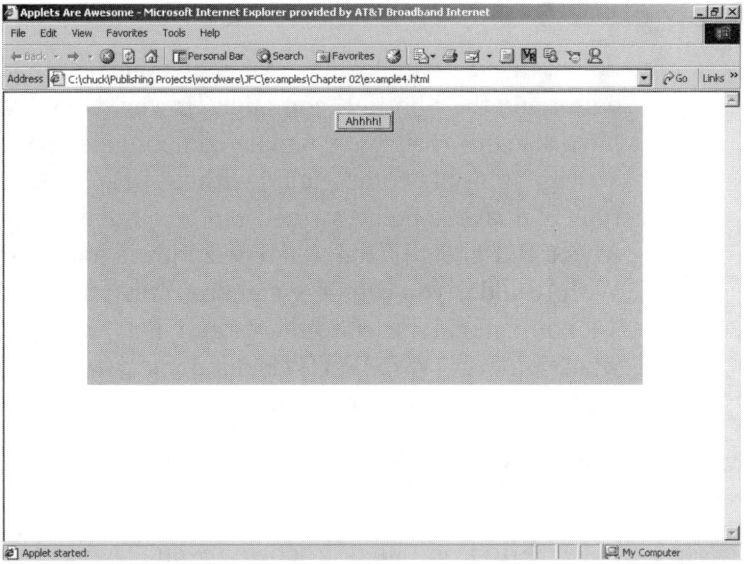

Figure 2.6 Illustration of Example 2.4

The biggest difference between this example and the previous examples is the addition of the "public boolean action (Event evt, Object objme)" code.

This function is designed to be called when the user clicks something in the applet. The Event object that is passed contains information about the event that occurred, including what triggered the event and what component was targeted by the event. Inside this function I simply placed an if statement that asked if the target was, indeed, our button. If it is, then change the caption of the button.

Example 2.5

So far, these examples have all been done with a simple text editor and the Sun JDK compiler. However, our examples have also only had a few simple components. Trying to arrange multiple components without being able to see what type of image is being formed can be quite difficult. This is where Borland's JBuilder can be an invaluable help to you. With JBuilder you can drag and drop Abstract Windowing Toolkit components onto the screen in a "what you see is what you get" (WYSIWYG) fashion. So now I would like to walk you through such an example using JBuilder.

Step 1: Obviously, you will need to launch JBuilder. Then start a new project.

Step 2: Select **File** from the drop-down menu. Then select **New.** You will be presented with the first screen of a wizard that will walk you through adding a new item to your project.

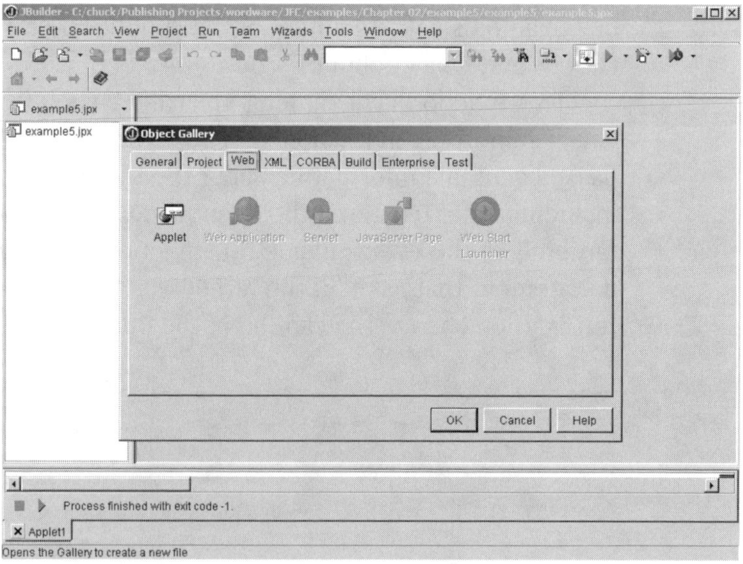

Figure 2.7 Object Gallery

For the purposes of this example, I will select **Application** from the General tab.

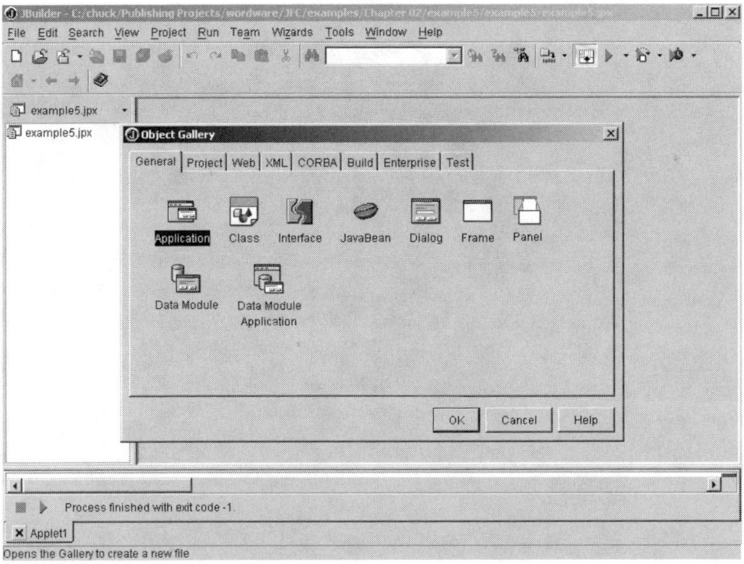

Figure 2.8 Adding an application

Step 3: JBuilder will now walk you through three simple screens as it prompts you for the settings you wish your application to have. For our purposes, I am choosing the default settings, as you see in Figures 2.9 through 2.11.

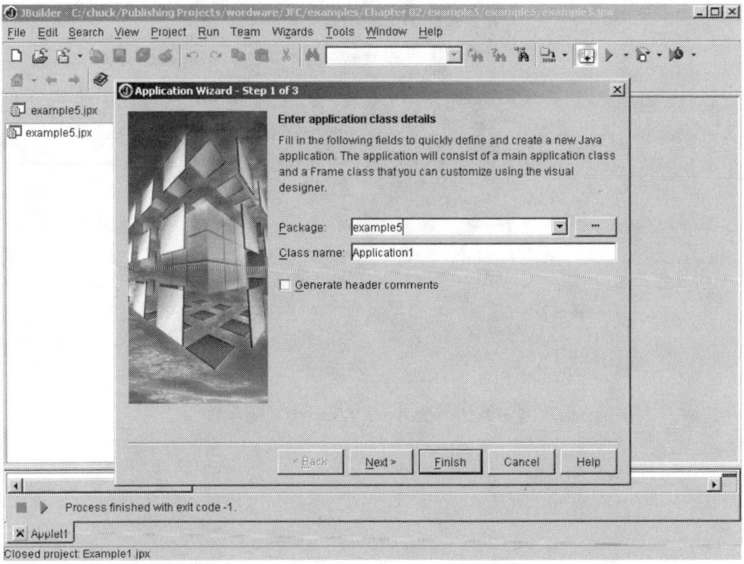

Figure 2.9 Application Wizard step 1

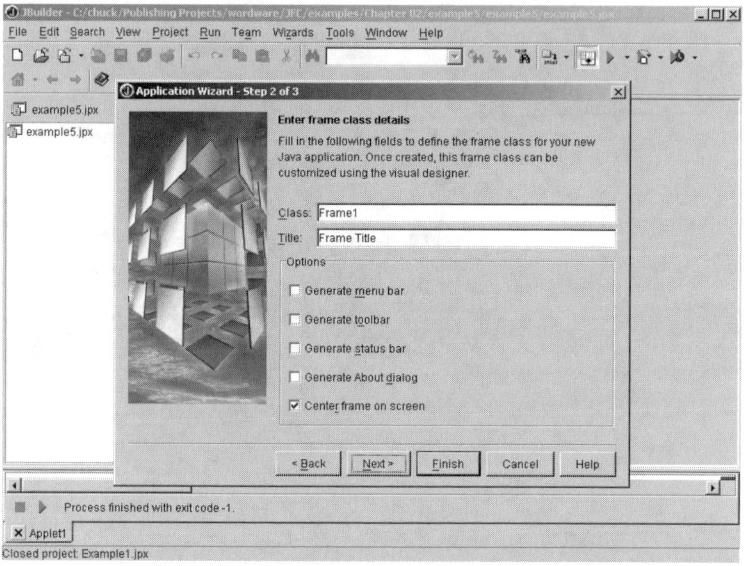

Figure 2.10 Application Wizard step 2

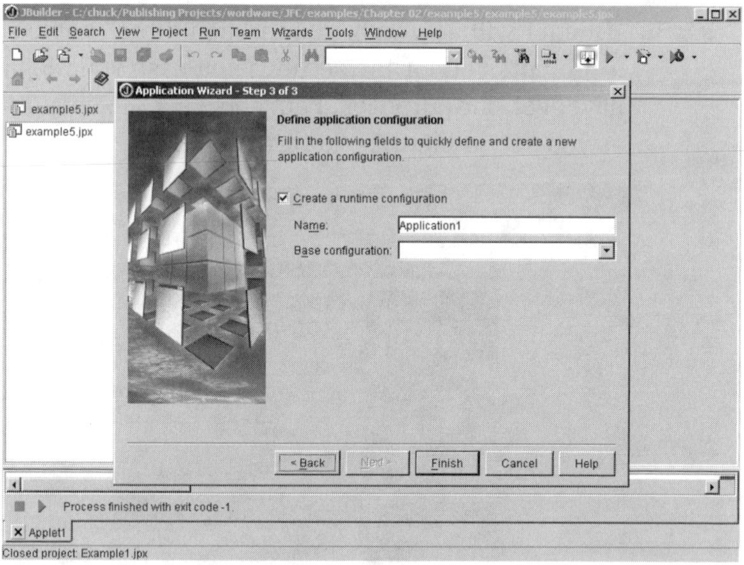

Figure 2.11 Application Wizard step 3

When you have completed the wizard, JBuilder will have built for you the basic framework for your application. You should note that at the bottom of the screen are various tabs. By default, you will be looking at the Source tab when the wizard is finished. However, you should change to the Design tab.

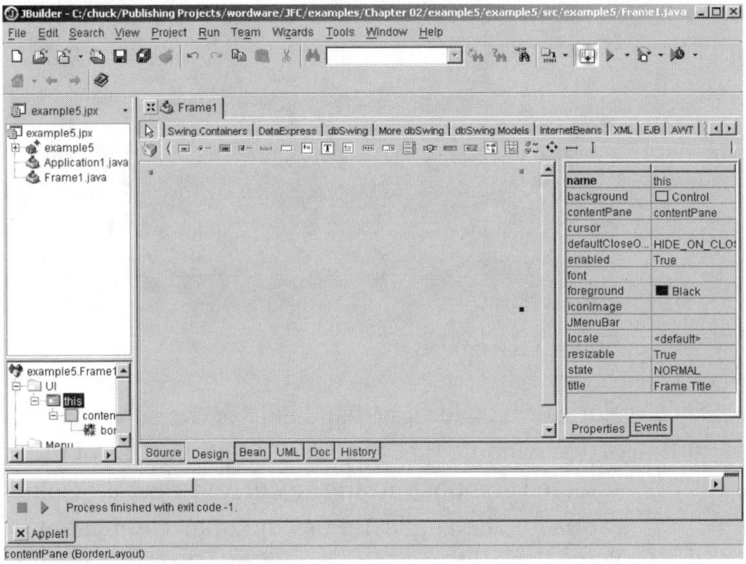

Figure 2.12 Design tab

Step 4: Note that the top has several tabs for a variety of different components, as well as arrows indicating that there are more components off screen. You will need to use those arrows to scroll until you see the AWT tab and then select that tab.

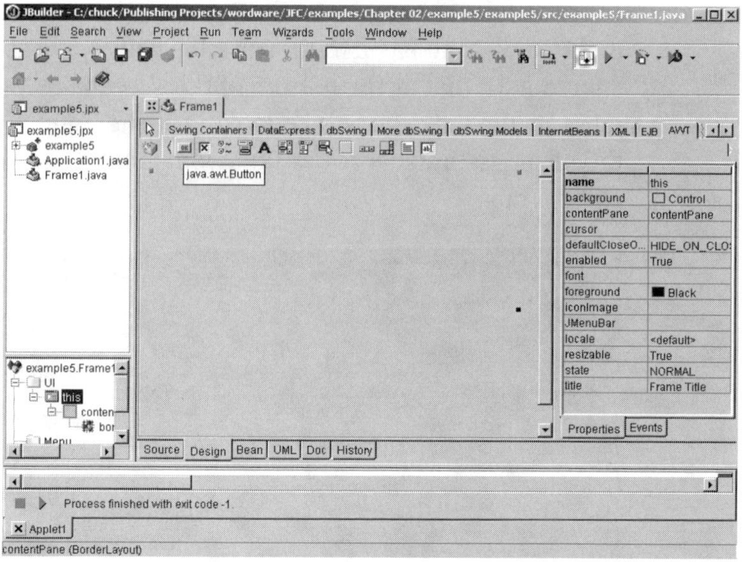

Figure 2.13 AWT tab

Step 5: Notice that the right-hand side of the screen has a Properties window that displays the properties of the currently selected component. In the current case it displays the properties for the application's container component, the frame. You will notice that the layout is set to the default of BorderLayout.

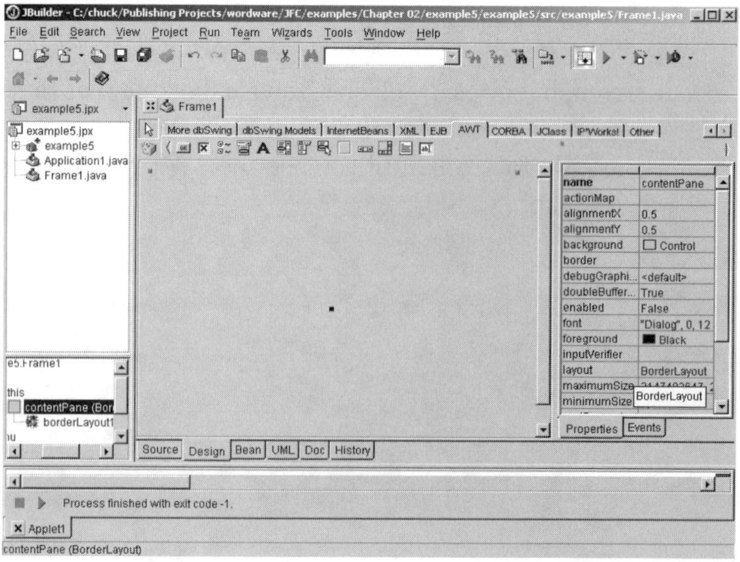

Figure 2.14 Default layout

Step 6: Place your mouse over any component's object and click once.

You can then draw the outline of one or more components on your screen. For this example, place an instance of the JBuilder Panel class in the center of the screen and set the panel's layout manager property to a grid of 2,2. You will then add four buttons to this panel. It should look like the image you see here.

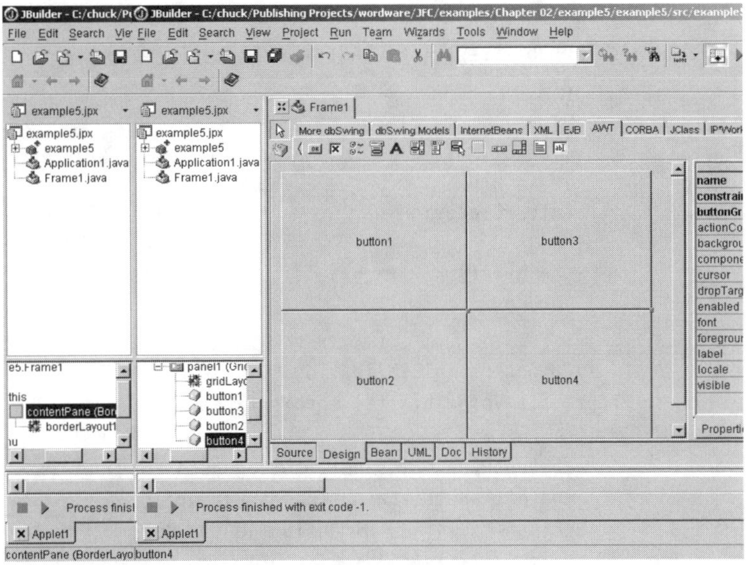

Figure 2.15 Grid layout

If you return to the Source tab of JBuilder, you can see the source code that JBuilder has created for you. That code is displayed below. Notice that the layouts, init, adding components, etc., are all done for you automatically. Also, the application termination code and other required code is done for you.

```
package example5;
import java.awt.*;
import java.awt.event.*;
import javax.swing.*;
public class Frame1 extends JFrame
{
```

```
JPanel contentPane;
BorderLayout borderLayout1 = new BorderLayout();
Panel panel1 = new Panel();
GridLayout gridLayout1 = new GridLayout(2,2);
Button button1 = new Button();
Button button2 = new Button();
Button button3 = new Button();
Button button4 = new Button();
//Construct the frame
public Frame1()
 {
  enableEvents(AWTEvent.WINDOW_EVENT_MASK);
  try
   {
    jbInit();
  }
  catch(Exception e)
 {
    e.printStackTrace();
  }
}
//Component initialization
private void jbInit() throws Exception
{
  contentPane = (JPanel) this.getContentPane();
  contentPane.setLayout(borderLayout1);
  this.setSize(new Dimension(400, 300));
  this.setTitle("Frame Title");
  panel1.setLayout(gridLayout1);
  button1.setLabel("button1");
  button2.setLabel("button2");
  button3.setLabel("button3");
  button4.setLabel("button4");
  contentPane.add(panel1, BorderLayout.CENTER);
  panel1.add(button1, null);
  panel1.add(button3, null);
  panel1.add(button2, null);
  panel1.add(button4, null);
}
//Overridden so we can exit when window is closed
protected void processWindowEvent(WindowEvent e)
{
  super.processWindowEvent(e);
  if (e.getID() == WindowEvent.WINDOW_CLOSING)
  {
```

```
        System.exit(0);
      }
    }
  }
```

You should realize that as your graphical user interface becomes increasingly complex, it will become more difficult to visualize the output of the code that you are writing. JBuilder handles the layout details for you. This makes JBuilder a very powerful tool for designing programs that have significant GUIs.

A Significant JBuilder Example

The examples you have seen so far in this chapter have been simple (so simple, in fact, as to be essentially of no practical value). The reason for this was to provide you with a gentle introduction to the concepts without burdening you with an excessive amount of code to deal with. It is important that a person be given an opportunity to work with a concept until he is comfortable with the essentials. However, it is equally important that you be able to apply this concept to some practical purpose. With that idea in mind, let's explore a practical example using JBuilder to create an AWT application. We are going to build a functioning calculator using JBuilder.

Example 2.6

Step 1: Start a new project. Add an Application object to that project.

Step 2: Make certain that the layout manager for the frame is a border layout.

Step 3: We are going to add two panels and a label to this application. One panel will be added to the center and named pnlnumbers. The second panel will be added to the east and named pnlbuttons. The label will be added to the north and named lbldisplay. The label should have its alignment set to right and its text set to "0". It would be hard to tell the difference between the two panels, so we will reset the background color of pnlnumbers to yellow. Your screen should look much like what is shown in Figure 2.16.

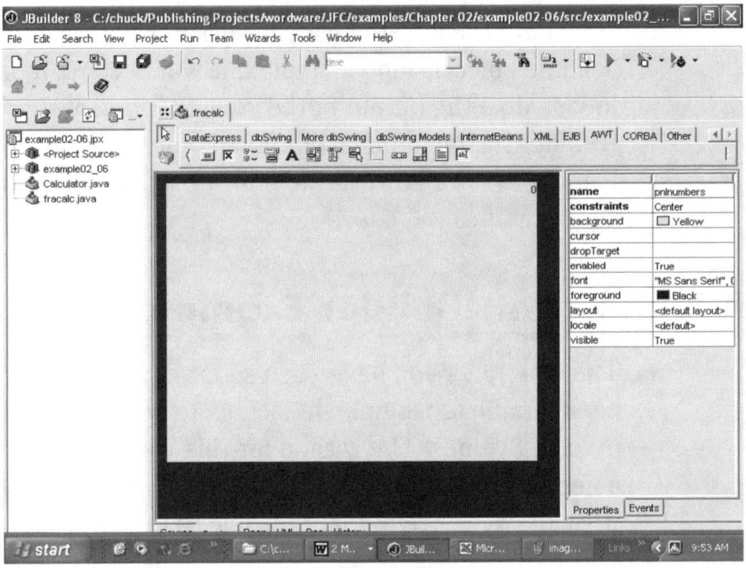

Figure 2.16 The calculator example

NOTE: Remember that for this chapter we are using components from the AWT tab, not the Swing tabs!

Step 4: Now set the pnlnumbers layout to a grid. Change the grid so that it is four rows by three columns. To change the rows and columns of the grid layout, you need to go to the Source tab in JBuilder and simply type in 4,3 in the parentheses following the grid. This is shown in Figure 2.17.

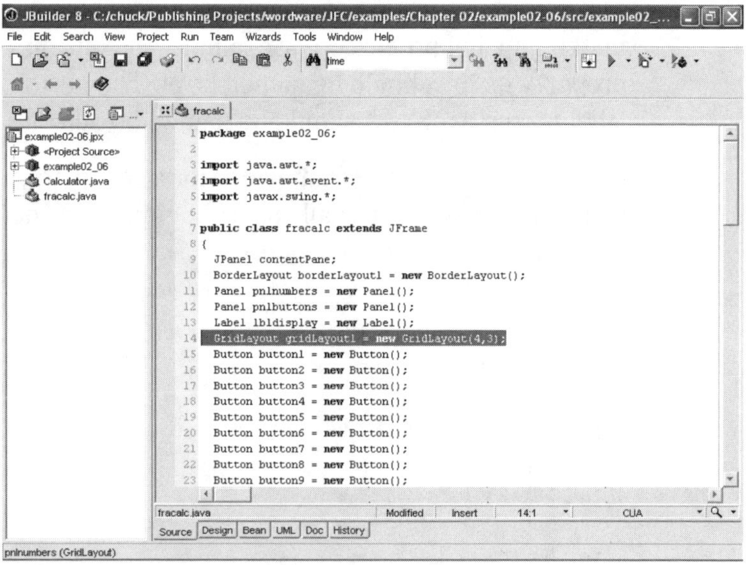

Figure 2.17 Changing the grid rows and columns

Step 5: Now we are going to change the pnlbuttons layout to a grid layout that is five rows by one column. We are also adding a series of buttons to both panels and setting the captions of those buttons. You can see this in Figure 2.18.

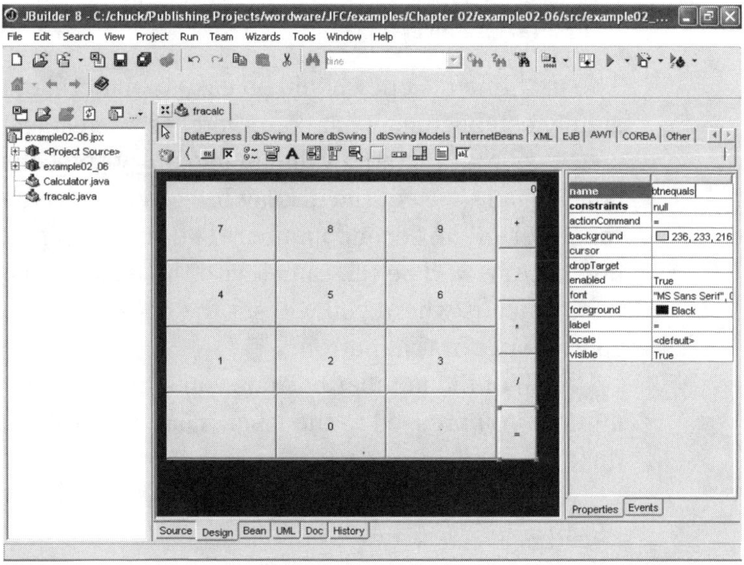

Figure 2.18 The button layout

Make certain that you change the name of each button to match its label property. For example, the button with a label property of “9” should be named btn9. The button with a label property of “+” should be named btnadd.

Step 6: Now that we have the framework for a calculator, it’s time to add some code! First of all, at the beginning of the class, we are going to add a few variables:

```
String temp;
float firstnumber;
float secondnumber;
float answer;
int operation;
int ADD = 0;
int SUBTRACT = 1;
int MULTIPLY = 2;
int DIVIDE = 3;
```

Now we move on to the operator buttons (+, –, *, /, and =). In each we will set the int operator equal to the appropriate integer value. The code for the add button is shown here:

```
operation = ADD;
 temp = lbldisplay.getText();
firstnumber= Float.valueOf(temp).floatValue();
lbldisplay.setText("0");
```

The first line of code should be easy to understand. We are simply establishing what operation has been selected. The next two lines take the value in lbldisplay and convert it to a float. Finally, we set the display back to zero so that the user can enter in the second number. The code in all four operation buttons will be the same, with the exception of the first line, which is where you will set the operation to one that is appropriate for that button.

Each of the number buttons will simply need to add the number you pressed to the label. That code will look like this:

```
temp = lbldisplay.getText();
temp = temp + "7";
lbldisplay.setText(temp);
```

Obviously, each button will have to be set to the appropriate number. The decimal button is set similarly to the number buttons. In the equals button we are going to have a bit more code:

```
temp = lbldisplay.getText();
secondnumber= Float.valueOf(temp).floatValue();
 if(operation == ADD)
   answer = firstnumber + secondnumber;
 if(operation == SUBTRACT)
    answer = firstnumber - secondnumber;
 if(operation == MULTIPLY)
   answer = firstnumber * secondnumber;
 if(operation == DIVIDE)
   answer = firstnumber / secondnumber;
temp = " " + answer;
lbldisplay.setText(temp);
```

All this code does is grab the current display, convert it to a float, and store it in the variable named secondnumber. Then we perform the appropriate mathematical operation. Finally, we display the answer. When you run this application, you can perform all the basic calculator operations, just like you see in Figure 2.19.

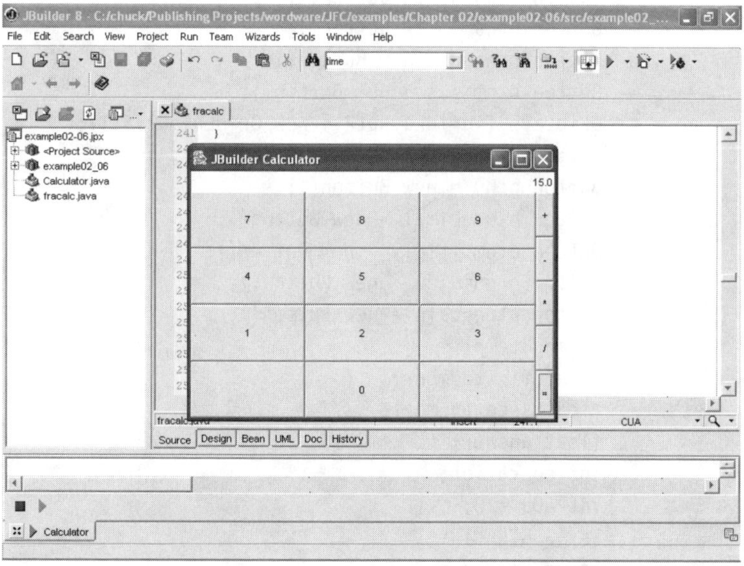

Figure 2.19 Running the Calculator example

For those readers not using JBuilder or who simply wish to see all of the source code, it is provided here.

NOTE: This is a long example.

```
package example02_06;
import java.awt.*;
import java.awt.event.*;
import javax.swing.*;
public class fracalc extends JFrame
{
  JPanel contentPane;
  BorderLayout borderLayout1 = new BorderLayout();
  Panel pnlnumbers = new Panel();
  Panel pnlbuttons = new Panel();
  Label lbldisplay = new Label();
  GridLayout gridLayout1 = new GridLayout(4,3);
  Button btn7 = new Button();
  Button btn2 = new Button();
  Button btn3 = new Button();
  Button btn1 = new Button();
  Button btn6 = new Button();
  Button btn5 = new Button();
  Button btn4 = new Button();
  Button btn8 = new Button();
  Button btn9 = new Button();
  Button btnadd = new Button();
  Button btnminus = new Button();
  GridLayout gridLayout2 = new GridLayout(5,1);
  Button btnplaceholder = new Button();
  Button btn0 = new Button();
  Button btndecimal = new Button();
  Button btnmultiply = new Button();
  Button btndivide = new Button();
  Button btnequals = new Button();
  String temp;
  float firstnumber;
  float secondnumber;
  float answer;
  int operation;
  int ADD = 0;
  int SUBTRACT = 1;
  int MULTIPLY = 2;
  int DIVIDE = 3;
```

```
//Construct the frame
 public fracalc()
 {
   enableEvents(AWTEvent.WINDOW_EVENT_MASK);
   try
   {
     jbInit();
   }
   catch(Exception e)
   {
     e.printStackTrace();
   }
 }
 //Component initialization
 private void jbInit() throws Exception
 {
   contentPane = (JPanel) this.getContentPane();
   contentPane.setLayout(borderLayout1);
   this.setSize(new Dimension(400, 300));
   this.setTitle("JBuilder Calculator");
   pnlnumbers.setBackground(Color.yellow);
   pnlnumbers.setLayout(gridLayout1);
   lbldisplay.setAlignment(Label.RIGHT);
   lbldisplay.setBackground(Color.white);
   lbldisplay.setText("0");
   pnlbuttons.setLayout(gridLayout2);
   btn7.setLabel("7");
   btn7.addActionListener(new fracalc_btn7_action
        Adapter(this));
   btn2.setLabel("2");
   btn2.addActionListener(new fracalc_btn2_action
        Adapter(this));
   btn3.setLabel("3");
   btn3.addActionListener(new fracalc_btn3_action
        Adapter(this));
   btn1.setLabel("1");
   btn1.addActionListener(new fracalc_btn1_action
        Adapter(this));
   btn6.setLabel("6");
   btn6.addActionListener(new fracalc_btn6_action
        Adapter(this));
   btn5.setLabel("5");
   btn5.addActionListener(new fracalc_btn5_action
        Adapter(this));
```

```
btn4.setLabel("4");
btn4.addActionListener(new fracalc_btn4_action
     Adapter(this));
btn8.setLabel("8");
btn8.addActionListener(new fracalc_btn8_action
     Adapter(this));
btn9.setLabel("9");
btn9.addActionListener(new fracalc_btn9_action
     Adapter(this));
btnadd.setLabel("+");
btnadd.addActionListener(new fracalc_btnadd_action
     Adapter(this));
btnminus.setLabel("-");
btnminus.addActionListener(new fracalc_btnminus_action
     Adapter(this));
btn0.setLabel("0");
btndecimal.setLabel(".");
btndecimal.addActionListener(new fracalc_btndecimal_action
     Adapter(this));
btnplaceholder.setLabel("");
btnmultiply.setLabel("*");
btnmultiply.addActionListener(new fracalc_btnmultiply_
     actionAdapter(this));
btndivide.setLabel("/");
btndivide.addActionListener(new fracalc_btndivide_action
     Adapter(this));
btnequals.setLabel("=");
btnequals.addActionListener(new fracalc_btnequals_action
     Adapter(this));
contentPane.add(pnlnumbers, BorderLayout.CENTER);
pnlnumbers.add(btn7, null);
pnlnumbers.add(btn8, null);
pnlnumbers.add(btn9, null);
pnlnumbers.add(btn4, null);
pnlnumbers.add(btn5, null);
pnlnumbers.add(btn6, null);
pnlnumbers.add(btn1, null);
pnlnumbers.add(btn2, null);
pnlnumbers.add(btn3, null);
pnlnumbers.add(btnplaceholder, null);
pnlnumbers.add(btn0, null);
pnlnumbers.add(btndecimal, null);
contentPane.add(pnlbuttons, BorderLayout.EAST);
pnlbuttons.add(btnadd, null);
pnlbuttons.add(btnminus, null);
```

```
    contentPane.add(lbldisplay, BorderLayout.NORTH);
    pnlbuttons.add(btnmultiply, null);
    pnlbuttons.add(btndivide, null);
    pnlbuttons.add(btnequals, null);
  }
  //Overridden so we can exit when window is closed
  protected void processWindowEvent(WindowEvent e)
  {
    super.processWindowEvent(e);
    if (e.getID() == WindowEvent.WINDOW_CLOSING)
    {
      System.exit(0);
    }
  }
  void btnadd_actionPerformed(ActionEvent e)
  {
   operation = ADD;
   temp = lbldisplay.getText();
   firstnumber= Float.valueOf(temp).floatValue();
   lbldisplay.setText("0");
  }
  void btnminus_actionPerformed(ActionEvent e)
  {
    operation = SUBTRACT;
    temp = lbldisplay.getText();
    firstnumber= Float.valueOf(temp).floatValue();
    lbldisplay.setText("0");
  }
  void btnmultiply_actionPerformed(ActionEvent e)
  {
    operation = MULTIPLY;
    temp = lbldisplay.getText();
    firstnumber= Float.valueOf(temp).floatValue();
    lbldisplay.setText("0");
  }
  void btndivide_actionPerformed(ActionEvent e)
  {
   operation = DIVIDE;
   temp = lbldisplay.getText();
   firstnumber= Float.valueOf(temp).floatValue();
  lbldisplay.setText("0");
 }
  void btn7_actionPerformed(ActionEvent e)
  {
     temp = lbldisplay.getText();
```

```
    temp = temp + "7";
    lbldisplay.setText(temp);
  }
  void btn9_actionPerformed(ActionEvent e)
  {
    temp = lbldisplay.getText();
    temp = temp + "9";
    lbldisplay.setText(temp);
  }
  void btn8_actionPerformed(ActionEvent e)
  {
    temp = lbldisplay.getText();
    temp = temp + "8";
    lbldisplay.setText(temp);
  }
  void btn6_actionPerformed(ActionEvent e)
  {
    temp = lbldisplay.getText();
    temp = temp + "6";
    lbldisplay.setText(temp);
  }
  void btn5_actionPerformed(ActionEvent e)
  {
    temp = lbldisplay.getText();
    temp = temp + "5";
    lbldisplay.setText(temp);
  }
  void btn4_actionPerformed(ActionEvent e)
  {
    temp = lbldisplay.getText();
    temp = temp + "4";
    lbldisplay.setText(temp);
  }
  void btn3_actionPerformed(ActionEvent e)
  {
    temp = lbldisplay.getText();
    temp = temp + "3";
    lbldisplay.setText(temp);
  }
  void btn2_actionPerformed(ActionEvent e)
  {
    temp = lbldisplay.getText();
    temp = temp + "2";
    lbldisplay.setText(temp);
  }
```

```
  void btn1_actionPerformed(ActionEvent e)
  {
    temp = lbldisplay.getText();
    temp = temp + "1";
    lbldisplay.setText(temp);
  }
  void btndecimal_actionPerformed(ActionEvent e)
  {
    temp = lbldisplay.getText();
    temp = temp + ".";
    lbldisplay.setText(temp);
  }
  void btnequals_actionPerformed(ActionEvent e)
  {
    temp = lbldisplay.getText();
    secondnumber= Float.valueOf(temp).floatValue();
     if(operation == ADD)
       answer = firstnumber + secondnumber;
     if(operation == SUBTRACT)
        answer = firstnumber - secondnumber;
     if(operation == MULTIPLY)
       answer = firstnumber * secondnumber;
     if(operation == DIVIDE)
       answer = firstnumber / secondnumber;
    temp = " " + answer;
    lbldisplay.setText(temp);
    }
}
class fracalc_btnadd_actionAdapter implements java.awt.event
     .ActionListener
{
  fracalc adaptee;
  fracalc_btnadd_actionAdapter(fracalc adaptee)
  {
    this.adaptee = adaptee;
  }
  public void actionPerformed(ActionEvent e)
  {
    adaptee.btnadd_actionPerformed(e);
  }
}
class fracalc_btnminus_actionAdapter implements java.awt.event
     .ActionListener
{
  fracalc adaptee;
```

```
  fracalc_btnminus_actionAdapter(fracalc adaptee)
  {
    this.adaptee = adaptee;
  }
  public void actionPerformed(ActionEvent e)
  {
    adaptee.btnminus_actionPerformed(e);
  }
}
class fracalc_btnmultiply_actionAdapter implements java.awt
     .event.ActionListener
{
  fracalc adaptee;
  fracalc_btnmultiply_actionAdapter(fracalc adaptee)
  {
    this.adaptee = adaptee;
  }
  public void actionPerformed(ActionEvent e)
  {
    adaptee.btnmultiply_actionPerformed(e);
  }
}
class fracalc_btndivide_actionAdapter implements java.awt.event
     .ActionListener
{
  fracalc adaptee;
  fracalc_btndivide_actionAdapter(fracalc adaptee)
  {
    this.adaptee = adaptee;
  }
  public void actionPerformed(ActionEvent e)
  {
    adaptee.btndivide_actionPerformed(e);
  }
}
class fracalc_btn7_actionAdapter implements java.awt.event
     .ActionListener
{
  fracalc adaptee;

  fracalc_btn7_actionAdapter(fracalc adaptee)
  {
    this.adaptee = adaptee;
  }
  public void actionPerformed(ActionEvent e)
```

```
  {
    adaptee.btn7_actionPerformed(e);
  }
}
class fracalc_btn9_actionAdapter implements java.awt.event
     .ActionListener
{
  fracalc adaptee;
  fracalc_btn9_actionAdapter(fracalc adaptee)
  {
    this.adaptee = adaptee;
  }
  public void actionPerformed(ActionEvent e)
  {
    adaptee.btn9_actionPerformed(e);
  }
}
class fracalc_btn8_actionAdapter implements java.awt.event
     .ActionListener
{
  fracalc adaptee;
  fracalc_btn8_actionAdapter(fracalc adaptee)
  {
    this.adaptee = adaptee;
  }
  public void actionPerformed(ActionEvent e)
  {
    adaptee.btn8_actionPerformed(e);
  }
}
class fracalc_btn6_actionAdapter implements java.awt.event
     .ActionListener
{
  fracalc adaptee;
  fracalc_btn6_actionAdapter(fracalc adaptee)
  {
    this.adaptee = adaptee;
  }
  public void actionPerformed(ActionEvent e)
  {
    adaptee.btn6_actionPerformed(e);
  }
}
class fracalc_btn5_actionAdapter implements java.awt.event
     .ActionListener
```

```
{
  fracalc adaptee;
  fracalc_btn5_actionAdapter(fracalc adaptee)
  {
    this.adaptee = adaptee;
  }
  public void actionPerformed(ActionEvent e)
  {
    adaptee.btn5_actionPerformed(e);
  }
}
class fracalc_btn4_actionAdapter implements java.awt.event
     .ActionListener
{
  fracalc adaptee;
  fracalc_btn4_actionAdapter(fracalc adaptee)
  {
    this.adaptee = adaptee;
  }
  public void actionPerformed(ActionEvent e)
  {
    adaptee.btn4_actionPerformed(e);
  }
}
class fracalc_btn3_actionAdapter implements java.awt.event
     .ActionListener
{
  fracalc adaptee;
  fracalc_btn3_actionAdapter(fracalc adaptee)
  {
    this.adaptee = adaptee;
  }
  public void actionPerformed(ActionEvent e)
  {
    adaptee.btn3_actionPerformed(e);
  }
}
class fracalc_btn2_actionAdapter implements java.awt.event
     .ActionListener
{
  fracalc adaptee;
  fracalc_btn2_actionAdapter(fracalc adaptee)
  {
    this.adaptee = adaptee;
  }
```

```
  public void actionPerformed(ActionEvent e)
{
    adaptee.btn2_actionPerformed(e);
  }
}
class fracalc_btn1_actionAdapter implements java.awt.event
     .ActionListener
{
  fracalc adaptee;
  fracalc_btn1_actionAdapter(fracalc adaptee)
  {
    this.adaptee = adaptee;
  }
  public void actionPerformed(ActionEvent e)
  {
    adaptee.btn1_actionPerformed(e);
  }
}
class fracalc_btndecimal_actionAdapter implements java.awt
     .event.ActionListener
{
  fracalc adaptee;
  fracalc_btndecimal_actionAdapter(fracalc adaptee)
  {
    this.adaptee = adaptee;
  }
  public void actionPerformed(ActionEvent e)
  {
    adaptee.btndecimal_actionPerformed(e);
  }
}
class fracalc_btnequals_actionAdapter implements java.awt.event
     .ActionListener
{
  fracalc adaptee;
  fracalc_btnequals_actionAdapter(fracalc adaptee)
  {
    this.adaptee = adaptee;
  }
  public void actionPerformed(ActionEvent e)
  {
    adaptee.btnequals_actionPerformed(e);
  }
}
```

This example is of practical value as well as instructional value. In this example you saw the use of a variety of components, containers, operations, etc. You essentially saw the essence of using AWT to create graphical user interfaces with JBuilder.

Summary

This chapter has provided you with a basic overview of AWT. If you have not previously had any significant exposure to the Abstract Windowing Toolkit, it is important to ensure that you understand all the important concepts of this chapter. You have been introduced to components and containers as well as layout managers. You have seen how AWT and containers can be used in both applications and applets. You have also seen several examples of using AWT. You should, at this point, have a basic understanding of the Abstract Windowing Toolkit.

Review Questions

1. What are the five layout managers?
2. What two components are actually subclasses of the Window class?
3. Which component must be associated with a frame?
4. What are the zones of a border layout manager?
5. What is the top-level component of an applet?
6. List the nine noncontainer AWT components.
7. What is the default layout manager for the Frame class?
8. What event is called when a user clicks on a button?
9. The Applet is a subtype of what class?
10. What is the default layout manager for the Applet class?

Chapter 3

User Input

This chapter covers the following:

- JTextField
- JPasswordField
- JLabel
- JTextArea
- The EditorKit
- JTextPane
- JEditorPane
- JButton

Introduction

Now that you have had a brief introduction to the Abstract Windowing Toolkit, it is time to dive right into Swing. A good place to start seems to be with providing a means for user input. In any application, getting input from the user is of paramount importance. This is true for console applications and AWT applications, as well as for JFC/Swing applications. But users have grown accustomed to having a wide variety of options for entering input. Fortunately, within the Java Foundation Classes, there are several Swing components that are ideal for a user to enter information in. You could conceivably use several different components for user input; however, some are better suited than others. The components in question are JTextField, JLabel, JTextArea, JPasswordField, JTextPane, and JEditorPane.

In this chapter you are introduced to these components and how to use them. Table 3.1 summarizes the purpose of each of these classes.

Table 3.1 Input components

Class	Purpose
JTextField	To allow the entry and editing of a single line of text
JPasswordField	To allow the entry of passwords and to display on the screen a password character, such as an asterisk
JLabel	To allow read-only display to the user
JTextArea	To allow the entry and editing of multiple lines of text
JTextPane	To allow the entry and editing of multiple lines of text along with a variety of formatting options
JEditorPane	To allow the entry and editing of several formats of text including HTML and rich text (RTF)

These components are all designed to allow a user to provide input to a program. Each component differs either in how the input is entered or in the type of input it can take.

JTextField

The JTextField is the most basic of the user entry fields. It allows the user to type in and edit a single line of text. This component inherits from java.swing.text.jTextComponent, which in turn inherits from java.swing.component. The JTextComponent is a base class for many of the components that we discuss in this chapter. The JTextField class was designed to be compatible with the java.awt.TextField class, but it does have capabilities not found in the java.awt.TextField class. We explore a few of those capabilities in this section. The most important methods of the JTextField class and their uses are summarized in Table 3.2. This table is important because many of these methods are shared with other components covered in this chapter.

Table 3.2 JTextField methods

Method	Purpose
getHorizontal-Alignment	`public int getHorizontalAlignment()` This function simply returns the horizontal alignment of the text. Valid keys: JTextField.LEFT, JTextField.CENTER, JTextField.RIGHT, JTextField.LEADING, and JTextField.TRAILING
setHorizontal-Alignment	`public void setHorizontalAlignment(int alignment)` This function is the corollary to the previous function. It is used to set the horizontal alignment of the text. Valid keys: JTextField.LEFT, JTextField.CENTER, JTextField.RIGHT, JTextField.LEADING (the default), and JTextField.TRAILING
getColumns	`public int getColumns()` This function simply returns the number of columns in this JTextField.
setColumns	`public void setColumns(int columns)` This function is used to set the number of columns in this JTextField.
setFont	`public void setFont(Font f)` This function is used to set the current font.
addAction-Listener	`public void addActionListener(ActionListener l)` This function adds the specified action listener to receive action events from this JTextField.
removeAction-Listener	`public void removeActionListener(Action Listener l)` This function will remove the specified action listener so that it no longer receives action events from this JTextField.
copy	`public void copy()` This function is used to transfer a copy of the currently selected range in the associated text model to the system clipboard, leaving the contents in the text model.
paste	`public void paste()` This function transfers a copy of the contents of the system clipboard into the associated text model. If there is a selection in the associated

Method	Purpose
paste (cont.)	view, it is replaced with the contents of the clipboard.
getText	`public String getText()` This function is used to retrieve the text contained in this text component.
setText	`public void setText(String t)` This method sets the text of this text component to the specified text. If the text is null or empty, it has the effect of simply deleting the old text.

There are certainly other methods besides the ones you see in this table; however, these methods are the ones most often used with the JTextField. Remember that the purpose of this component is simply to allow the user to enter a single line of text. This means that most of the methods summarized in the preceding table should be, in one way or another, concerned with accomplishing that goal. For example, the getText method allows you to retrieve code inside your application. Of course, the setText method allows you to place code into a JTextField. The various other methods are mostly concerned with formatting the JTextField so that it displays the text in a manner that suits you.

In addition to the methods provided by the class, there are several different constructors for the class. They are summarized in Table 3.3.

Table 3.3 JTextField constructors

Constructor	Purpose
JTextField()	This constructor simply creates a new JTextField.
JTextField(String text)	This constructor creates a new JTextField but one that is initialized with the specified text.
spalphaJTextField(int columns)	This constructor builds a new empty JTextField with the specified number of columns.
JTextField(String text, int columns)	This constructor builds a new JTextField that is initialized with the specified text and a specific number of columns.

Now that you have read a little about the JTextField class, it would probably be best if you saw an example that used this JTextField in action.

Example 3.1

This example simply shows you some of the uses of the JTextField class. I will walk you through the example using JBuilder. However, if you do not have JBuilder (even an earlier version will do), then simply skip to the listing of the source code and enter that code in your favorite text editor and compile as you would any other Java program, using the Sun Java Development Kit compiler.

Note: In all JBuilder examples I provide the complete source code so that readers not using JBuilder can use any Java compiler they wish. The complete code is also provided so that if you have trouble making an example work, you can compare your code against the example source code.

Note: This example walks you through every single step of using JBuilder to create an application. This is provided for those readers who have not previously used JBuilder. Most subsequent examples in this book will not spell out every one of these steps, so if you forget the steps, just refer back to this example. If you are not familiar with JBuilder, I strongly recommend that you get a copy of *Charlie Calvert's Learn JBuilder* (Wordware Publishing). It is perhaps the best book around for learning how to work with JBuilder.

Step 1: Open JBuilder and start a new project. You will need to use whatever location and name suits you; the images here show the settings on my machine. The following images show the steps through the New Project Wizard. However, except for the path and project names, you can just use the default settings if you like.

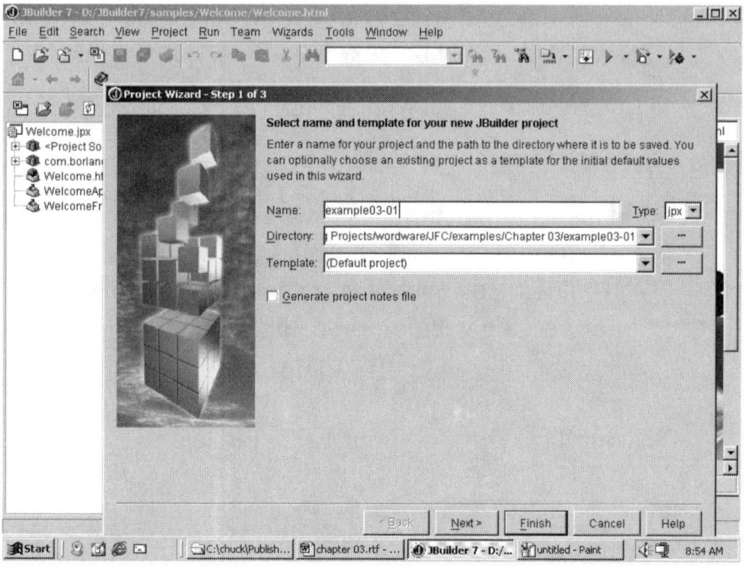

Figure 3.1 Project Wizard step 1

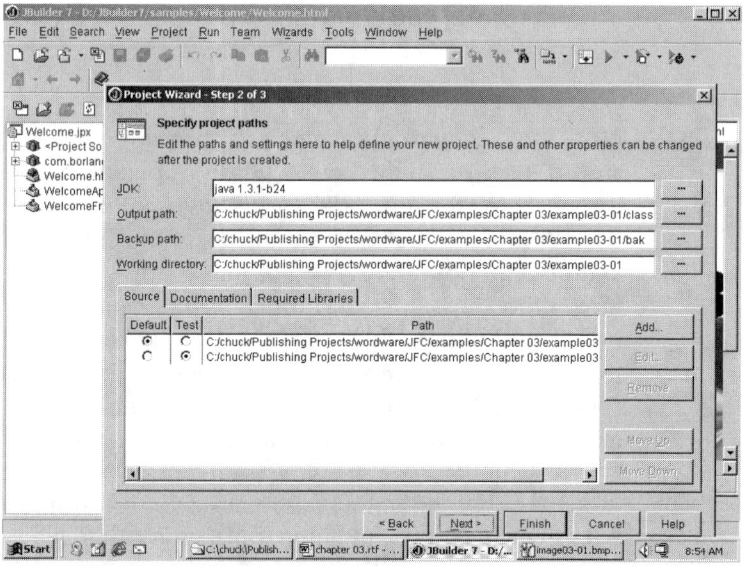

Figure 3.2 Project Wizard step 2

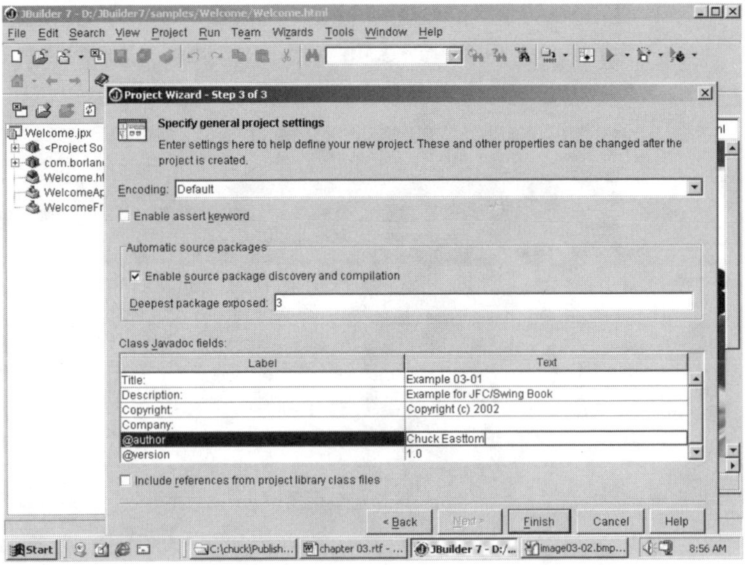

Figure 3.3 Project Wizard step 3

Step 2: Now that you have started a JBuilder project, you can add a number of different types of source files to it. When you choose a type of source file, you will get all the basic code for it already written for you. For our purposes in this example, simply choose **Application**.

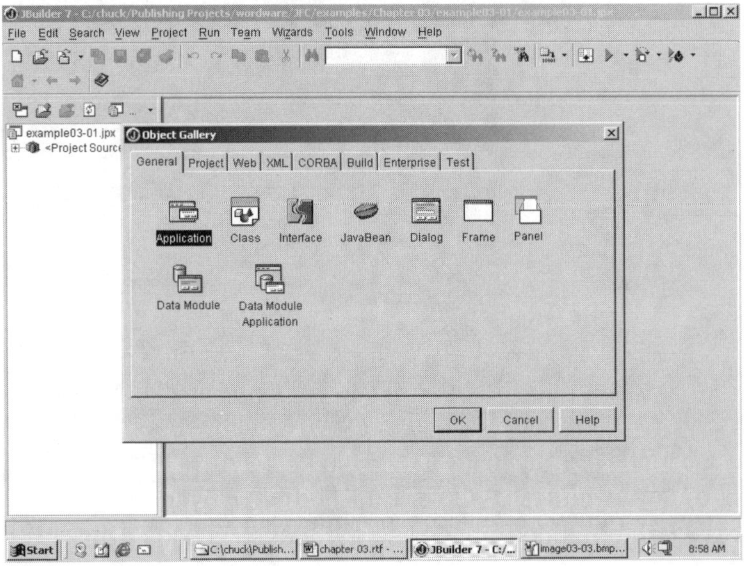

Figure 3.4 Choosing Application

This will in turn take you through the wizard for the particular object you chose. In our case, you can use the default settings shown in the following images.

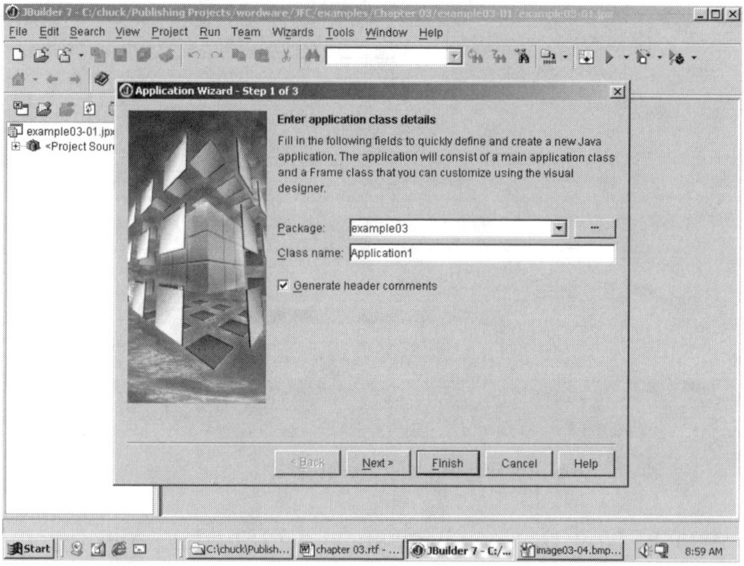

Figure 3.5 Application Wizard step 1

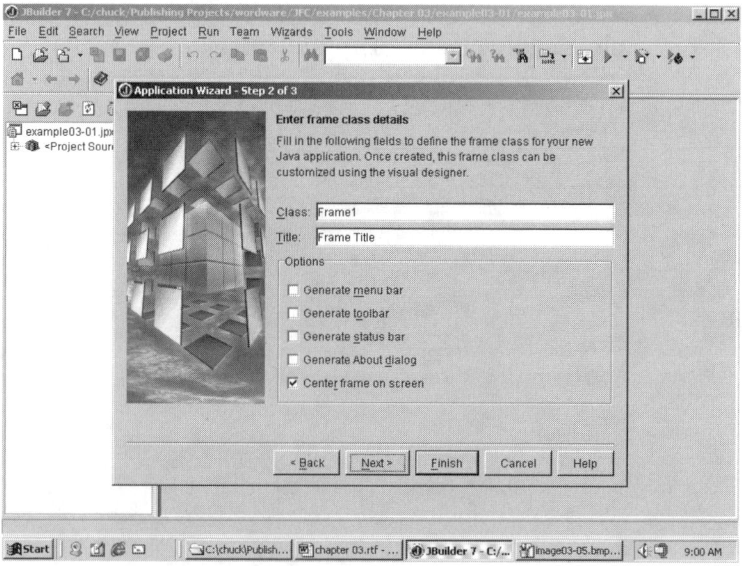

Figure 3.6 Application Wizard step 2

Notice on this screen that you can request several items to be added to your application. We won't use those here (but we do later). However, notice that you can have JBuilder create the code for such items as toolbars and About dialogs. That is quite a useful feature.

When you have completed this wizard, you will be looking at the framework for the source code. Notice that code for a Frame class is included. Recall that with applications there must be some container class to place component classes in. This is not true with applets since the browser itself provides a container.

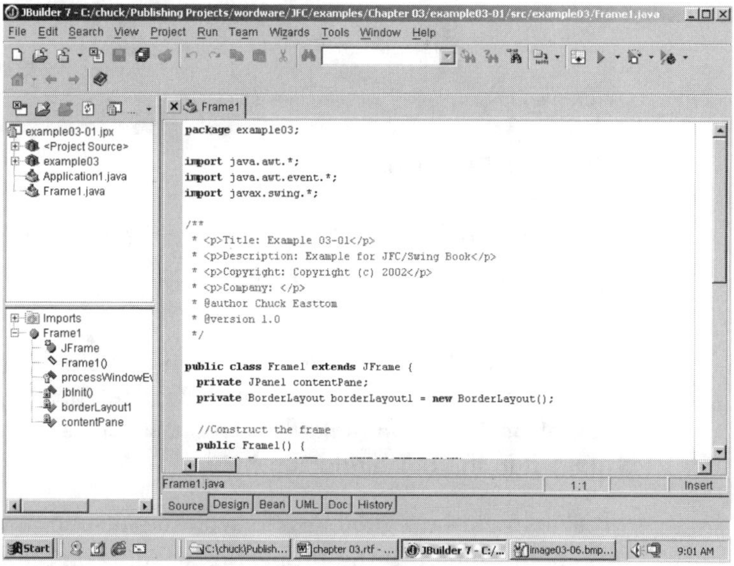

Figure 3.7 A container

Step 3: You could, of course, simply add in your code in this code window. However, it's much faster and easier to add the components on the design window. Click on the **Design** tab at the bottom of the screen to see a window where you can place components directly on the frame.

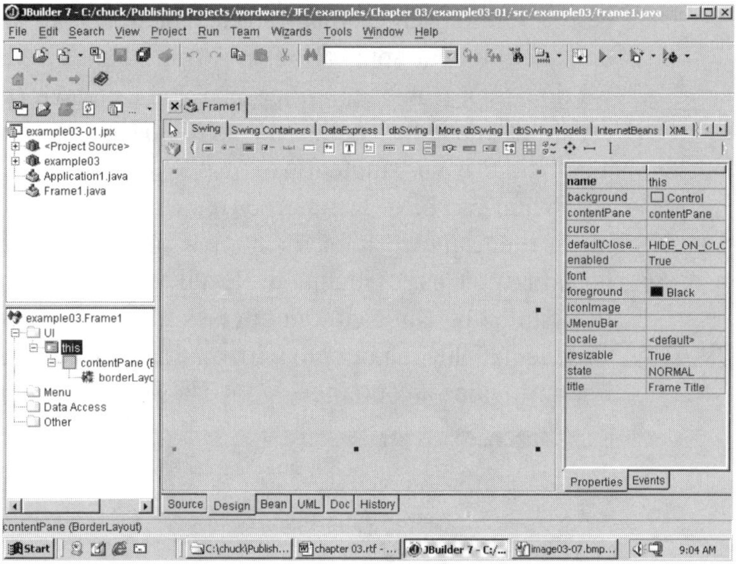

Figure 3.8 Design tab

The sixth component from the left is the JTextField. We are going to place two of them on the screen.

Note: The frame is a border layout by default. If you keep this layout, don't place your JTextField in the center or it will dominate the screen. In this example, I place it in the north and south.

It also might be a good idea for you to pause for a few moments and view the Properties window on the right side of the screen. There are a number of properties of the JTextField that you can set here. Most are fairly self-explanatory (alignment, background, tooltiptext, text, etc.).

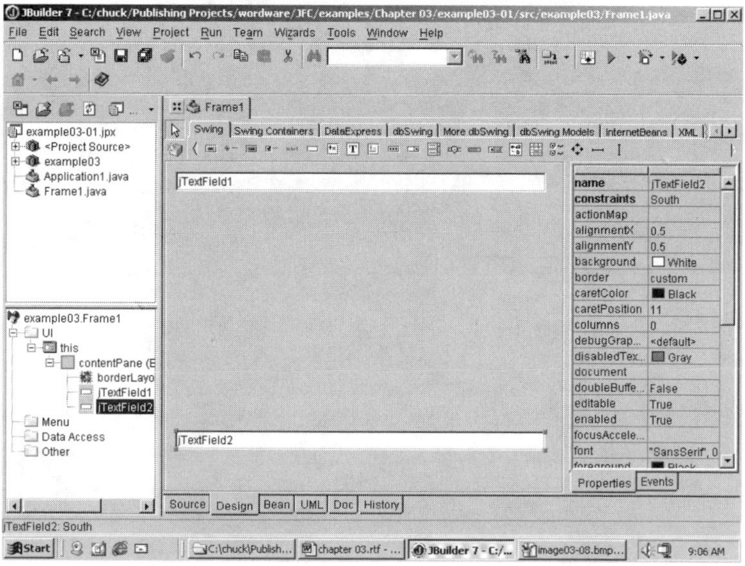

Figure 3.9 Placing two JTextFields

Step 4: Let's return to the code window to enter some code. If you simply double-click on one JTextField, the action event for that JTextField will be added to your source code, and you will be taken directly to it (now that's convenient!).

I am adding just one line of code to this action event:

```
jTextField2.setText(jTextField1.getText());
```

When I type something in the first JTextField and press the Enter key, it is copied into the second JTextField. This may not be particularly exciting code, but it does demonstrate the essentials of JTextFields. Specifically, it demonstrates the getText and setText methods and some of the helpful features of JBuilder. The getText and setText methods are, by far, the most commonly used methods of the JTextField class.

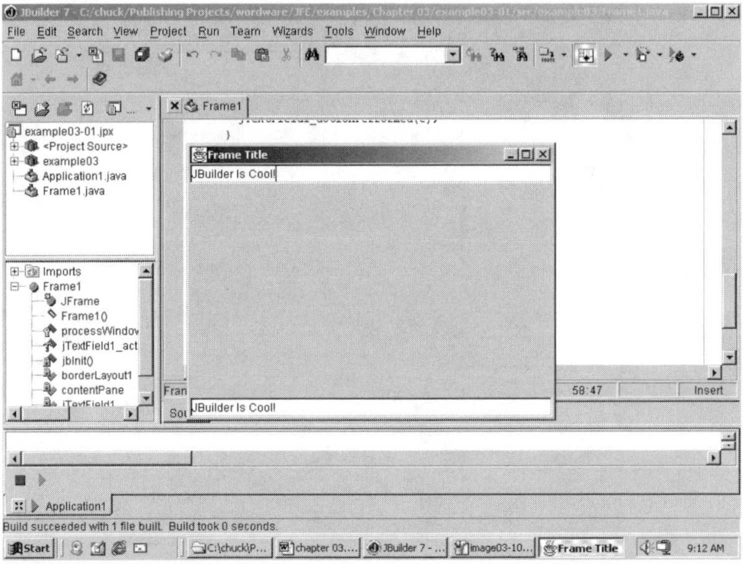

Figure 3.10 Using JTextField

For those of you who don't have JBuilder or if you simply want to check your own code, here is the complete source code:

```
package example03;
import java.awt.*;
import java.awt.event.*;
public class Frame1 extends JFrame
{
  private JPanel contentPane;
  private BorderLayout borderLayout1 = new BorderLayout();
  private JTextField jTextField1 = new JTextField();
  private JTextField jTextField2 = new JTextField();
  //Construct the frame
  public Frame1()
{
    enableEvents(AWTEvent.WINDOW_EVENT_MASK);
    try
     {
      jbInit();
    }
    catch(Exception e)
   {
      e.printStackTrace();
    }
```

```
}
//Component initialization
private void jbInit() throws Exception
 {
  contentPane = (JPanel) this.getContentPane();
  jTextField1.setText("jTextField1");
  jTextField1.addActionListener(new java.awt.event
       .ActionListener()
 {
    public void actionPerformed(ActionEvent e)
   {
      jTextField1_actionPerformed(e);
    }
  });
  contentPane.setLayout(borderLayout1);
  this.setSize(new Dimension(400, 300));
  this.setTitle("Frame Title");
  jTextField2.setText("jTextField2");
  contentPane.add(jTextField1, BorderLayout.NORTH);
  contentPane.add(jTextField2, BorderLayout.SOUTH);
}
protected void processWindowEvent(WindowEvent e)
{
  super.processWindowEvent(e);
  if (e.getID() == WindowEvent.WINDOW_CLOSING)
 {
    System.exit(0);
  }
}
void jTextField1_actionPerformed(ActionEvent e)
{
   jTextField2.setText(jTextField1.getText());
 }
}
```

As you can see, JBuilder generates a lot of code for you. This is very useful, as it allows you to concentrate on the actual task at hand without having to worry about the basics. Now it's time to take a look at a few other input components.

JPasswordField

The JPasswordField class is rather straightforward. Its purpose is to provide the user with a place to type in passwords. It is very much like JTextField except for the manner in which it displays text. Rather than display the keys being pressed to the screen, it displays a password character. It shares most of its methods with JTextField. In fact, the JPasswordField component inherits from JTextField. That means it has all the methods that JTextField has, plus a few additional methods. Methods that are unique to this class are summarized in the following table.

Table 3.4 JPasswordField methods

Method	Purpose
setEchoChar(char c)	This method sets the echo character for this JPasswordField. This is probably the most important method for this class.
char getText()	This is a method that has been deprecated. As of Java 2 platform v1.2, it was replaced by getPassword(). That means it's not meant to be used any longer but will still work.
char[] getPassword()	This is the method used to return the text contained in this component.
char getEchoChar()	This is the method for retrieving the character to be used for echoing.
append(string)	This function takes a string and simply appends it to the existing text.

These methods are all concerned with how to display a password without letting onlookers read it from the screen. Remember that this class also has all of the methods it inherited from JTextField. In addition to these methods, the JPasswordField has a number of constructor options. Each one is used to construct a JPasswordField with slightly different parameters. Table 3.5 summarizes these constructors.

Table 3.5 JPasswordField constructors

Constructor	Purpose
JPasswordField()	This constructor builds a new, blank JPasswordField with no columns.
JPasswordField(Document doc, String txt, int columns)	This constructor builds a new JPasswordField that uses the given text storage model and the specified number of columns.
JPasswordField(int columns)	This constructor will build a new, empty JPasswordField with the specified number of columns.
JPasswordField(String text)	This constructor builds a new JPasswordField initialized with the specified text.
JPasswordField(String text, int columns)	This constructor will build a new JPasswordField initialized with the specified text and the specified number of columns.

Since this component is almost identical in function to JTextField, there is not an explicit example of its use provided here. That would be redundant and a waste of space. Instead, an example provided later in this chapter combines several of these rather simple components into a single example, illustrating the use of all of them.

JLabel

The JLabel class is relatively simple, compared to other classes, but quite important. This class allows you to provide read-only text to the user. Labels are quite useful in identifying the other visual components in your application. For example, if you want a user to type her name in a JTextField, it might be a good idea to have a JLabel next to it that reads "Enter Name." This class is probably the simplest one that you encounter in this chapter. However, unlike many components in this chapter, this component inherits directly from JComponent and not from JTextComponent. This means there are several properties and methods that JLabel does not share with other components in this chapter. Its most commonly used methods are summarized in Table

3.6. Since the label is most often set when the application is started and left unchanged, I also include the constructor methods here.

Table 3.6 JLabel methods

Method	Purpose
icon getDisabledIcon()	This function is used to return the value of the disabledIcon property if this property has been set. If it hasn't been set and the value of the icon property is an ImageIcon, we compute a "grayed out" version of the icon and update the disabledIcon property with that.
icon getIcon()	This method will return the graphic image, if any, that the label displays.
string getText()	This method simply returns the text string that the label displays.
void setIcon(Icon icon)	This function is used to set the icon this component will display.
void setText(String text)	This method is used to set the text this component will display.

These methods are rather straightforward in their purpose. They are used to set or retrieve the text or the image that the JLabel is to display at run time. The JLabel is a rather simple component whose sole purpose is to display text or images to the user in a static, or read-only, format. In addition to the methods shown in the preceding table, the JLabel has, of course, several constructor options. These are summarized in Table 3.7.

Table 3.7 JLabel constructors

Constructor	Purpose
JLabel()	This constructor is used to create a JLabel instance with nothing currently displayed.
JLabel(String text)	This constructor creates a JLabel with the specified text.
JLabel(String text, int horizontalAlignment)	This constructor creates a JLabel instance with the specified text and the specified horizontal alignment.

Constructor	Purpose
JLabel(Icon image)	This constructor will create a JLabel instance, which is displaying the specified image.
JLabel(Icon image, int horizontalAlignment)	This constructor will create a JLabel instance with the specified image and the specified horizontal alignment.
JLabel(String text, Icon icon, int horizontalAlignment)	This constructor will create a JLabel instance with the specified text, image, and horizontal alignment.

As with the JPasswordField, this component is very easy to use. It is so easy to use, in fact, that providing a separate example just for it would be a waste. Later in this chapter there is an example that demonstrates the JLabel, JPasswordField, and several other components.

JTextArea

As mentioned earlier in this chapter, JTextArea is simply a multiline version of JTextField. With this component, you can display multiple lines of text rather than the single line of text that JTextField allows you to display. There are several instances where this can be useful. For example, if you are creating an application to track employee data and you want a notes field, JTextArea would be perfect for allowing the user to enter several lines of text. Like many of the components discussed in this chapter, JTextArea inherits from javax.swing.text.jTextComponent.

AWT had a version of this component simply called TextArea. It inherently handled scrolling (if the text went beyond the bounds of the component); however, JTextArea does not. Instead it implements the Swing Scrollable interface. This allows it to be placed inside a JScrollPane if scrolling behavior is desired. This class shares many of the methods found in JTextField. The following table summarizes some methods that are either unique to JTextArea or implemented a bit differently.

Table 3.8 JTextArea methods

Method	Purpose
void append(String str)	This method will append the text passed to it to the end of the document.
int getLineCount()	This method returns the number of lines currently contained in JTextArea.
Boolean getLineWrap()	This method returns the line-wrapping policy of the text area — true if line wrapping is on, false if not.
int getColumns()	This method will simply return the number of columns in JTextArea.
int getRows()	This method will return the number of rows in JTextArea as an integer value.
void setLineWrap (boolean wrap)	This method is used to set the line-wrapping policy of JTextArea — true for line wrapping on, false for off.

As you can see, most of these methods are concerned with setting the format of the text in the JTextArea component, particularly with items such as number of rows, number of columns, and line wrapping. Other methods such as getText and setText are the same as they are with the JTextField class.

In addition to the methods shown (and others that you can find in the JBuilder help files), there are several different constructors for this class, each with its own purpose. Table 3.9 summarizes those for you.

Table 3.9 JTextArea constructors

Constructor	Purpose
JTextArea()	This constructor creates a new instance of the JTextArea class without any default text in it (i.e., one that is blank).
JTextArea(Document doc)	This constructor will create a new JTextArea with the given document model.
JTextArea(String text)	This constructor is used to create a new JTextArea with the specified text displayed.
JTextArea(int rows, int columns)	This constructor creates a new empty JTextArea with the specified number of rows and columns.

Given that the various input components are quite similar, I will not give you an individual example of each. Instead, I will wait and give you an example of all of them together in an application.

Example 3.2

Recall that several of the components covered so far were not given individual example programs. You were told that a later example would cover all of them. Here is that example program, which shows you the use of several of the component classes discussed so far. You will see how to use the JTextField, JLabel, and JTextArea all in one application. Again, if you do not have JBuilder (earlier versions such as 4.0, 5.0, and 6.0 will work, although I am using 7.0), then simply skip to the source code section of this example and enter that code in your favorite text editor. Compile it from the command line/shell using the Sun JDK compiler.

Step 1: The first step is to start a new project, as you did in the previous example. I won't show you all those steps here; simply choose **File** and **New Project**, and then follow the wizard. After your project is complete, you can then choose **File** and **New**. Then select **Application** in order to add a new basic source file to your project.

Step 2: Use the Design tab at the bottom of the screen so that you can graphically place various components on the screen. This is exactly how we placed the components in the previous example. Then change the layout manager to a FlowLayout. The various layout managers are discussed in more detail in the next chapter. For now, you simply need to understand that the layout manager determines how the other components will be laid out on the screen.

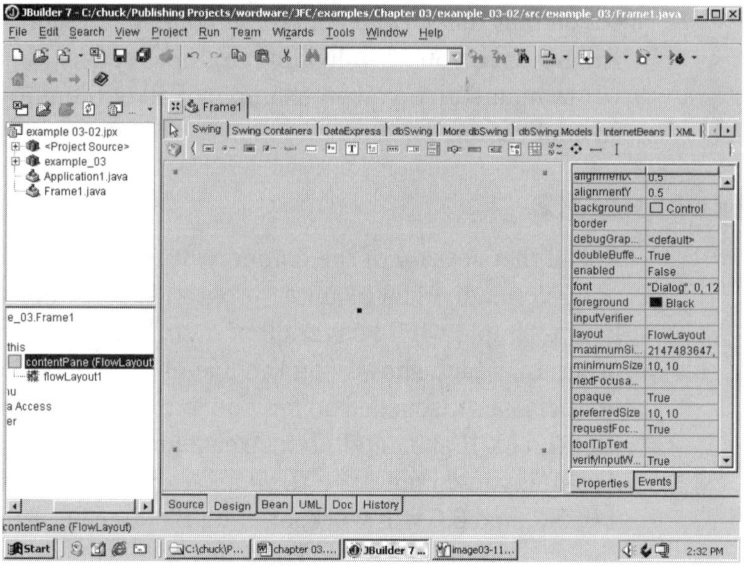

Figure 3.11 Layout manager

The goal now is to place various components on the screen so that we can see how to use them. We place one JLabel (with its text changed, as you see in the following image), one JTextArea, and one JTextField on the screen, as you can see in Figure 3.12.

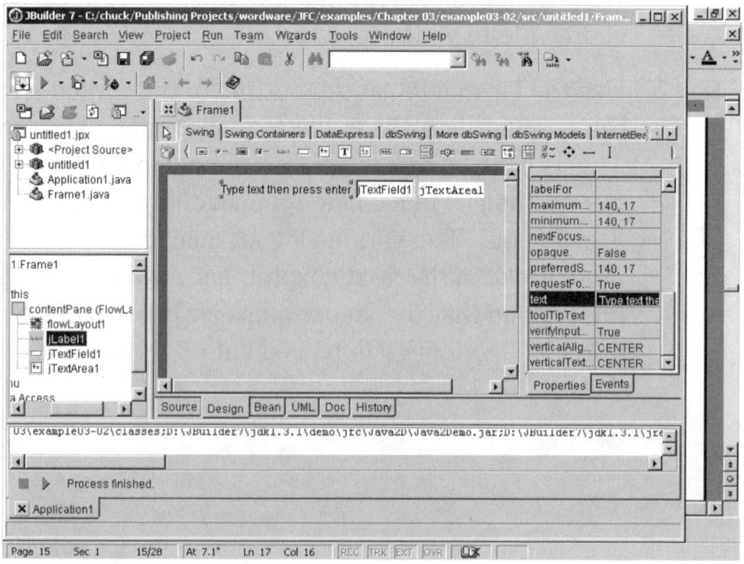

Figure 3.12 Component layout

Step 3: Double-click on the text area, and you will be taken to its action event. Place the single line of code you see here:

```
  void jTextField1_actionPerformed(ActionEvent e)
{
    jTextArea1.append(jTextField1.getText());
  }
```

Now every time you press the Enter key on the JTextField1, its contents will be appended to JTextArea1, as you can see in Figure 3.13.

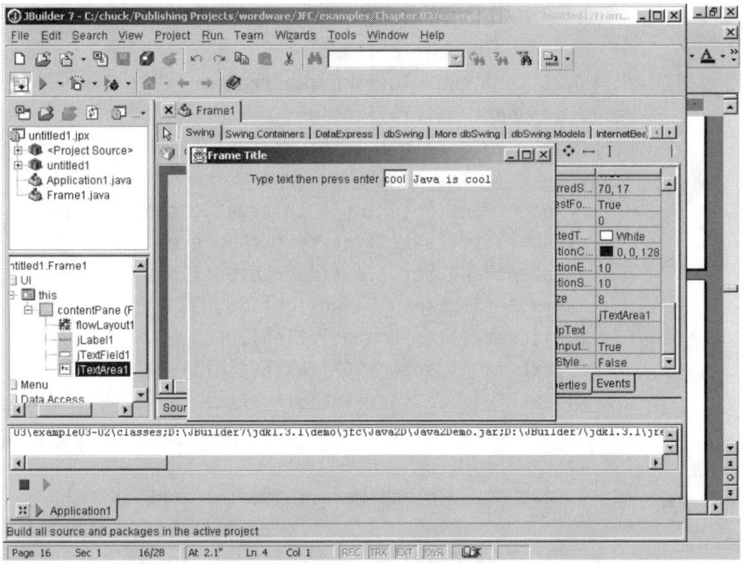

Figure 3.13 Using JLabel, JTextField, and JTextArea

Those readers not using JBuilder can simply type the following code into their favorite text editor and compile it:

```
package untitled1;
import java.awt.*;
import java.awt.event.*;
import javax.swing.*;
public class Frame1 extends JFrame
{
  private JPanel contentPane;
  private JLabel jLabel1 = new JLabel();
  private FlowLayout flowLayout1 = new FlowLayout();
```

```
private JTextField jTextField1 = new JTextField();
private JTextArea jTextArea1 = new JTextArea();
//Construct the frame
public Frame1()
{
  enableEvents(AWTEvent.WINDOW_EVENT_MASK);
  try
  {
    jbInit();
  }     // end of try block
  catch(Exception e)
  {
    e.printStackTrace();
  }     //end of catch block
}       // end of frame constructor
//Component initialization
private void jbInit() throws Exception
{
  contentPane = (JPanel) this.getContentPane();
  jLabel1.setText("Type text then press enter");
  contentPane.setLayout(flowLayout1);
  this.setSize(new Dimension(400, 300));
  this.setTitle("Frame Title");
  jTextField1.setText("jTextField1");
  jTextField1.addActionListener(new java.awt.event
       .ActionListener()
 {
    public void actionPerformed(ActionEvent e)
   {
      jTextField1_actionPerformed(e);
    }
  });
  jTextArea1.setText("jTextArea1");
  contentPane.add(jLabel1, null);
  contentPane.add(jTextField1, null);
  contentPane.add(jTextArea1, null);
}
//Overridden so we can exit when window is closed
protected void processWindowEvent(WindowEvent e)
{
  super.processWindowEvent(e);
  if (e.getID() == WindowEvent.WINDOW_CLOSING)
  {
    System.exit(0);
  }     // end of if
```

```
  }      // end of function

  void jTextField1_actionPerformed(ActionEvent e)
  {
    jTextArea1.append(jTextField1.getText());
  }     // end of action performed
}       // end of class
```

The EditorKit

You will notice that the next two classes have methods that make use of something called the EditorKit. It therefore seems prudent to introduce you to that item before you see the classes that use it. This class establishes the set of things needed by a text component to be a functioning editor for some type of text content. A kit can safely store an editing state as an instance of the kit. The kit will be dedicated to a text component. New kits will normally be created by cloning a prototype kit. The kit will have its setComponent method called to establish its relationship with a JTextComponent.

JTextPane

JTextPane bears some similarities to JTextArea, as it can also hold multiline text. However, the reason you would use JTextPane is its formatting. With JTextPane you can format the text on a character-by-character basis, much like a word processor. Essentially, this class provides you with a text editor. This class has a variety of methods that allow you to do this formatting. This class inherits from JEditorPane, which in turn inherits from JTextComponent. Of course, it shares many methods with JTextField and JTextArea as well. Table 3.10 summarizes those fields that are unique to JTextPane.

Table 3.10 JTextPane methods

Method	Purpose
Style addStyle(String nm, Style parent)	This method is used to add a new style into the logical style hierarchy.
Style getLogicalStyle()	This method will return the logical style assigned to the paragraph represented by the current position of the caret, or null.
Style getStyle(String nm)	This method will return a named non-null style previously added.
getCharacterAttributes()	This method will return the character attributes in effect at the current location of the caret, or null.
getParagraphAttributes()	This method is used to return the current paragraph attributes in effect at the location of the caret, or null if none.
insertIcon(Icon g)	This method is used to insert an icon into the document as a replacement for the currently selected content.
removeStyle(String nm)	This method removes a named non-null style previously added to the document.
setDocument(Document doc)	This method is used to set the editor with a text document.
setLogicalStyle(Style s)	This method is used to set the logical style to use for the paragraph at the current caret position.
protected EditorKitcreate-DefaultEditorKit()	This method will create the default editor kit (PlainEditorKit) for when the component is first created.
protected StyledEditorKitget-StyledEditorKit()	This method will retrieve the editor kit.

Some of these methods may seem strange to you. You probably noticed that several of these methods either take or return an item of type Style. Style is an interface that is essentially a collection of attributes to associate with an element in a document. Other customized attributes that get associated with the element will effectively be name-value pairs that live in a hierarchy, and if a name (key) is not found locally, the request is forwarded to the parent. Commonly used attributes are separated out to facilitate alternative implementations that are more efficient.

Unlike the other user input classes that we have examined, JTextPane only has two constructors, summarized in Table 3.11.

Table 3.11 JTextPane constructors

Constructor	Purpose
JTextPane()	This constructor is the default, with no arguments constructor, and is used to create a blank JTextPane.
JTextPane(StyledDocument doc)	This constructor is used to create a new JTextPane with a specified document model.

This particular component is not used as frequently as some of the other components. In fact, you can program for several years and never have any occasion to use it. For that reason, this book does not delve deeply into its usage. However, this essential introduction is provided so that you will have at least some basic knowledge of what a JTextPane is and what it can do.

JEditorPane

This component is very similar to the JTextPane. However, rather than allowing you to edit basic text, it allows you to choose between text, HTML, and RTF (rich text format) styles. Note that it enables you to do HTML, allowing you to create an HTML editor. This class inherits from javax.swing.text.JTextComponent.

As you might guess, this class shares several methods with JTextPane. Those methods, which it does not share with JTextPane and implements differently, are summarized in Table 3.12. These methods primarily deal with how to load text into the JEditorPane.

Table 3.12 JEditorPane methods

Method	Purpose
void setText(String t)	The setText method is used to initialize the component from a string. In this case, the current EditorKit will be used, and the content type will be expected to be of this type.
read	The read method is used to initialize the component from a reader. Note that if the content type is HTML, relative references (i.e., for things like images) can't be resolved unless the <base> tag is used or the Base property of HTMLDocument is set.
void setPage(String url)	The setPage method is used to initialize the component from a URL. In this case, the content type will be determined from the URL, and the registered EditorKit for that content type will be set.
void addHyperlinkListener (HyperlinkListener listener)	This method adds a hyperlink listener for notification of any changes (for example, when a link is selected and entered).
void fireHyperlinkUpdate (HyperlinkEvent e)	This method notifies all listeners that have registered interest for notification on this event type.
URL getPage()	This method returns the current URL being displayed.
EditorKit getEditorKit()	This method retrieves the currently installed kit for handling content.
protected InputStreamgetStream(URL page)	This method retrieves a stream for the given URL, which is about to be loaded by the setPage method.
void read(InputStream in, Object desc)	This method initializes from a stream.

JEditorPane is another component that, while quite useful, is not often encountered. You may program in Java for years without having an occasion to use this component. In this book, we are trying to get you up to speed on the most commonly used aspects of JFC and Swing as quickly as possible.

However, less common components, such as this one, are introduced so that you are at least familiar with them.

JButton

The JButton component is not, strictly speaking, a user input component. However, its use is so widespread that it had to be introduced early in this book, since you use it in subsequent chapters. Also, one could make an argument, albeit a rather weak one, that the JButton allows a user to commit input. In any case, the JButton is the Swing/JFC version of the AWT button. The JButton inherits from javax.swing.AbstractButton, which in turn inherits from JComponent.

The use of this component should be rather obvious. You place a button on your screen and the user clicks it with the mouse in order to cause some action to occur. This button has a number of properties and events that you will undoubtedly find quite useful. The most commonly used properties and methods are summarized in Table 3.13.

Table 3.13 JButton methods and properties

Property/Method	Purpose
text	This property allows you to set the text that the user will see.
foreground	This property allows you to set the color of the font.
background	This property allows you to set the color of the button.
font	This property allows you to choose various fonts for the button's text.
icon	This property allows you to display an icon on the button.
tooltipText	This property allows you to create brief sections of text that display automatically when the user's mouse hovers over the button.
actionPerformed	This is the primary event associated with the JButton and is executed when the button is clicked.

Property/Method	Purpose
setText(String)	This method allows you to change the text that the button displays.
getText()	This method returns a string containing the text on the button.
hasFocus()	This property is true if the button currently has focus and false if not.

Of course, there are more properties for the JButton than this, but these are the ones you will use most often. You should be familiar with these properties and methods so that you can appropriately use the JButton. If you are using JBuilder, many of these can be set via the Properties window. The JButton also has a number of different constructors that you can use to create a variety of different types of JButtons. Those constructors are summarized in Table 3.14.

Table 3.14 JButton constructors

Constructor	Purpose
JButton()	This constructor creates a blank button (i.e., a button with no set text or icon).
JButton(Action a)	This constructor creates a button where properties are taken from the action supplied.
JButton(Icon icon)	This constructor creates a button that displays an icon.
JButton(String text)	This constructor creates a button with text.
JButton(String text, Icon icon)	This constructor is used to create a button with initial text and an icon.

Chapter 6 discusses events and event handling in great detail. You probably have an intuitive idea of how a button works, since you have undoubtedly used many buttons in software. Let's take a look at an example that should help you see what you can do with a JFC/Swing button.

Example 3.3

Step 1: Start a new project and add a standard application to it, just as you have done with the previous examples.

Step 2: On the design screen, change the container's layout to **Flow**. Don't worry, layout managers will be explained in detail in Chapter 4.

Step 3: Place a single button on the screen.

Step 4: We are now going to change several of its properties. Change the text to Java and the background and foreground to any color you find appropriate. (Just click on the background or foreground properties, and you will get a small window that allows you to mix colors.)

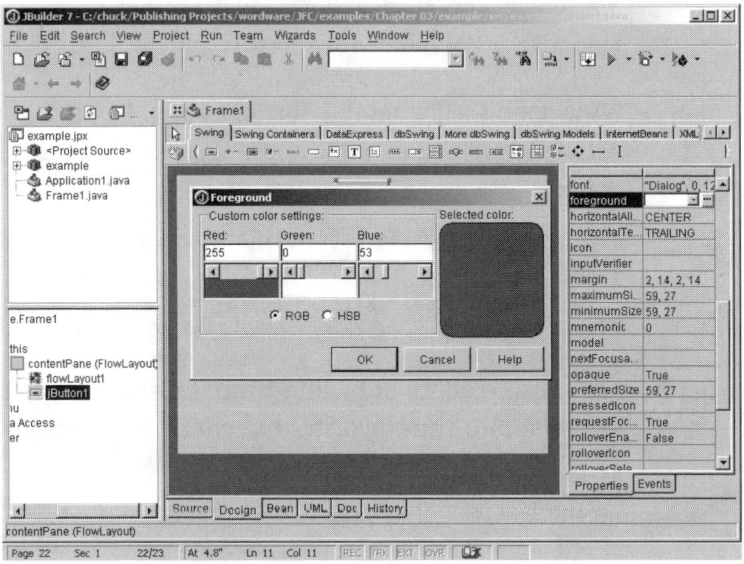

Figure 3.14 JButton properties

I also changed the font to SansSerif and bold. When you are done changing these properties, your button should look like Figure 3.15.

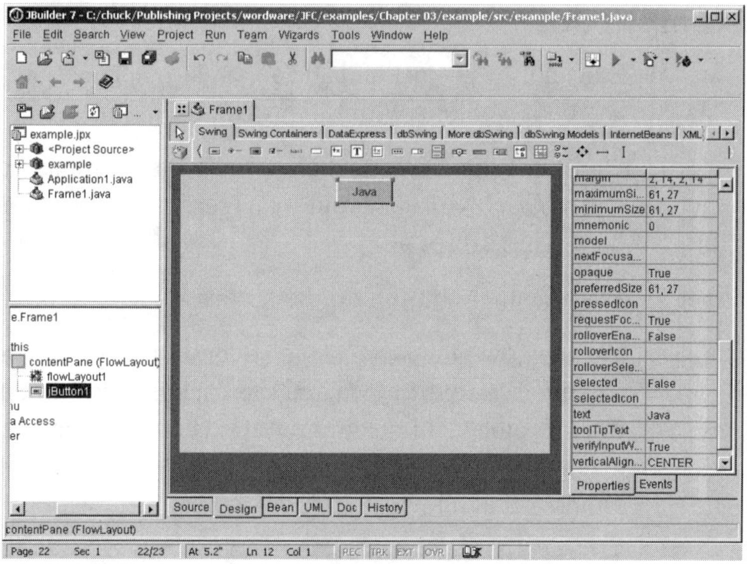

Figure 3.15 The finished JButton

Step 5: Now double-click on the button to be taken to its actionPerformed event. Simply type in one single line of code:

```
  void jButton1_actionPerformed(ActionEvent e)
{
      jButton1.setText("Is Cool");
  }
```

Step 6: For those readers not using JBuilder, simply type the following code into your favorite text editor and compile it:

```
package example;
import java.awt.*;
import java.awt.event.*;
import javax.swing.*;
public class Frame1 extends JFrame
{
  private JPanel contentPane;
  private FlowLayout flowLayout1 = new FlowLayout();
  private JButton jButton1 = new JButton();
  //Construct the frame
  public Frame1()
  {
    enableEvents(AWTEvent.WINDOW_EVENT_MASK);
```

```
    try
    {
      jbInit();
    }     // end of try block
    catch(Exception e)
    {
      e.printStackTrace();
    }     // end of catch block
  }       // end of constructor
  //Component initialization
  private void jbInit() throws Exception
 {
    contentPane = (JPanel) this.getContentPane();
  // The following lines set the properties for the JButton
    jButton1.setBackground(new Color(212, 171, 200));
    jButton1.setFont(new java.awt.Font("SansSerif", 1, 12));
    jButton1.setForeground(new Color(255, 0, 53));
    jButton1.setText("Java");
    jButton1.addActionListener(new java.awt.event
         .ActionListener()
   {
      public void actionPerformed(ActionEvent e)
      {
        jButton1_actionPerformed(e);
      }
    });
    contentPane.setLayout(flowLayout1);
    this.setSize(new Dimension(400, 300));
    this.setTitle("Frame Title");
    contentPane.add(jButton1, null);
  }
  //Overridden so we can exit when window is closed
  protected void processWindowEvent(WindowEvent e)
  {
    super.processWindowEvent(e);
    if (e.getID() == WindowEvent.WINDOW_CLOSING)
   {
      System.exit(0);
    }     // end of if
  }       // end of processWindowEvent
  void jButton1_actionPerformed(ActionEvent e)
{
       jButton1.setText("Is Cool");
  }      // end of action performed event
}// end of class
```

Step 7: Run your application. When it first starts, the button should read "Java," and then when you click it, the caption should change to "Is Cool."

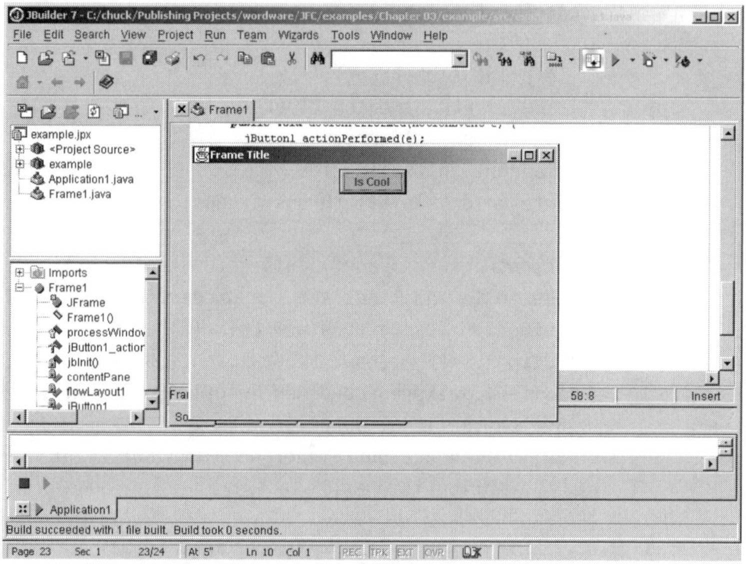

Figure 3.16 Clicking the JButton

Obviously, there are more JButton properties and methods, and you are introduced to those as they are needed in our examples throughout this book. However, this example should show you the basics of the JButton and give you a good feel for its use.

Summary

This chapter summarized the most basic user input and display classes. These classes create components that allow you to display text to the user in a variety of formats and get textual input from the user in an equally varied set of formats. These are fundamental classes; it is hard to imagine a Java programmer writing many applications without using them. It is, therefore, imperative that you become intimately familiar with them. The JTextField component is, by far, the most commonly used, with JTextArea and JPasswordField tying for a close second.

Review Questions

1. What two classes listed in this chapter do not allow multiline display?
2. What class would you use to display HTML?
3. What class would you use if you did not want the actual keystrokes to be shown on the screen?
4. List two methods of the JTextField component.
5. List two methods of the JPasswordField component.
6. What is the primary difference between JTextField and JTextArea?
7. What is the EditorKit?
8. How would you add text at the end of a JTextArea?
9. Name one difference between the AWT TextArea and the JFC JTextArea.
10. What is the primary difference between JTextPane and JTextArea?

Chapter 4

Look and Feel

This chapter covers the following:

- Layout managers
- BorderLayout
- GridLayout
- XYLayout
- FlowLayout
- VerticalFlowLayout
- BoxLayout2
- CardLayout
- OverlayLayout
- GridbagLayout
- PaneLayout
- Look and feel

Introduction

One of the most important aspects of the graphical user interface is the ability to alter the way an application looks, as well as the way it feels. The look and feel of your application will have a tremendous impact on a user's impression of it. JFC/Swing provides several methods and classes to help you with this. The first are the layout manager classes. These layout managers allow you to set the way in which components on a container will be arranged. We have already used a layout manager in the last chapter without providing much explanation. This chapter provides you with a thorough explanation and several examples of layout managers.

It is also important to be able to set the way an application feels. With AWT, the components were all generated in accordance with the operating system on which they were running. JFC allows you to set the type of appearance that you want, and your component will appear that way regardless of the operating system. If you simply right-click on a component, you will see an option called “Look and Feel,” which gives you three options: Metal, CDE/Motif, and Windows. I explore these options later in this chapter.

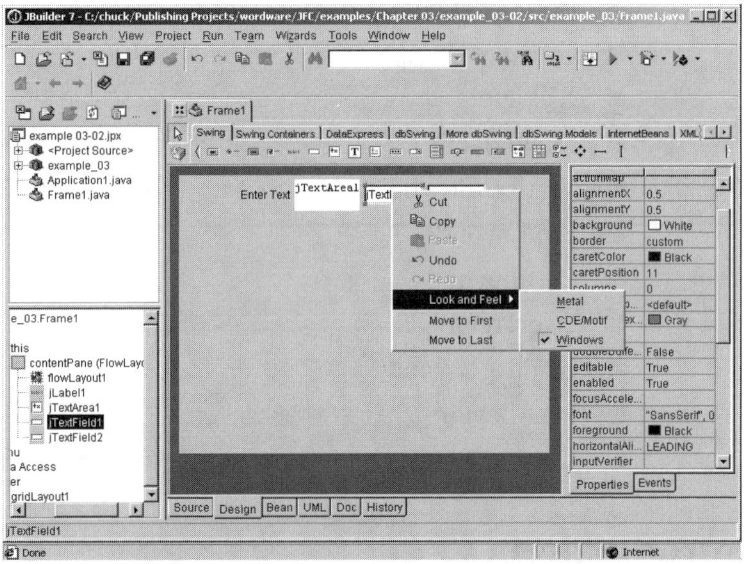

Figure 4.1 Look and feel options

Layout Managers

Your components should be displayed in some type of format. A layout manager allows you to alter the display. With JFC, there are ten layout managers. With AWT, there are five (GridLayout, GridbagLayout, etc.). Each of these proscribes a different layout sequence for components added to the container using the given layout manager. The following table summarizes the layout managers and their basic purpose.

Table 4.1 JFC layout managers

Layout Manager	Purpose
BorderLayout	This layout manager is very common. It arranges a container's components in areas named North, South, East, West, and Center. The components in North and South are given their preferred height and stretched across the full width of the container. The components in East and West are given their preferred width and stretched vertically to fill the space between the North and South areas. You will encounter the BorderLayout manager in a variety of situations.
BoxLayout2Layout	This layout manager allows multiple components to be laid out either vertically or horizontally. The components will not wrap; thus, a vertical arrangement of components will stay vertically arranged when the frame is resized.
CardLayout	CardLayout places components on top of each other in a stack, similar to a deck of cards. You see only one component at a time.
FlowLayout	FlowLayout arranges components in rows from left to right and then top to bottom, using each component's normal size. FlowLayout lines up as many components as it can in a row and then moves to a new row. This simple layout manager is the default layout manger for some containers; however, its layout is, at least in many cases, too simple for a truly appealing graphical user interface.

Layout Manager	Purpose
GridLayout	The GridLayout manager places components in a grid of cells that are in rows and columns. GridLayout expands each component to fill the available space within its cell. This particular layout manager is very common. You should be sure that you are well acquainted with it, since you will see it frequently.
GridbagLayout	The GridbagLayout manager is similar to GridLayout but more flexible. GridbagLayout positions components horizontally and vertically on a dynamic rectangular grid. The rows do not have to have the same number of cells.
OverlayLayout	This layout manager is similar to the CardLayout manager in that it places the components on top of each other. However, unlike CardLayout, several components can be visible at the same time if you make each component in the container transparent.
PaneLayout	PaneLayout allows you to specify the size of a component in relation to its sibling components.
VerticalFlowLayout	The VerticalFlowLayout manager arranges components in columns from top to bottom and left to right, using each component's default size. This layout manager arranges as many components as it can in a column and then moves to a new column.
XYLayout	XYLayout is not a standard Java layout manager. If you are using the Sun JDK rather than JBuilder, you will not have access to this particular layout manager; it is only available with JBuilder. XYLayout places the components in a container at specific x,y coordinates, thus the name. In this coordinate system the point of origin (0,0) is the upper left-hand corner. This is the only layout manager mentioned in this chapter that is *not* part of the Java SDK.

All the various layout manager classes implement the Layout interface. That interface defines the common methods that all layout managers implement. The following table summarizes those methods.

Table 4.2 Layout interface methods

Method	Purpose
void addLayoutComponent (String name, Component comp)	This method is used to add the specified component with the specified name to the layout. You really cannot work with layout managers without adding components to them, so this is the most commonly used method of the Layout interface.
void layoutContainer (Container parent)	This method will lay out the container in the specified panel.
void removeLayout-Component(Component comp)	This method is used to remove the specified component from the layout.
dimension minimum-LayoutSize(Container parent)	This method calculates the minimum size dimensions for the specified panel given the components in the specified parent container.
dimension preferred-LayoutSize(Container parent)	This method calculates the preferred size dimensions for the specified panel given the components in the specified parent container.

These are just a few methods, but they contain all the functionality you might need in order to effectively utilize any particular layout manager. Of course, like all classes, you will need to instantiate one of the layout manager classes in order to use that particular layout manager. You create a layout manager the same way you create an instance of any other Java class. Here is an example:

```
private GridLayout gridLayout1 = new GridLayout(4,1);
```

We have created an instance of the GridLayout manager, named gridLayout1. Our GridLayout manager has four rows and one column.

Your application, or applet, might have more than one container component in it. You will need to associate a specific container with a specific layout manager. All container components have a method, setLayout, that allows you to associate a specific layout with a specific container. Here is an example:

```
contentPane.setLayout(gridLayout1);
```

You can see that associating a specific layout with a particular container component is rather simple. The difficulties arise with choosing the correct layout manager for a specific situation and in properly manipulating that layout manager. Let's take a look at the various layout managers, how they are implemented, and what situations are most appropriate for their use. Examples are provided for the most commonly used layout managers.

BorderLayout

The BorderLayout manager arranges the components into five zones. There is a rather large Center zone and smaller zones for North, South, East, and West. This layout manager is frequently used to place container components that will in turn host other components. Figure 4.2 depicts the layout arrangement for you.

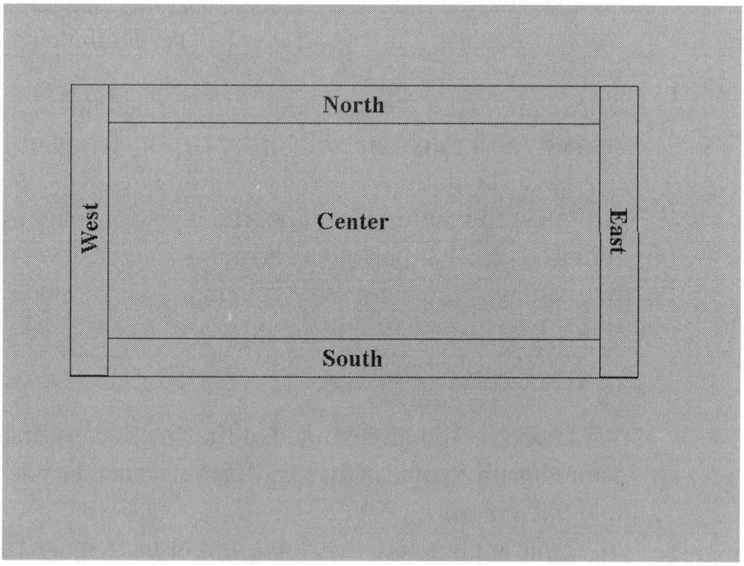

Figure 4.2 BorderLayout

GridLayout

As previously mentioned, the GridLayout manager arranges components in a grid with each row having the same number of cells. The number of rows and columns is determined by two numbers passed to the GridLayout manager when it is instantiated. The first number indicates the rows, and the second indicates the columns. So if you write:

```
GridLayout mygrid = new GridLayout(4,2),
```

...you are declaring a grid layout with four rows and two columns. One place where this is of particular use is with a calculator application. Since the buttons must be arrayed in a grid format, the GridLayout manager is perfect for this situation. The following example is a bit long but gives you a good example of the various uses of the GridLayout manager, as well as BorderLayout.

Example 4.1

Step 1: Open a new project with JBuilder. (Again, users without JBuilder can simply skip to the source code and enter that into their favorite text editor and compile it.)

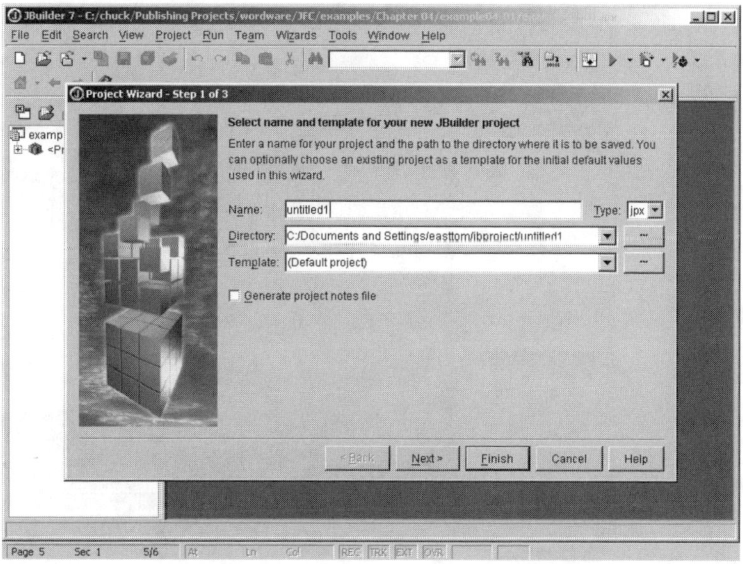

Figure 4.3 Example 4.1

Step 2: Add a standard application to the project. You can use the default settings for this.

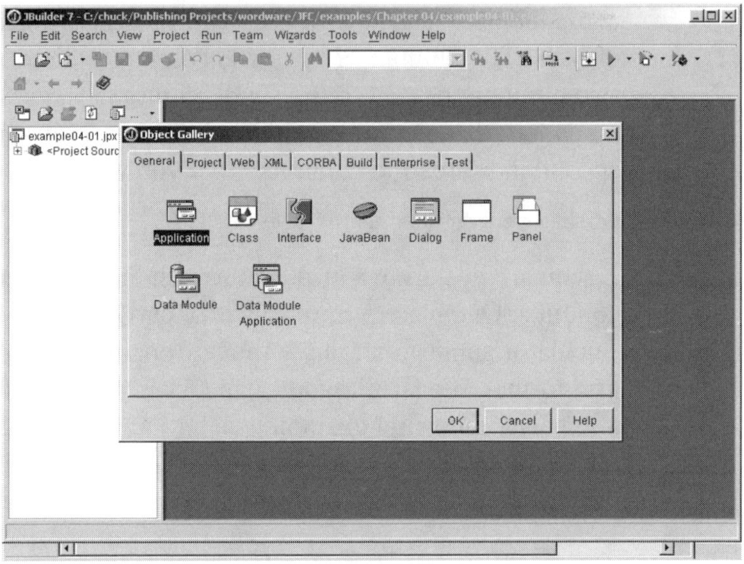

Figure 4.4 Example 4.1

Step 3: Use the Design tab to set the BorderLayout manager.

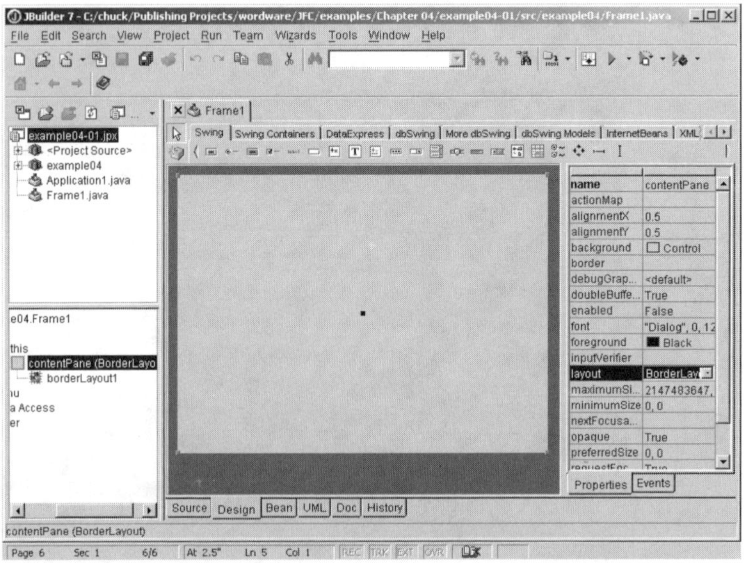

Figure 4.5 Example 4.1

Step 4: After you have set the BorderLayout manager, place the panels in the Center and East regions (you will find the JPanel control on the second tab with the caption Swing Containers). Each of the panels should use the grid layout. You can then go into the code and alter the rows and columns like this:

```
private GridLayout gridLayout1 = new GridLayout(5,1);
private GridLayout gridLayout2 = new GridLayout(3,4);
```

Note: Chapter 5 discusses containers at some length; for now just place them in the required places.

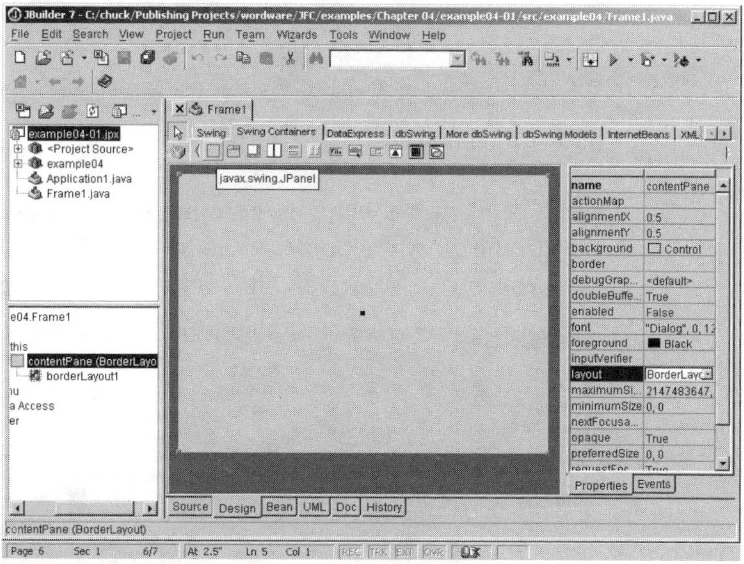

Figure 4.6 Example 4.1

Note: It will probably be easier to see where the panels are if you set each of them with a different background color. This may not be the most visually appealing layout, but it will help you remember where you put things!

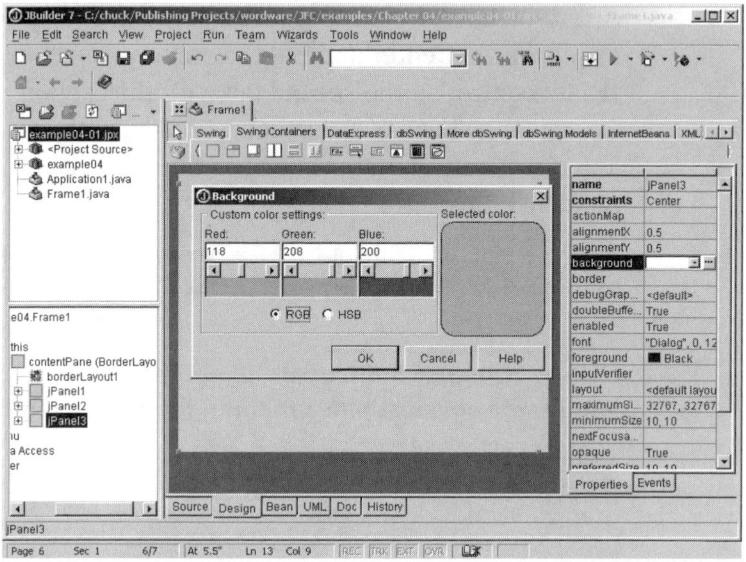

Figure 4.7 Example 4.1

Step 5: Place a label with a white background and a default caption of "0" in the North region. Set the label's horizontal alignment property to **White** and its border type to **Etched**.

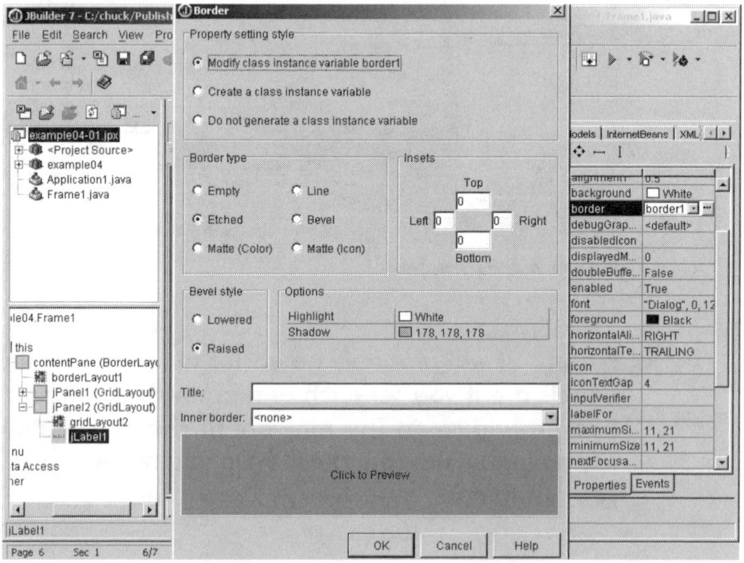

Figure 4.8 Example 4.1

Step 6: We are now going to add a few buttons to this display. The buttons on the panel in the East side of the screen are going to contain the function buttons for our calculator; therefore, we will make an array of buttons called btnfunction.

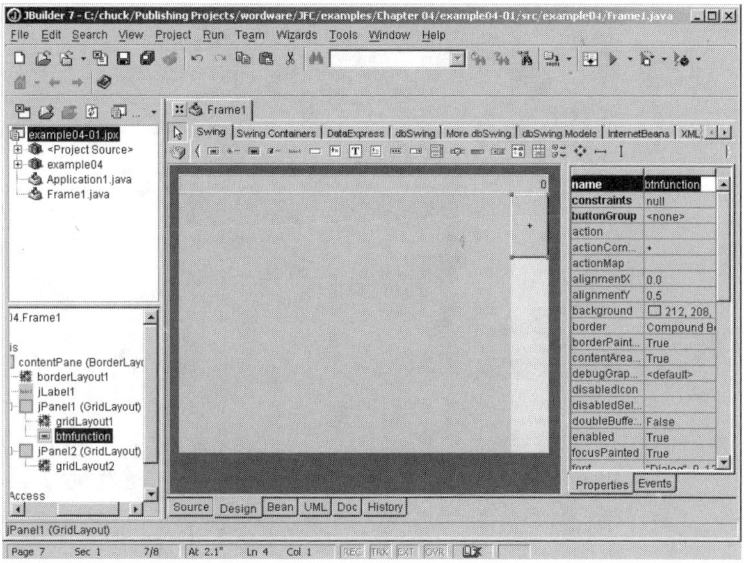

Figure 4.9 Calculator buttons

Note: You can simply right-click on the first button, choose Copy, and then paste it four times. Then simply change the captions as you see here.

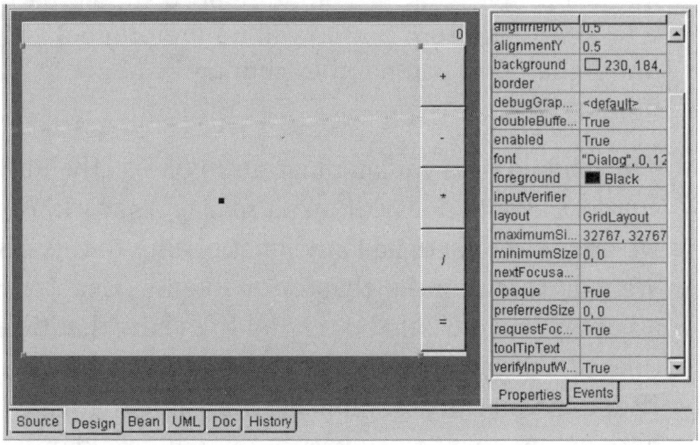

Figure 4.10 Calculator buttons 2

To add the buttons to the Center panel, you will do much the same thing. Start with a button named btnnumber and then create an array. Then you can change the captions, as you see in this image:

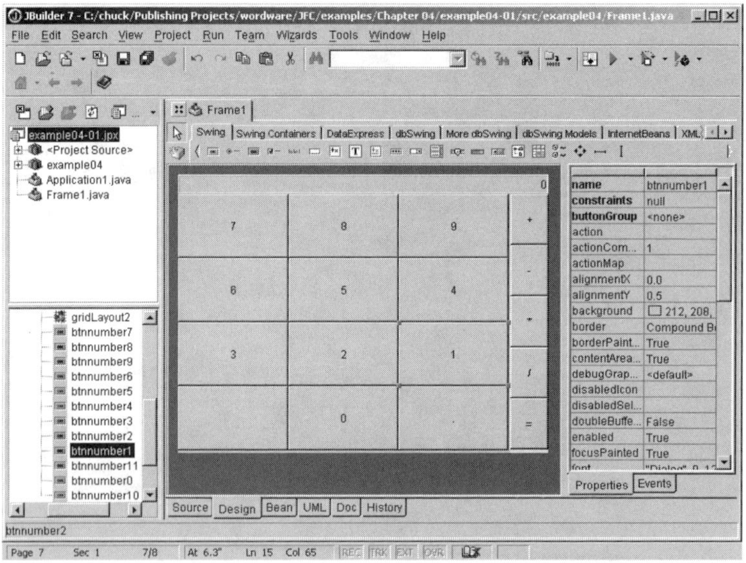

Figure 4.11 Number buttons

Warning: You are going to have to move the buttons around until the number button matches the text field. In other words, btnnumber1 must be the button with the text property of "1". Btnnumber10 should be the "." button. The zero button will be the original bnnumber, and you need to change its name to btnnumber0.

This should give you an illustration of exactly how the BorderLayout and GridLayout managers work. At this point, we are not going to add any functionality to this calculator. We will do that in the chapter on events (Chapter 6), since all of that code would be related to events that take place (like pressing a button). For those readers not using JBuilder, you can accomplish everything that has been done here by opening your favorite text editor and entering the code you see here:

```
package example04;
import java.awt.*;
import java.awt.event.*;
import javax.swing.*;
import javax.swing.border.*;
public class Frame1 extends Jframe
 {
  private JPanel contentPane;
  private BorderLayout borderLayout1 = new BorderLayout();
  private Border border1;
  private JLabel jLabel1 = new JLabel();
  private JPanel jPanel1 = new JPanel();
  private JPanel jPanel2 = new JPanel();
  private JButton btnfunction = new JButton();
  private GridLayout gridLayout1 = new GridLayout(5,1);
  private GridLayout gridLayout2 = new GridLayout(4,3);
  private JButton btnfunction1 = new JButton();
  private JButton btnfunction2 = new JButton();
  private JButton btnfunction3 = new JButton();
  private JButton btnfunction4 = new JButton();
  private JToggleButton btnnumber0 = new JToggleButton();
  private JToggleButton btnnumber1 = new JToggleButton();
  private JToggleButton btnnumber2 = new JToggleButton();
  private JToggleButton btnnumber3 = new JToggleButton();
  private JToggleButton btnnumber4 = new JToggleButton();
  private JToggleButton btnnumber5 = new JToggleButton();
  private JToggleButton btnnumber6 = new JToggleButton();
  private JToggleButton btnnumber7 = new JToggleButton();
  private JToggleButton btnnumber8 = new JToggleButton();
  private JToggleButton btnnumber9 = new JToggleButton();
  private JToggleButton btnnumber10 = new JToggleButton();
  private JToggleButton btnnumber11 = new JToggleButton();
  //Construct the frame
  public Frame1()
 {
    enableEvents(AWTEvent.WINDOW_EVENT_MASK);
    try
  {
      jbInit();
    }
    catch(Exception e)
   {
      e.printStackTrace();
    }
  }
```

```
//Component initialization
private void jbInit() throws Exception
{
  contentPane = (JPanel) this.getContentPane();
  border1 = new EtchedBorder(EtchedBorder.RAISED,
      Color.white,new Color(178, 178, 178));
  contentPane.setLayout(borderLayout1);
  this.setSize(new Dimension(400, 300));
  this.setTitle("Frame Title");
  jLabel1.setBackground(Color.white);
  jLabel1.setBorder(border1);
  jLabel1.setHorizontalAlignment(SwingConstants.RIGHT);
  jLabel1.setText("0");
  jPanel1.setBackground(new Color(230, 255, 105));
  jPanel1.setLayout(gridLayout1);
  jPanel2.setBackground(new Color(230, 184, 255));
  jPanel2.setLayout(gridLayout2);
  btnfunction.setText("+");
  btnfunction1.setText("-");
  btnfunction2.setText("*");
  btnfunction3.setText("/");
  btnfunction4.setText("=");
  btnnumber0.setText("0");
  btnnumber1.setText("1");
  btnnumber2.setText("2");
  btnnumber3.setText("3");
  btnnumber4.setText("4");
  btnnumber5.setText("5");
  btnnumber6.setText("6");
  btnnumber7.setText("7");
  btnnumber8.setText("8");
  btnnumber10.setText(".");
  btnnumber9.setText("9");
  contentPane.add(jLabel1, BorderLayout.NORTH);
  contentPane.add(jPanel1, BorderLayout.EAST);
  contentPane.add(jPanel2, BorderLayout.CENTER);
  jPanel2.add(btnnumber7, null);
  jPanel2.add(btnnumber8, null);
  jPanel2.add(btnnumber9, null);
  jPanel2.add(btnnumber6, null);
  jPanel2.add(btnnumber5, null);
  jPanel2.add(btnnumber4, null);
  jPanel2.add(btnnumber3, null);
  jPanel2.add(btnnumber2, null);
  jPanel2.add(btnnumber1, null);
```

```
    jPanel2.add(btnnumber11, null);
    jPanel2.add(btnnumber0, null);
    jPanel2.add(btnnumber10, null);
    jPanel1.add(btnfunction, null);
    jPanel1.add(btnfunction1, null);
    jPanel1.add(btnfunction2, null);
    jPanel1.add(btnfunction3, null);
    jPanel1.add(btnfunction4, null);
  }
  //Overridden so we can exit when window is closed
  protected void processWindowEvent(WindowEvent e)
  {
    super.processWindowEvent(e);
    if (e.getID() == WindowEvent.WINDOW_CLOSING) {
      System.exit(0);
    }
  }
}
```

Now I don't doubt that seeing all of this code may seem rather daunting to you. Not to worry — it will all be explained. In fact, the code itself is rather simple; there just happens to be a lot of it. There are really only two sections that comprise the bulk of the code. The first is at the beginning of the Frame class. At this point, all the components that will be used are declared. Their declarations are much like the instantiation of any other object variable. The next section is the jbInit function. This is where the items are initialized. The dimensions are set and layout managers are associated with specific components. If you examine this code one line at a time, it's really not that complicated. Since we have not yet put any functionality into this program, jbInit is the only real function in the program. We don't have any functions to handle action or manipulate data yet (but you will in Chapter 6!).

XYLayout

The XYLayout manager is useful when you need to have components in a specific and exacting location. With this layout manager, you specify the x and y coordinates of where you wish a component to be placed, thus the name. Let's take a look at an example.

Example 4.2

Step 1: Start a new project and add a standard Application object to it. Do this in exactly the same manner as you did with previous examples.

Step 2: Set the background container's layout manager to **XY.** (If you use the default settings when you add an Application object, a frame is also added and used as a container for other components.)

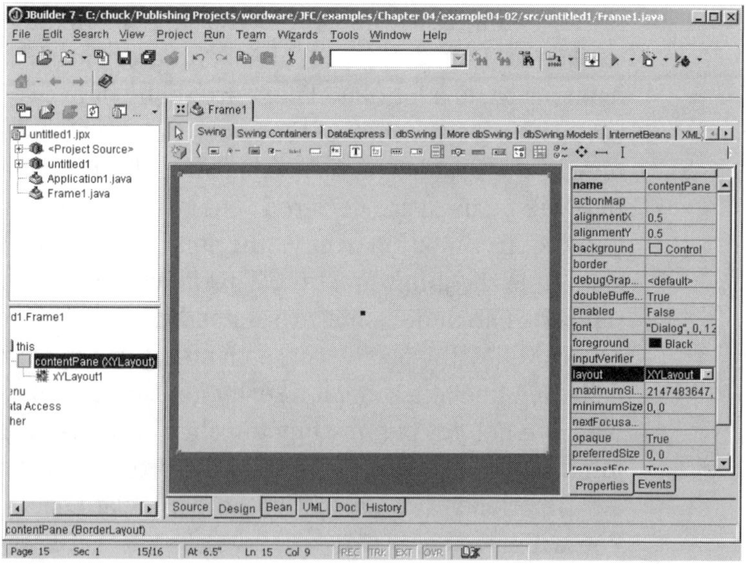

Figure 4.12 XYLayout manager

Step 3: For demonstration purposes, place three different buttons on the screen. Notice that you can move them around anywhere you want them to be.

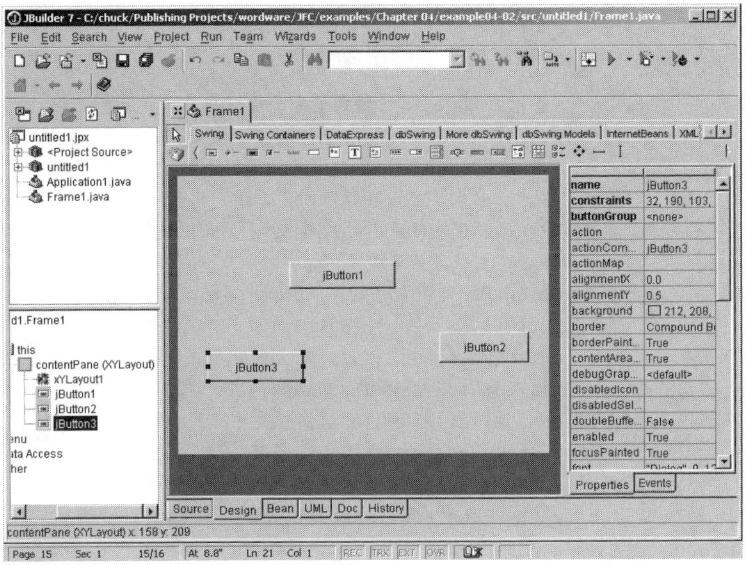

Figure 4.13 XY example

This is why people choose the XYLayout manager — because you can place a component in an exact location.

The following code is generated for you:

```
package untitled1;
import java.awt.*;
import java.awt.event.*;
import javax.swing.*;
import com.borland.jbcl.layout.*;
public class Frame1 extends JFrame
{
  private JPanel contentPane;
  private XYLayout xYLayout1 = new XYLayout();
  private JButton jButton1 = new JButton();
  private JButton jButton2 = new JButton();
  private JButton jButton3 = new JButton();

  //Construct the frame
  public Frame1()
{
```

```
    enableEvents(AWTEvent.WINDOW_EVENT_MASK);
    try
  {
      jbInit();
    }
    catch(Exception e)
  {
      e.printStackTrace();
    }
  }
  //Component initialization
  private void jbInit() throws Exception
 {
    contentPane = (JPanel) this.getContentPane();
    jButton1.setText("jButton1");
    contentPane.setLayout(xYLayout1);
    this.setSize(new Dimension(400, 300));
    this.setTitle("Frame Title");
    jButton2.setText("jButton2");
    jButton3.setText("jButton3");
    contentPane.add(jButton1,  new XYConstraints(120, 93,
         114, 29));
    contentPane.add(jButton2,   new XYConstraints(281, 169,
         97, 33));
    contentPane.add(jButton3,  new XYConstraints(32, 190,
         103, 32));
  }
  //Overridden so we can exit when window is closed
  protected void processWindowEvent(WindowEvent e)
{
    super.processWindowEvent(e);
    if (e.getID() == WindowEvent.WINDOW_CLOSING)
    {
      System.exit(0);
    }
  }
}
```

The only part of this code that is really interesting from our perspective is the code specific to the XYLayout manager. This really consists of two types of expressions, the first of which establishes the use of the XYLayout manager. That is done with the following line of code:

```
contentPane.setLayout(xYLayout1);
```

When other components are added, they are given specific x and y coordinates. They will each be given four numbers. The first two are the x and y coordinates of the upper left-hand corner of the component; then we have the x and y coordinates for the lower right-hand corner of the component.

```
contentPane.add(jButton1,  new XYConstraints(120, 93,
     114, 29));
contentPane.add(jButton2,  new XYConstraints(281, 169,
     97, 33));
contentPane.add(jButton3,  new XYConstraints(32, 190,
     103, 32));
```

The XYLayout manager is yet another example of the advantage of using JBuilder. Not only do you have access to additional layout managers such as this one, but it would be difficult for you to visualize exactly where components are going to be based strictly on x and y coordinates. With JBuilder, you can simply place them in a graphical environment.

FlowLayout

The FlowLayout manager is one of the simplest. Components are simply placed on the screen from left to right until a row is filled, and then the next row is started. This usually does not lend itself to an attractive layout.

VerticalFlowLayout

The VerticalFlowLayout manager is virtually identical to the FlowLayout manager, except components are arranged in vertical columns until a column is filled and then the next column is started. The following example shows both the FlowLayout and the VerticalFlowLayout.

Example 4.3

Step 1: Start a new project and add a standard Application object to it.

Step 2: Leave the background frame with its default border layout.

Step 3: Place a JPanel (remember that you can get this from the Swing Containers tab) to the West end and one to the East end. Recall that altering the background colors of the panels will make it easier for you to remember where you placed them.

Step 4: Set the West panel's layout manager to **VerticalFlow** and the East panel's layout manger to **Flow**. Now add three buttons to each panel. You should see something like what is displayed in Figure 4.14.

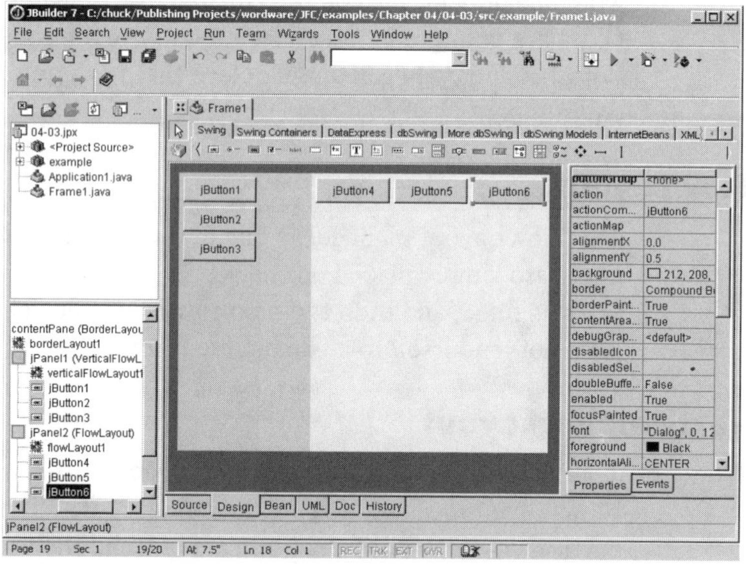

Figure 4.14 VerticalFlowLayout

As you can see, the primary difference is that the FlowLayout is horizontal in orientation, whereas the VerticalFlowLayout manager is, of course, vertical.

If you are not using JBuilder, you can simply enter the following code into your favorite text editor:

```
package example;
import java.awt.*;
import java.awt.event.*;
import javax.swing.*;
import com.borland.jbcl.layout.*;
public class Frame1 extends JFrame
{
  private JPanel contentPane;
  private BorderLayout borderLayout1 = new BorderLayout();
  private JPanel jPanel1 = new JPanel();
  private JPanel jPanel2 = new JPanel();
  private FlowLayout flowLayout1 = new FlowLayout();
  private VerticalFlowLayout verticalFlowLayout1 = new
       VerticalFlowLayout();
  private JButton jButton1 = new JButton();
  private JButton jButton2 = new JButton();
  private JButton jButton3 = new JButton();
  private JButton jButton4 = new JButton();
  private JButton jButton5 = new JButton();
  private JButton jButton6 = new JButton();
  //Construct the frame
  public Frame1()
 {
    enableEvents(AWTEvent.WINDOW_EVENT_MASK);
    try
    {
      jbInit();
    }
    catch(Exception e)
  {
      e.printStackTrace();
    }
  }
  //Component initialization
  private void jbInit() throws Exception
 {
    contentPane = (JPanel) this.getContentPane();
    contentPane.setLayout(borderLayout1);
    this.setSize(new Dimension(400, 300));
    this.setTitle("Frame Title");
    jPanel1.setBackground(new Color(212, 208, 160));
    jPanel1.setLayout(verticalFlowLayout1);
```

```
        jPanel2.setBackground(new Color(212, 255, 200));
        jPanel2.setLayout(flowLayout1);
        jButton1.setText("jButton1");
        jButton2.setText("jButton2");
        jButton3.setText("jButton3");
        jButton4.setText("jButton4");
        jButton5.setText("jButton5");
        jButton6.setText("jButton6");
        contentPane.add(jPanel1, BorderLayout.WEST);
        jPanel1.add(jButton1, null);
        jPanel1.add(jButton2, null);
        jPanel1.add(jButton3, null);
        contentPane.add(jPanel2, BorderLayout.EAST);
        jPanel2.add(jButton4, null);
        jPanel2.add(jButton5, null);
        jPanel2.add(jButton6, null);
      }
      //Overridden so we can exit when window is closed
      protected void processWindowEvent(WindowEvent e)
      {
        super.processWindowEvent(e);
        if (e.getID() == WindowEvent.WINDOW_CLOSING)
         {
          System.exit(0);
        }
      }
    }
```

BoxLayout2

The BoxLayout2 manager inherits directly from java.lang.object, so you don't inherit from AWT or Component classes. This layout manager allows multiple container objects to be arranged either vertically or horizontally. Unlike the FlowLayout and VerticalFlowLayout managers, this layout manager's components do not wrap. That means their positions will not change when the container is resized.

CardLayout

The CardLayout manager allows only one component at a time to be viewed, rather like a deck of cards. You can flip through the components, viewing one component at a time. Usually the components themselves are container components. You change the "cards" by using something like the code you see here:

```
CardLayout cl = (CardLayout)(nameofcontainerwithcard
     layout.getLayout());
cl.show(nameofcontainerwithcardlayout,"nameofcontainer
     youwanttoshow");
```

Let's take a look at an example that illustrates this layout manager.

Example 4.4

Step 1: Start a new project and add an Application object to it, just as you did in previous examples.

Step 2: On the Design tab, set the layout to **Card**.

Step 3: Place two panels on the screen. Make each a different color, and place a button on each. The button and the colors are just so you can tell when we flip through the various components.

Step 4: When you first run the project, you will see something like what is shown in the following figure.

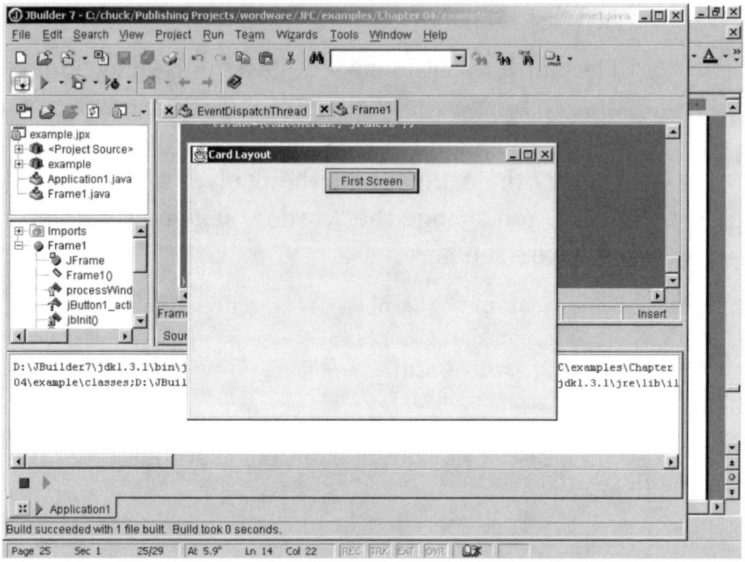

Figure 4.15

After pressing the button, you will see something like what is shown in this figure.

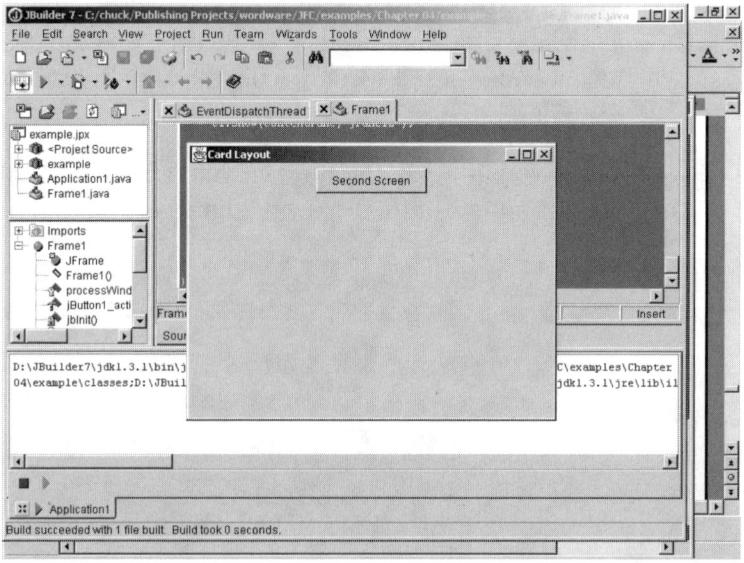

Figure 4.16

For those readers not using JBuilder, simply enter the following code into your favorite text editor and compile it:

```
package example;
import java.awt.*;
import java.awt.event.*;
import javax.swing.*;
public class Frame1 extends JFrame
{
  private JPanel contentPane;
  private CardLayout cardLayout1 = new CardLayout();
  private JPanel jPanel1 = new JPanel();
  private JButton jButton1 = new JButton();
  private JPanel jPanel2 = new JPanel();
  private JButton jButton2 = new JButton();
  private JPanel jPanel3 = new JPanel();
  private JButton jButton3 = new JButton();
  //Construct the frame
  public Frame1()
  {
    enableEvents(AWTEvent.WINDOW_EVENT_MASK);
    try
    {
      jbInit();
    }     // end of try
    catch(Exception e)
    {
      e.printStackTrace();
    }     // end of catch
  }
  //Component initialization
  private void jbInit() throws Exception
  {
    contentPane = (JPanel) this.getContentPane();
    contentPane.setLayout(cardLayout1);
    this.setSize(new Dimension(400, 300));
    this.setTitle("Card Layout");
    jPanel1.setBackground(new Color(212, 255, 211));
    jButton1.setText("First Screen");
    contentPane.add(jPanel1, "jPanel1");
    jPanel1.add(jButton1, null);
    jButton2.setText("Second Screen");
    contentPane.add(jPanel2, "jPanel2");
    jPanel2.add(jButton2, null);
```

```
    jButton1.addActionListener(new java.awt.event
         .ActionListener() {
   public void actionPerformed(ActionEvent e)
   {
        jButton1_actionPerformed(e);
  }     //end of action performed
    });
  }
  //Overridden so we can exit when window is closed
  protected void processWindowEvent(WindowEvent e)
   {
    super.processWindowEvent(e);
    if (e.getID() == WindowEvent.WINDOW_CLOSING)
    {
      System.exit(0);
    }
  }

  void jButton1_actionPerformed(ActionEvent e)
  {
    try
    {
     CardLayout cl = (CardLayout)(contentPane.getLayout());
     cl.show(contentPane,"jPanel2");
    }// end of try
    catch(Exception err)
    {
      err.printStackTrace();
      jButton1.setText(err.toString());
    }// end of catch
  }
}
```

As you can see, the CardLayout manager is rather simple to use. Don't let all the code scare you. Basically, all that is happening is the components are being created, initialized, and associated with the desired containers.

OverlayLayout

The OverlayLayout manager places items on top of each other, much like a CardLayout. However, unlike a CardLayout, the various items can be seen at the same time. With this exception, it behaves very much like the previously described CardLayout manager.

GridbagLayout

A GridbagLayout is virtually identical to a grid layout, except the various rows do not have to have the same number of cells. With this one exception, it is almost identical to the GridLayout manager that you previously used in the calculator example.

PaneLayout

This layout manager allows you to specify the size of a component in relation to its sibling components. Each component is very much like the panes in a window (thus the name); however, the size of each component is determined in relation to the sizes of the other components being displayed. Let's look at an example that illustrates this.

Example 4.5

Step 1: Start a new project and add a new Application object to it, as you have done with all previous examples.

Step 2: Set the layout manager of the container to **Pane**. Then add four buttons. When you run it, you will see something like the following:

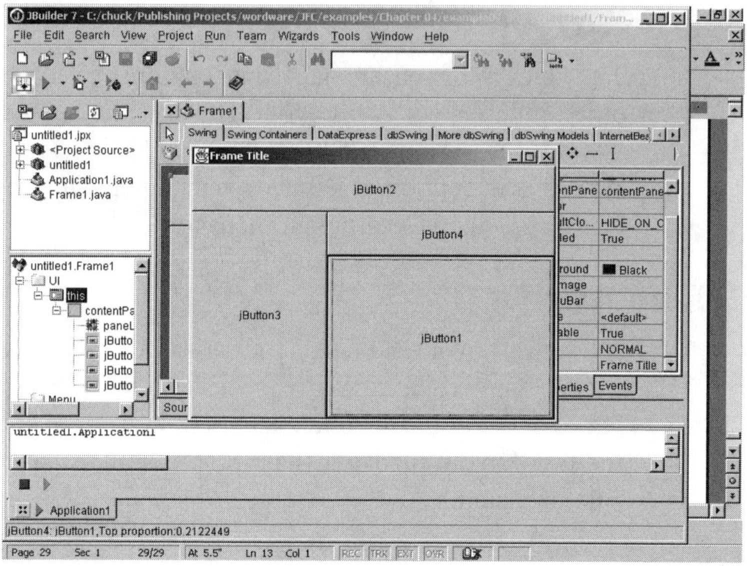

Figure 4.17

Notice how each button is in a separate pane. You can resize the components at design time. The other components will simply resize to match. Whatever arrangement you select, the entire screen will be occupied.

For those readers not using JBuilder, you can, as always, simply enter the following code into your favorite text editor and compile it:

```
package untitled1;
import java.awt.*;
import java.awt.event.*;
import javax.swing.*;
import com.borland.jbcl.layout.*;
public class Frame1 extends JFrame
{
  private JPanel contentPane;
  private PaneLayout paneLayout1 = new PaneLayout();
  private JButton jButton1 = new JButton();
  private JButton jButton2 = new JButton();
  private JButton jButton3 = new JButton();
  private JButton jButton4 = new JButton();
  //Construct the frame
  public Frame1()
  {
```

```
    enableEvents(AWTEvent.WINDOW_EVENT_MASK);
    try
    {
      jbInit();
    }// end of try
    catch(Exception e)
    {
      e.printStackTrace();
    }// end of catch block
  }
  //Component initialization
  private void jbInit() throws Exception
  {
    contentPane = (JPanel) this.getContentPane();
    jButton1.setText("jButton1");
    contentPane.setLayout(paneLayout1);
    this.setSize(new Dimension(400, 300));
    this.setTitle("Frame Title");
    jButton2.setText("jButton2");
    jButton3.setText("jButton3");
    jButton4.setText("jButton4");
    contentPane.add(jButton1,     new PaneConstraints
        ("jButton1", "jButton1", PaneConstraints.ROOT, 0.5f));
    contentPane.add(jButton2,      new PaneConstraints
        ("jButton2", "jButton1", PaneConstraints.TOP,
        0.26333332f));
    contentPane.add(jButton3,      new PaneConstraints
        ("jButton3", "jButton1", PaneConstraints.LEFT,
        0.23000002f));
    contentPane.add(jButton4,      new PaneConstraints
        ("jButton4", "jButton1", PaneConstraints.TOP,
        0.4244898f));
  }
  //Overridden so we can exit when window is closed
  protected void processWindowEvent(WindowEvent e)
  {
    super.processWindowEvent(e);
    if (e.getID() == WindowEvent.WINDOW_CLOSING)
    {
      System.exit(0);
    }
  }
}
```

Look and Feel

As I mentioned at the beginning of this chapter, you can right-click on a component and select its look and feel. This setting is designed to help you make a component's visual interface conform to the standards of a given operating system. The three choices are Metallic, Windows, and CDE/Motif, as shown here:

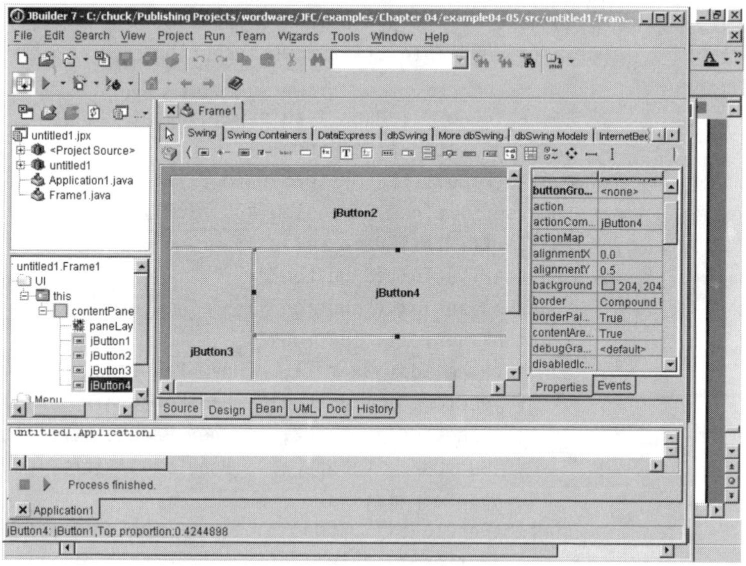

Figure 4.18 Metallic

Setting the look and feel of your components can give them a particular appearance that can make them seem more congruous with a given target operating system.

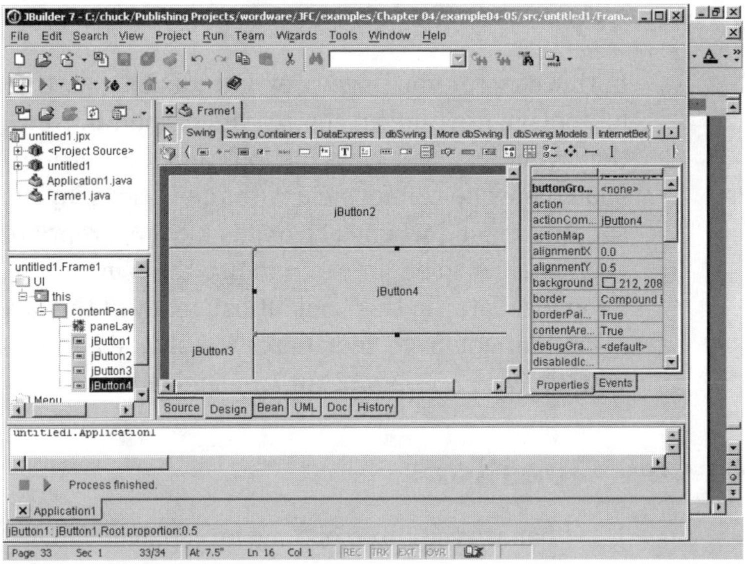

Figure 4.19 Windows

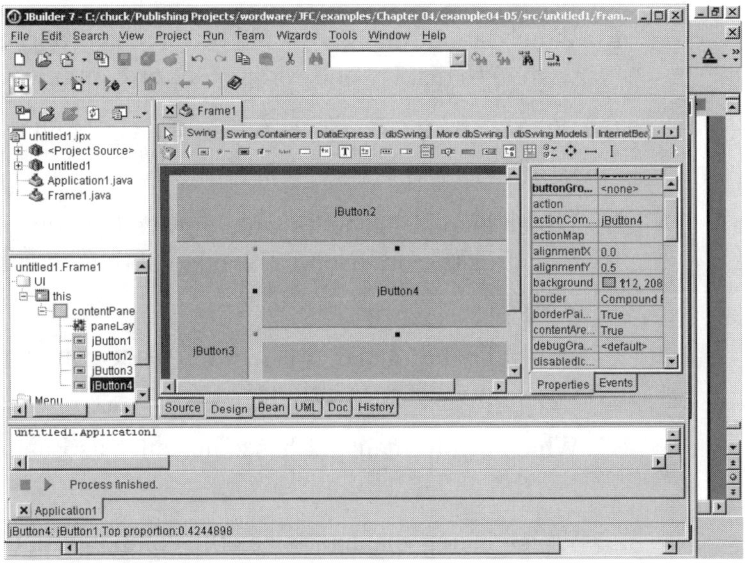

Figure 4.20 CDE/Motif

Summary

In this chapter you have been introduced to two very powerful tools in creating an appropriate graphical user interface: the layout managers and the look and feel setting. You should now be comfortable with the various layout managers and understand when each one is most appropriately used. You should also be prepared to use them in various settings. Examples later in this book utilize many of the layout managers that you have seen here. You should also be familiar with the various options for look and feel.

Review Questions

1. What are the three options for look and feel?
2. How many layout mangers are there in AWT?
3. How many layout mangers are there in JFC?
4. Which layout manger would be most appropriate if you wished to display one component or container at a time?
5. What is the difference between the Grid and the Gridbag?
6. Which layout managers simply place the components one after the other until the edge of the container is reached?
7. Which layout manager is used to place components in an exact coordinate position?
8. Which layout manager has zones such as East and North?
9. Which layout manager sizes the components in relation to the size of the other components on the container?
10. List five of the layout managers found in JFC.

Chapter 5

Container Components

This chapter covers the following:

- JPanel
- JTabbed Pane
- JScroll Pane
- JSplit Pane
- JBox

Introduction

In the last chapter you were introduced to layout managers. Layout managers are applied to various container components (like the frame and the panel). These containers were presented to you, quite briefly, with no real explanation of their function and use. This chapter endeavors to rectify that situation. Containers are much like any other component. They are simply Java classes with methods, properties, etc. Container components are simply components whose purpose is to contain or hold other components. There are several reasons to do this, the most obvious being to organize components in logical groupings. Another reason would be to arrange other components in a specific format by working with specific layout managers, such as the CardLayout manager that you saw in the last chapter. It should also be pointed out that all graphical components *must* be on some container component.

There are a number of container components that you can use in your applications and applets. If you are using JBuilder, you can find these on the second tab of the design screen marked Swing Containers, shown in Figure 5.1.

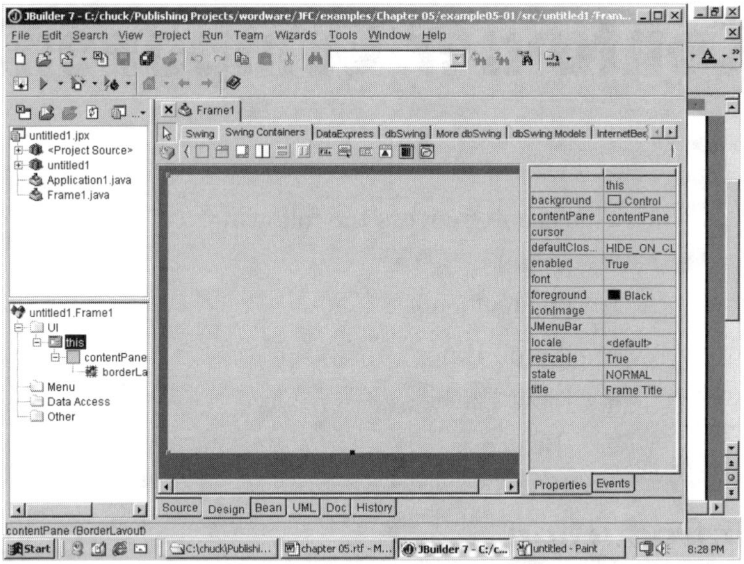

Figure 5.1 Container components

There are, in fact, six container components available to you in JFC. The tab that you see in the image shows more than six components. However, the other six components are not simply containers, but rather they support other functionality, such as drop-down menus and toolbars. Those components are dealt with in a subsequent chapter. Each of the six container components and their basic purpose are summarized in Table 5.1.

Table 5.1 Container components

Container	Purpose
JPanel	This is a good general-purpose lightweight component that is simply used to contain other components. You will see this component frequently.
JTabbedPane	This component allows you to tab between several containers.

Container	Purpose
JScrollPane	This component simply provides a scrollable view of a component.
JSplitPane	This container provides a pane that is split, either vertically or horizontally, and the split can be moved.
JBox (both vertical and horizontal)	This is a basic lightweight container that utilizes the BoxLayout manager.

The JPanel is certainly the most commonly encountered container component and is often used as a simple general-purpose container. In fact, it was used in the previous chapter. The three variations of the Pane component clearly have their own specialized purposes. Perhaps the most specialized and least frequently encountered containers are the two variations of the JBox container.

JPanel

As previously mentioned, this component is the most commonly used container. For that reason, it bears much closer scrutiny than the other container components. At first glance, it is relatively easy to use. You simply place one on your designer screen, set its layout manager, and then place components on it. If you are not using JBuilder, then just declare an instance of it, set its layout manager, and add components to it. Either way, its use is rather straightforward. This is primarily due to the fact that its interface is uncluttered. It has no panes, splits, or tabs to complicate matters. This component, like many of the containers, inherits from the JComponent class. The JPanel uses the FlowLayout manager by default, but you can set it to use any layout manager you wish.

You saw this component used extensively in the last chapter and should have a good idea of how it is used. The JPanel component, like all components, has a plethora of methods and properties. However, many are either not frequently used or more appropriately explained in a later chapter. Those properties and methods that are commonly used are summarized in the following table.

Table 5.2 JPanel properties and methods

Property/Method	Purpose
layout	As you saw in the previous chapter, this property allows you to choose the layout manager for any container.
background	This property was shown in Chapter 3. It allows you to change the background color.
border	This property allows you to change the border of the panel.
tooltipText	This is a property that many components have. It allows you to set a pop-up tooltip for the component.
add	This is a method that all containers have and allows you to add components to the container.
isShowing	This property is also common to most components, and it returns true if the component is currently showing.
remove	This method is common to all containers and allows you to remove components from the container.

Most of these methods and properties can be accessed via the Properties window in JBuilder, or you can access them directly in code. In addition to the methods shown, there are a few different ways to construct a JPanel. The various constructors available for this class are shown in Table 5.3.

Table 5.3 JPanel constructors

Constructor	Purpose
JPanel()	This constructor will create a JPanel with a double buffer and the default FlowLayout.
JPanel(boolean isDoubleBuffered)	This will create a JPanel with the default FlowLayout and the specified buffering strategy.
JPanel(LayoutManager layout)	This constructor will create a JPanel with the specified layout manager. This is probably the most commonly used constructor with this class.
JPanel(LayoutManager layout, boolean isDoubleBuffered)	This constructor creates a JPanel with the specified layout manager and buffering strategy.

As you have already seen in the previous chapter, the Panel component is a relatively easy-to-use, basic all-purpose container. Most of its methods are also relatively straightforward and easy to use. Since you have already seen this container, and you indeed see it used frequently throughout this book, it would be redundant to provide an additional full-length example here.

JTabbedPane

As the name implies, the JTabbedPane container is designed to present items to the user in a series of tabs. Like most containers, this class inherits directly from JComponent. It is frequently quite convenient to provide users with a series of tabs, each of which contains a set of logically grouped components. For example, if you wish to write an application to track employees, you might have one tab with personal information, another with current job position information, and another with job history. I'm sure you can imagine even more situations in which a tabbed display would be convenient for the user.

This container simply allows the user to select which set of components they might wish to view by clicking on a particular tab. This container is actually rather easy to use, although it has some particular properties and methods of which you should be aware. Those properties and methods are listed in the following table.

Table 5.4 JTabbedPane properties and methods

Property/Method	Purpose
tabPlacement	This property determines where to place the tabs.
model	This property displays the currently selected model.
Componentadd(Component component)	This method is used to add a component with a tab title defaulting to the name of the component.

Property/Method	Purpose
Componentadd(Component component, int index)	This method adds a component at the specified tab index with a tab title defaulting to the name of the component.
void add(Component component, Object constraints)	This method is used to add a component to the tabbed pane.
void add(Component component, Object constraints, int index)	This method will add a component at the specified tab index.
component add(String title, Component component)	This method is used to add a component with the specified tab title.
void addTab(String title, Icon icon, Component component)	This method will add a component represented by a title and/or icon, either of which can be null.
addTab(String title, Component component)	This method simply adds a tab represented by a title and no icon.
addTab(String title, Icon icon, Component component, String tip)	This method adds a tab as well as an icon and a tooltip.
getTabCount	This method returns the current number of tabs.
getTitleAt(int index)	The method returns the title for a tab located at the index that you pass to it.
remove(Component component)	This method will remove a specific component from the container.
remove(int index)	This method will remove the tab at the index you pass to it.
removeall()	This method removes all tabs.

You may have noticed a lot of add methods. This is simply because there are a variety of ways in which you might add a component to the JTabbedPane. Swing tries to accommodate as many of those methods as possible. Even the list provided here is not comprehensive; it simply contains the main add component methods. This table is not an exhaustive list, nor is it meant to be. However, it should provide you with a summary of some of the more commonly used properties and methods of the JTabbedPane class. The next step is obviously to walk you through an example that illustrates the various uses of the JTabbedPane class.

Example 5.1

Step 1: Begin a project and add a new application to it, as you have done in all the previous examples.

Step 2: Add the tabbed pane container to the Center section of the application's frame container. You will also need to add two tabs to the tabbed pane container. You won't see the frames until they have some component on them, and it's easiest to do that in code. So go to the Code tab and add the following code to the jbInit() function:

```
JButton mybutton = new JButton("Click Me");
JButton mybutton2 = new JButton("No Click Me");
jTabbedPanel.addTab("tab 1",mybutton);
jTabbedPanel.addTab("tab 2",mybutton2);
```

Now you should be able to go back to the Design tab and see something like what is shown in Figure 5.2.

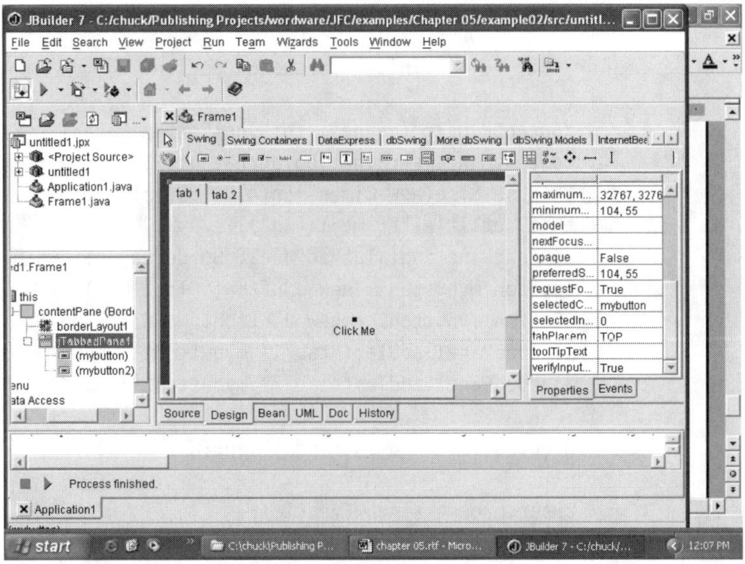

Figure 5.2 The tabbed pane

For those of you not using JBuilder, you can simply type the following code into your favorite text editor and compile it:

```
package untitled1;
import java.awt.*;
import java.awt.event.*;
import javax.swing.*;
public class Frame1 extends JFrame
{
  private JPanel contentPane;
  private BorderLayout borderLayout1 = new BorderLayout();
  private JTabbedPane jTabbedPane1 = new JTabbedPane();
  //Construct the frame
  public Frame1()
  {
    enableEvents(AWTEvent.WINDOW_EVENT_MASK);
    try
    {
      jbInit();
    }
    catch(Exception e)
    {
      e.printStackTrace();
    }
  }
  private void jbInit() throws Exception
  {
    contentPane = (JPanel) this.getContentPane();
    contentPane.setLayout(borderLayout1);
    this.setSize(new Dimension(400, 300));
    this.setTitle("Frame Title");
    contentPane.add(jTabbedPane1, BorderLayout.CENTER);
    JButton mybutton = new JButton("Click Me");
    JButton mybutton2 = new JButton("No Click Me");
    jTabbedPane1.addTab("tab 1",mybutton);
    jTabbedPane1.addTab("tab 2",mybutton2);
  }
  protected void processWindowEvent(WindowEvent e)
  {
    super.processWindowEvent(e);
    if (e.getID() == WindowEvent.WINDOW_CLOSING)
    {
      System.exit(0);
    }
  }
}
```

Step 3: Run the program. You should see images much like what is depicted in Figures 5.3 and 5.4.

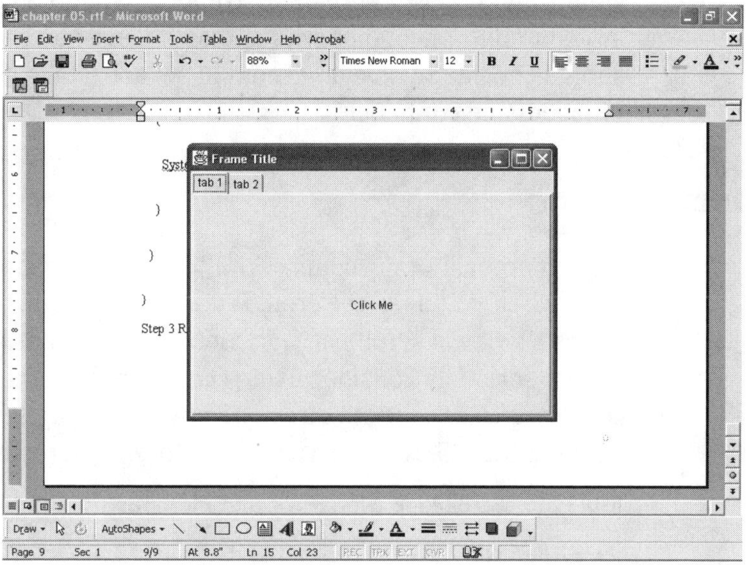

Figure 5.3 First tab

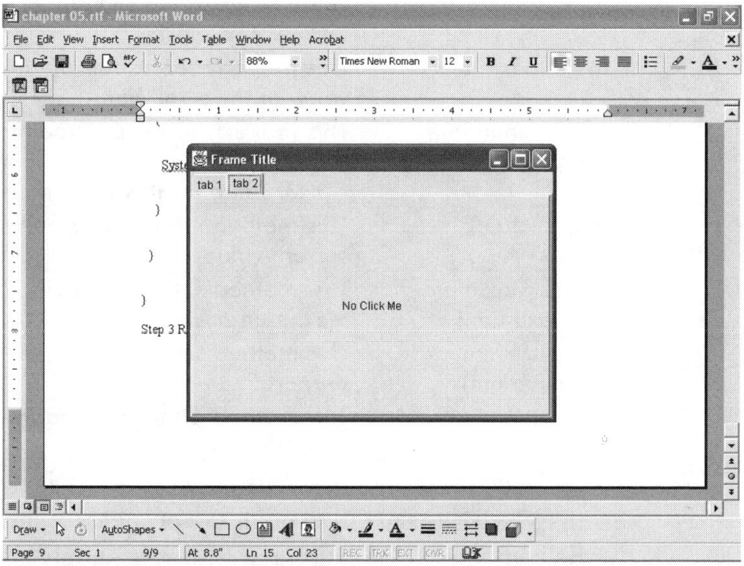

Figure 5.4 Second tab

As you can see, the tabbed pane allows you to place more components on an individual screen than you normally would, and this is its greatest strength. When you have a large number of components to display on a screen, you should consider displaying them in separate tabs using the JTabbedPane container.

JScrollPane

As you probably can surmise, the JScrollPane container is used when you need to scroll. If you feel that your container needs a vertical scroll bar, horizontal scroll bar, or both, you should seriously consider using the JScrollPane. Again, this container class inherits directly from java.swing.JComponent. Table 5.5 summarizes many of the methods.

Table 5.5 JScrollPane properties and methods

Property/Method	Purpose
int getBlockIncrement (int direction)	This method returns an integer, which is the amount to change the scroll bar's value by when the container receives an up/down request.
int getMaximum()	This property represents the maximum value of the scroll bar.
int getMinimum()	This property represents the minimum value supported by the scroll bar. The typical value for this property is zero.
int getValue()	This method returns the scroll bar's current value.
void setMaximum (int maximum)	This method sets the container's maximum property.
void setMinimum (int minimum)	This method sets the container's minimum property.
void setValue(int value)	This method is the scroll bar's value.

As with the other tables in this book, this one is not meant as an exhaustive coverage of all the properties and methods of the container in question but rather is simply a summary of the most commonly used methods and properties. You can also choose whether the horizontal and vertical scroll bars should always appear, appear when needed, or never appear.

In JBuilder this is quite simply a matter of setting a property, as you can see in Figure 5.5.

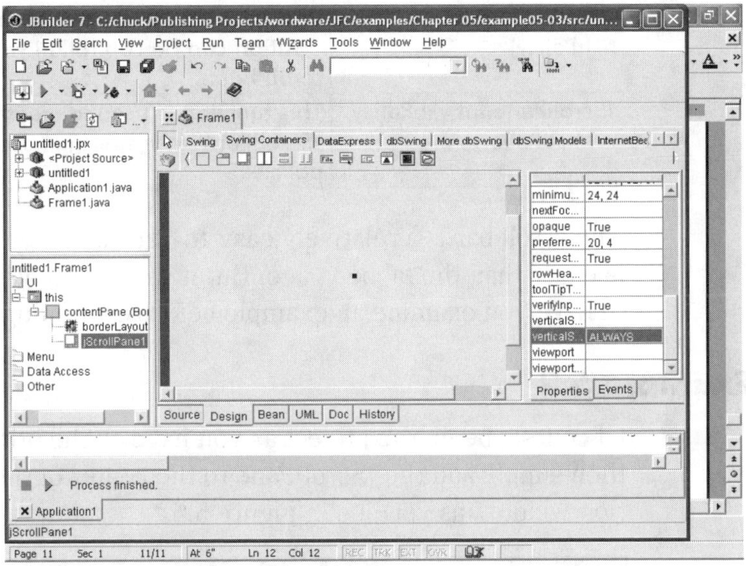

Figure 5.5 Displaying scroll bars

As with all other Java classes, the JScrollPane has several different constructors from which to choose. Table 5.6 lists the various constructors and summarizes each one's purpose.

Table 5.6 JScrollPane constructors

Constructor	Purpose
JScrollPane()	This constructor is the simplest and just creates an empty JScrollPane where both horizontal and vertical scroll bars appear when needed.
JScrollPane (Component view)	This constructor is used to create a JScrollPane that displays the contents of the specified component, where both horizontal and vertical scroll bars appear whenever the component's contents are larger than the view.

Constructor	Purpose
JScrollPane (Component view, int vsbPolicy, int hsbPolicy)	This constructor will create a JScrollPane that displays the view component in a viewport whose view position can be controlled with a pair of scroll bars.
JScrollPane(int vsbPolicy, int hsbPolicy)	This function is used to create an empty JScrollPane with specified scroll bar policies.

The scroll bar is a relatively easy-to-use container; in fact, it is easer than the tabbed pane. But it would still be prudent to have you examine an example before continuing on.

Example 5.2

Step 1: Of course, begin the project as you have all the others. You then simply add the JScrollPane to the center of the application window, as you see in Figure 5.6.

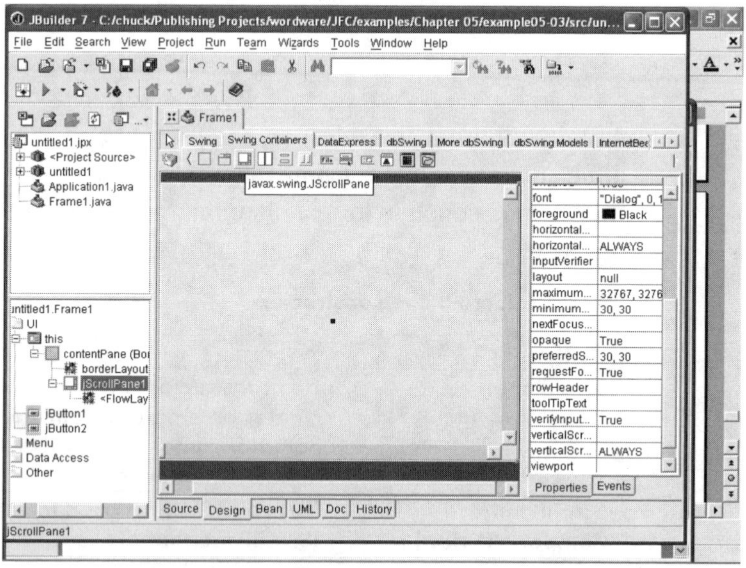

Figure 5.6 Placing the scroll pane

Step 2: Now we will need a few components on the scroll pane in order to see it scrolling when we run it. So I suggest placing two buttons at different places on the container, as you see in Figure 5.7.

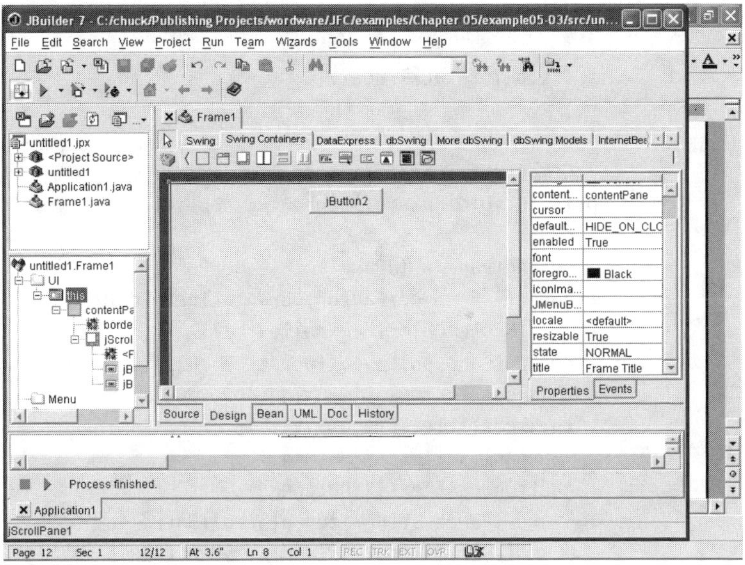

Figure 5.7 Placing buttons on the scroll pane

You will end up with source code much like what you see here:

```
package untitled1;
import java.awt.*;
import java.awt.event.*;
import javax.swing.*;
import javax.swing.border.*;
public class Frame1 extends JFrame
{
  private JPanel contentPane;
  private BorderLayout borderLayout1 = new BorderLayout();
  private JButton jButton1 = new JButton();
  private JScrollPane jScrollPane1 = new JScrollPane();
  private JButton jButton2 = new JButton();
  private Border border1;
  //Construct the frame
  public Frame1()
  {
    enableEvents(AWTEvent.WINDOW_EVENT_MASK);
    try
```

```
    {
      jbInit();
    }
    catch(Exception e)
    {
      e.printStackTrace();
    }
  }
  //Component initialization
  private void jbInit() throws Exception
  {
    contentPane = (JPanel) this.getContentPane();
    border1 = BorderFactory.createLineBorder
        (SystemColor.controlText,1);
    contentPane.setLayout(borderLayout1);
    this.setSize(new Dimension(400, 300));
    this.setTitle("Frame Title");
    jButton1.setText("jButton1");
    jButton2.setText("jButton2");
    jScrollPane1.setHorizontalScrollBarPolicy
         (JScrollPane.HORIZONTAL_SCROLLBAR_ALWAYS);
    jScrollPane1.setVerticalScrollBarPolicy
         (JScrollPane.VERTICAL_SCROLLBAR_ALWAYS);
    jScrollPane1.setViewportBorder(border1);
    contentPane.add(jScrollPane1, BorderLayout.CENTER);
    jScrollPane1.setLayout(new FlowLayout());
    jScrollPane1.getViewport().add(jButton1,null);
    jScrollPane1.getViewport().add(jButton2, null);
  }
  protected void processWindowEvent(WindowEvent e)
  {
    super.processWindowEvent(e);
    if (e.getID() == WindowEvent.WINDOW_CLOSING)
    {
      System.exit(0);
    }
  }
}
```

Note: By this time, you should notice some very close correlations between what happens in the Properties box in JBuilder and the code that is generated for you. For example, when you select the Vertical Scroll Bar property and set it to Always, the following code is generated:

```
jScrollPane1.setVerticalScrollBarPolicy(JScrollPane
     .VERTICAL_SCROLLBAR_ALWAYS);
```

This illustrates the essence of what makes JBuilder such a valuable tool for any Java development. It will generate the Java code for you while you concentrate on the actual problem you are trying to solve and making a visually appealing graphical user interface.

JSplitPane

As the name suggests, this particular container allows you to split the container into two different regions, both of which are resizable. I personally find this configuration to be aesthetically pleasing in many situations, so I use this container frequently. Like the other container classes mentioned in this chapter, this class inherits directly from java.swing.JComponent. The following table summarizes its major properties and methods.

Table 5.7 JSplitPane methods and properties

Method/Property	Purpose
Divider_size	This property sets the size of the divider that splits the two panes. The default is 5.
Divider_location	This property sets the location of the divider that splits the two panes.
StringDIVIDER	This method is used to add a component that will represent the divider.
Int HORIZONTAL_SPLIT	Horizontal split indicates that the division of the panes is horizontal.
Int VERTICAL_SPLIT	This indicates that the panes are split vertically.
String RIGHT	This method is used to add a component to the right of the other components.
String BOTTOM	This method is used to add a component below the other components.
String TOP	This method is used to add a component above the other component.

This list of methods and properties is not comprehensive, but it does cover the essential methods and properties that you will need in order to effectively utilize the JSplitPane. Table 5.8 summarizes the constructors for this particular class.

Table 5.8 JSplitPane constructors

Constructor	Purpose
JSplitPane()	This constructor creates a JSplitPane configured to arrange the child components side by side horizontally, using two buttons for the components.
JSplitPane(int newOrientation)	This constructor builds a JSplitPane configured with the specified orientation and no continuous layout.
JSplitPane(int newOrientation, boolean newContinuousLayout)	This constructor will create a JSplitPane with the specified orientation and a continuous layout.
JSplitPane(int newOrientation, boolean newContinuousLayout, Component newLeftComponent, Component newRight-Component)	This constructor will create a JSplitPane with the specified orientation and the specified components.
JSplitPane(int newOrientation, Component newLeftComponent, Component newRight-Component)	This constructor will create a JSplitPane with the specified orientation and the specified components that do not do continuous redrawing.

This diverse set of constructors allows you, the programmer, to select the type of split pane you wish to use and how it will be displayed and utilized. This component is quite simple to use (actually easier than the tabbed pane), so let's take a look at an example using this component.

Example 5.3

Step 1: You will need to start a new project. You will also need to add a new application.

Step 2: Place the split pane container on the application's frame. You should see something much like what is depicted in Figure 5.8.

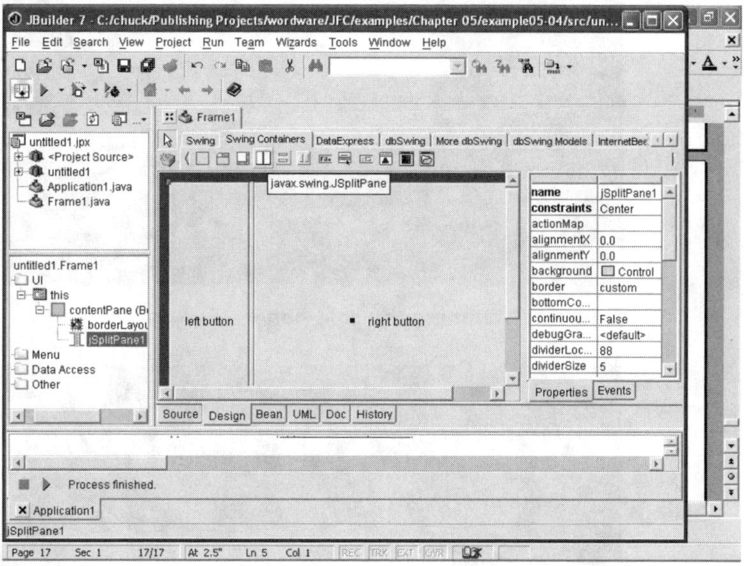

Figure 5.8 The split pane

Notice that you already have two panes and each is labeled. When you run the application as it is now, you can easily move the panes back and forth, resizing them. This is clearly shown in Figures 5.9 and 5.10.

Figure 5.9 Running the split pane

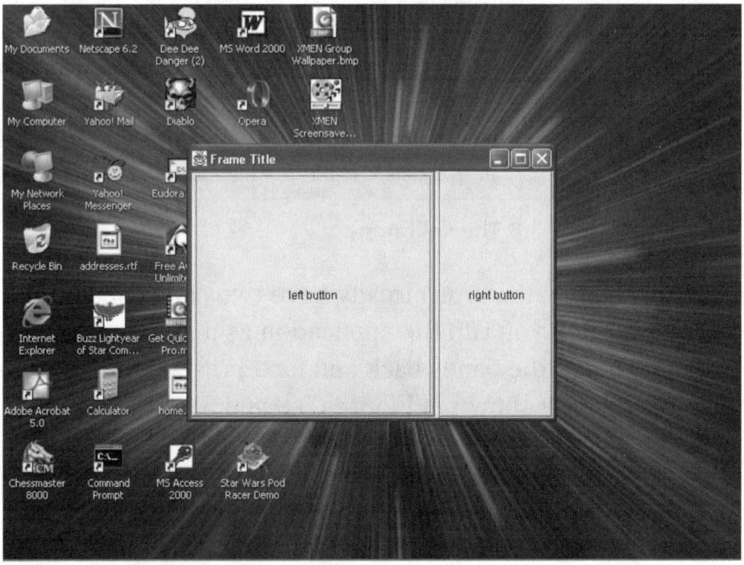

Figure 5.10 Resizing the split pane

The entire purpose of this container component is to provide you with a resizable container that has separate panes. You can even place components on the different panes, and they will be moved with the pane.

For those of you not using JBuilder and having to do all this by hand, here is the source code:

```
package untitled1;
import java.awt.*;
import java.awt.event.*;
import javax.swing.*;
public class Frame1 extends JFrame
{
  private JPanel contentPane;
  private BorderLayout borderLayout1 = new BorderLayout();
  private JSplitPane jSplitPane1 = new JSplitPane();

  //Construct the frame
  public Frame1()
  {
    enableEvents(AWTEvent.WINDOW_EVENT_MASK);
    try
    {
      jbInit();
    }
    catch(Exception e)
    {
      e.printStackTrace();
    }
  }
  //Component initialization
  private void jbInit() throws Exception
  {
    contentPane = (JPanel) this.getContentPane();
    contentPane.setLayout(borderLayout1);
    this.setSize(new Dimension(400, 300));
    this.setTitle("Frame Title");
    contentPane.add(jSplitPane1, BorderLayout.CENTER);
  }
  //Overridden so we can exit when window is closed
  protected void processWindowEvent(WindowEvent e)
  {
    super.processWindowEvent(e);
    if (e.getID() == WindowEvent.WINDOW_CLOSING)
    {
      System.exit(0);
    }
  }
}
```

As you can see, this particular container is rather interesting. Splitting the display area into two separate and sizable (at least relative to each other) segments is one way to give the user more control over the focus area. This container can be a great enhancement to the user friendliness of your graphical interface.

JBox

On your JBuilder Swing Containers toolbar there are actually two JBox containers, one vertical and one horizontal. As the name suggests, this container uses the box layout as its default layout manager. Frankly, I do not see this particular container used very much in the code that I have examined during my career. The container is sometimes used to create invisible areas that affect the overall layout. Essentially, if you need a given area of your GUI to remain blank, you might wish to consider the JBox container. Its most commonly used methods are summarized in Table 5.9.

Table 5.9 JBox methods

Method	Purpose
component createGlue()	This method creates an invisible component that can be useful in a box whose visible components have a maximum width (for a horizontal box) or height (for a vertical box). This component is essentially a "glue" for the other components.
Box createHorizontalBox()	This method creates a box that displays its components from left to right.
component createHorizontalGlue()	This method creates a horizontal glue component.
component createHorizontalStrut (int width)	This method creates an invisible, fixed-width component.
Box createVerticalBox()	This method creates a box that displays its components from top to bottom.
component createRigid-Area(Dimension d)	This method creates an invisible component that's always the specified size.

As I mentioned earlier, this particular container is not used as frequently as the others.

Summary

This chapter has given you a solid coverage of the containers available to you in Swing. Containers play a vital role in creating graphical user interfaces. Choosing the proper container for a given situation is absolutely vital. You will only be able to choose the proper container if you understand the various containers, their purpose, and their usage. If you worked through the examples in this chapter, you should have the requisite knowledge to effectively use Swing containers. If you did not, please reread the chapter and try the examples again.

Review Questions

1. Name the Swing containers.
2. Which container is used most often?
3. What property would you set to make sure your scroll bar pane always displayes a vertical scroll bar?
4. Can you change the size of the divider in a split pane?
5. Which container would be used to create placeholders and connections between components?
6. How many versions of the JBox container does JBuilder have?
7. What method would you use to move the scroll bar?

Chapter 6

Handling Events

This chapter covers the following:

- Events
- Listeners
- Applying events
- Anonymous inner class adapters

Introduction

Hopefully in the preceding chapters you have noticed that events are frequently used to respond to actions by the user. You probably have an intuitive idea of what an event is, but a more formal definition might prove useful. An *event* is an action that is initiated by the user, another program, or another function. Such actions would include clicking the mouse, pressing a key, or even simply moving a mouse into a given area. When an action is initiated, an event is generated and sent to any available event handlers. These event handlers can then respond to the event appropriately. Event handlers are specialized classes designed to handle specific events.

Event handling with Swing and JFC is based on the earlier AWT event handling model. There are many similarities between the two approaches. If you are familiar with AWT event handling, you will probably need only a cursory examination of this chapter. If you do not have previous experience with AWT event handling, you may require a more thorough study of the material presented here.

Events

An event is anything that might occur. From a user's point of view, an event is any action such as clicking a button or moving a mouse over a given component. From a programmer's point of view, each event is a specialized class that is designed for that event. All events have as their root class the java.awt.AWTEvent class. AWTEvent is then subclassed to a variety of specific event classes, such as ActionEvent, WindowEvent, ItemEvent, KeyEvent, MouseEvent, etc. This means that each of the specific events will share a certain number of methods and properties.

The direct subclasses of AWTEvent and their purpose are summarized in Table 6.1.

Table 6.1 Subclasses of AWTEvent

Class	Purpose
ActionEvent	This is an event that indicates a component-defined action occurred. This event is generated by a component when a component-specific action occurrs, such as clicking a button. The event is then passed to every Action-Listener object that registered to receive such events using the component's addAction-Listener method.
AdjustmentEvent	The adjustment event emitted by adjustable objects is fired when one of these objects is adjusted.
AncestorEvent	This is an event reported to a child component that originated from an ancestor in the component hierarchy. In other words, it tells a child component that an event occurred with one of the parent components.
ComponentEvent	This is a low-level event that indicates a component moved, changed size, became visible or invisible, etc. This event is for notification purposes only. The component's action will take place regardless of what you may or may not do with this event.
HierarchyEvent	This event indicates some change to the component hierarchy to which a component belongs.

Class	Purpose
InputMethodEvent	This event fires when text is entered into an appropriate component. Anytime the text changes, for any reason, the input method sends an event.
InternalFrame-Event	InternalFrameEvent is a rather odd event. You will not see it used very frequently. It is an AWTEvent that adds support for JInternalFrame objects as the event source. This class has the same event types as WindowEvent.
InvocationEvent	This event will execute the run() method on a Runnable when dispatched by the AWT event dispatcher thread.
ItemEvent	This event indicates that an item was selected or deselected. You will see this associated frequently with list boxes.
TextEvent	This event indicates that an object's text changed.

Some of these classes are, in turn, parent classes for other events. This is another example of how Java uses object orientation to build specialized classes from a foundation of more general base classes in an ever-growing hierarchical class structure.

Since all events derive from the AWTEvent class, it would be prudent to examine some of its more common and useful methods. These are summarized in Table 6.2.

Table 6.2 AWTEvent methods

Method	Purpose
protected void consume()	This method is used to consume the event in question. Once consumed, an event is destroyed and cannot be propagated any further.
int getID()	This method is used to return the numeric value indicating the event type.
String toString()	This method will return a string representation of this event object.
protected void finalize()	This method is actually called by the garbage collector on an object when garbage collection determines that there are no more references to the object.
protected Boolean isConsumed()	This method will tell you whether or not the event in question has been consumed.

Method	Purpose
String paramString()	This method is used to return a string representing the state of this event.

This class has only two possible constructors. Those constructors are summarized in Table 6.3.

Table 6.3 AWTEvent constructors

Constructor	Purpose
AWTEvent(Event event)	This constructor is used to create an AWTEvent object from the parameters of a 1.0-style event.
AWTEvent(Object source, int id)	This constructor will create an AWTEvent object with the specified source object and type.

An understanding of the AWTEvent class and its direct subclasses can be instrumental in understanding how events in general work. It is not necessary that you memorize each of these tables or this chapter. It is, however, a good idea to be familiar with the material.

Listeners

When an event is fired, it is received by one or more listeners that act on the event. A *listener* is just a special class that is designed for the express purpose of listening for a specific event to occur. Event handling is accomplished through the use of listener interfaces, which are defined in the package java.awt.event. In Java there are a number of built-in interfaces as listeners for different types of event handling.

Applying Events

This general knowledge about events, what they are and how they work, is useful but incomplete. What is missing is an overview of how one goes about applying events in a program. The following is an overview of the basic steps for applying events:

1. Decide which GUI component to apply the event to.
2. Implement the appropriate listener interface or interfaces. The appropriate interfaces are those that correspond to that component.
3. Now apply the methods involved in the interface.

These steps would probably be more helpful if you were aware of the common interfaces. Below is a brief example and description of the most common interfaces.

- **Action listener**

  The action listener is associated with a variety of user actions but primarily with the clicking of a button. The function looks like this:

  ```
  public void actionPerformed(ActionEvent e)
  {
        //your code goes here
  }
  ```

- **Item listener**

  This function is called in response to a wide range of item events. For example, selecting an item from a list box will fire this event.

  ```
  public void itemStateChanged(ItemEvent e)
  {
        //your code goes here
  }
  ```

Using events in JBuilder is significantly simplified because JBuilder itself takes care of some of the work for you. JBuilder creates an EventAdapter class for that specific component/event and gives it an appropriate name, which corresponds to that particular component and event. This will occur simply by double-clicking on a particular component. If, for example, you double-click on a button, JBuilder will generate the action listener for you. JBuilder will also create a line of code in the jbInit() method that connects the component's event source through the EventAdapter to your event-handling method. This is accomplished by calling an addListener method of the component. All that's left for you to do is fill in the event-handling method that the action adapter calls when the event occurs.

Anonymous Inner Class Adapters

Anonymous inner classes are also frequently used by Java programmers as adapter classes. JBuilder can also generate these inner class event adapters. Inner classes have several advantages, including:

- The code is generated inline, thereby simplifying the code.
- No separate class is generated.
- The inner class has access to all variables in scope where it is declared, unlike the standard event adapters that have only public and package level access.

The particular types of inner class event adapters that JBuilder generates are known as anonymous adapters. This style of adapter avoids the creation of a separate adapter class. The resulting code is compact and elegant. For example, the following code is generated for a focusGained() event using an anonymous adapter:

```
jButton1.addFocusListener(new java.awt.event.FocusAdapter()
{
  public void focusGained(FocusEvent e)
{
   jButton1_focusGained(e);
  }
}
  void jButton1_focusGained(FocusEvent e)
{
  }
```

Compare this code with the standard adapter code sample shown previously. JBuilder generated that code using a standard adapter class. Both ways of using adapters provide the code to handle focusGained() events, but the anonymous adapter approach is more compact.

Summary

This chapter has introduced you to the concept of events, event listeners, and event handling. Events are the primary way in which you will be able to respond to the user's actions. The user's actions will often trigger a specific event. Your event listener will listen for that event to occur in relation to a specific component. Then your event handler will respond to that event. Events and event handling are the core of user interaction. We have seen in this chapter the basic structure of event handlers, adapter classes, and even anonymous inner adapter classes.

Review Questions

1. From a user's perspective, what is an event?
2. What is an event handler?
3. What is the parent class of all event classes?
4. List four common event classes.
5. What is a listener?
6. What are three advantages to using inner class adapters?
7. How many constructors are there for the AWTEvent class?

Chapter 7

User Choices

This chapter covers the following:

- JRadioButton
- JToggleButton
- JCheckBox
- JComboBox
- JList
- JSlider

Introduction

So far, this book has discussed issues regarding the structure of Swing components, containers, altering appearance, and even handling complex event structures. However, we have not yet addressed one of the core issues in designing graphical user interfaces. The entire reason why we, as programmers, develop rich GUI interfaces is to facilitate increased user interaction. We wish to give the user a feeling of being in control and able to make choices. With that in mind, it would seem self-evident that an integral part of any GUI toolkit, be it AWT, Swing, or some other approach, would be to allow the user to make choices. The Java Foundation Classes provide a number of visual components that allow the user to make choices. In this chapter we will explore these components.

Certainly, allowing the user to make choices is closely associated with the user input topics discussed in Chapter 3.

However, Chapter 3 was concerned with components that allowed the user to type in text. This chapter is concerned with components that allow the user to select from a set of choices that you have provided. We have all encountered software like this many times. When you go to an ATM to withdraw money, it is likely that you are presented with a series of options in certain increments, or you can type in a specific amount. Those predefined options are what this chapter is concerned with. Table 7.1 summarizes the components that we explore in this chapter and provides a brief description of their uses.

Table 7.1 User choice components

Component	Purpose
JRadioButton	A radio button allows a user to select between two or more mutually exclusive choices.
JCheckBox	A check box is used when you want a user to select one or more options that are not mutually exclusive.
JComboBox	The combo box presents a drop-down list and allows the user to select only one of the options.
JList	The list is very much like the combo box, except all the choices are already displayed. The box does not need to drop down.
JSlider	The slider allows the user to select one value from a predetermined range of values.
JToggleButton	A toggle button allows you to toggle between two mutually exclusive options.

Each of these components are thoroughly explored, with examples, throughout this chapter. These components are rather straightforward and easy to learn. However, they are essential to designing truly user-friendly interfaces.

JRadioButton

Radio buttons are ubiquitous components. Many applications make use of them on a regular basis. They are akin to the predetermined incremental values presented in ATMs that were mentioned earlier. A radio button looks like the image shown in Figure 7.1.

Figure 7.1 The radio button

The user is presented with a series of two or more radio buttons, and one option can be selected. This is what differentiates radio buttons from check boxes; the radio button allows the user to make a single, mutually exclusive choice. The JRadioButton class actually inherits from the JToggle-Button class. One could argue that it would have been prudent to first describe the JToggleButton class; however, the radio button is far more common. Radio buttons are used in conjunction with a button group component so that the appropriate buttons are grouped together. The most important methods and properties of the radio button are summarized in Table 7.2.

Table 7.2 JRadioButton methods and properties

Method/Property	Purpose
getText	This method retrieves the text in the radio button.
setText	This method will set the text displayed as a caption for the radio button.
toolTipText	This property sets a tooltip to be displayed when the user's mouse hovers over the radio button.
enabled	This property determines whether or not the radio button is enabled.
String paramString()	This function/method returns a string representation of this JRadioButton.

You, as a Java programmer, have several options with the JRadioButton constructor. When you create an instance of a JRadioButton, you can pass it a string that will be used as a caption, an icon that will be displayed, or neither, thus creating a blank radio button. Clearly, there are a number of functions common to all Swing and even AWT components. We do not explore those here. Instead, we work through a short example that demonstrates the essentials of using the radio button.

Example 7.1

Step 1: Create a new project and an application object, as you did in previous chapters.

Step 2: Set the layout manager for the screen to a GridLayout that is five rows by one column.

Step 3: Add three radio buttons to the application, and change their captions (text), as shown in Figure 7.2.

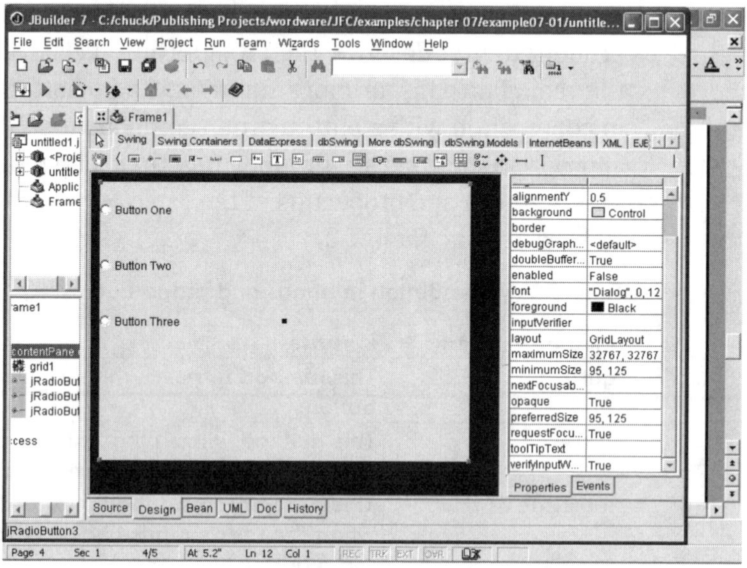

Figure 7.2 Radio button layout

Step 4: Add a button group. It won't display on the screen, but do not worry; it is there. When you select the buttonGroup property of the radio buttons, you will see the button group show up. This is shown in Figure 7.3. One by one, select each radio button and set its buttonGroup property to buttonGroup1.

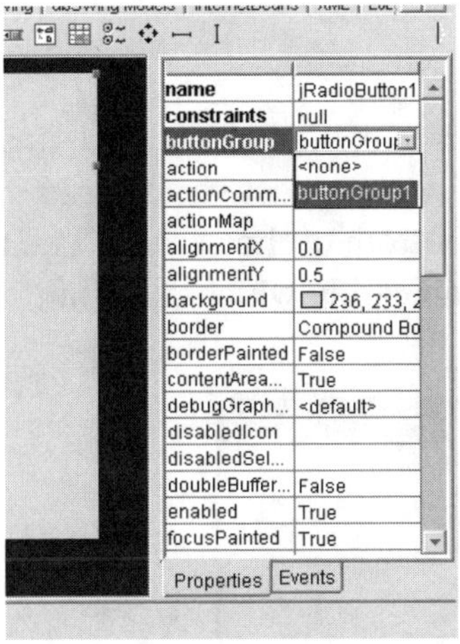

Figure 7.3 Selecting a button group

By assigning all of the radio buttons to the same group, you cause them to work in concert and be mutually exclusive.

Note: Using more than one button group on a screen allows you to have more than one grouping of radio buttons, with each group behaving as a cohesive unit but with no interaction between the groups.

Step 5: Add a single text field and a single button to the screen.

Step 6: At the beginning of the class, add a declaration for a private int called choice. Then in the action event of each radio button, you can set that int to reflect the button selected. For example, in radio button 1 you set the choice to 1.

Step 7: In the action event of the button, place the following code:

```
switch(choice)
  {
    case 1:
      jTextField1.setText("Hey, you pressed radio button 1");
      break;
    case 2:
      jTextField1.setText("You pressed radio button 2);
      break;
    case 3:
      jTextField1.setText("You have pressed radio button 3");
```

```
      break;
  }    // end of switch
```

When you run the application, you will see the image depicted in Figure 7.4. As you select various radio buttons, press the button at the bottom of the screen. The text field will display a message indicating which radio button you selected.

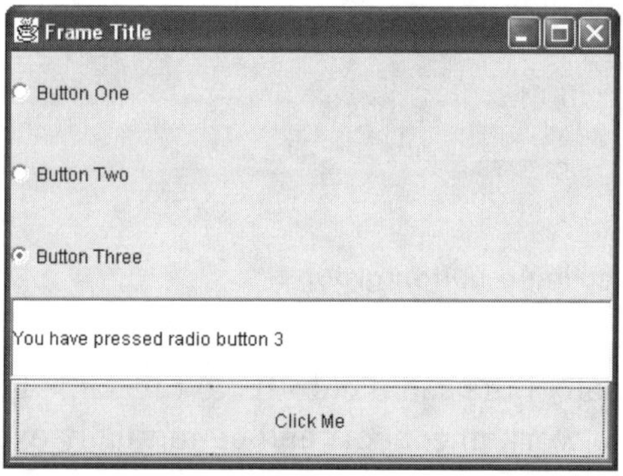

Figure 7.4 Illustration of Example 7.1

If you do not have JBuilder, you can enter the following code into your favorite text editor and compile it. You will get the same effect.

```
package untitled1;
import java.awt.*;
import java.awt.event.*;
import javax.swing.*;
public class Frame1 extends JFrame
{
  private JPanel contentPane;
  private GridLayout grid1 = new GridLayout(5,1);
  private JRadioButton jRadioButton1 = new JRadioButton();
  private JRadioButton jRadioButton2 = new JRadioButton();
  private JRadioButton jRadioButton3 = new JRadioButton();
  private ButtonGroup buttonGroup1 = new ButtonGroup();
  private JTextField jTextField1 = new JTextField();
  private int choice;
  private JButton jButton1 = new JButton();
  //Construct the frame
  public Frame1()
  {
```

```
    enableEvents(AWTEvent.WINDOW_EVENT_MASK);
    try
    {
      jbInit();
    }
    catch(Exception e)
    {
      e.printStackTrace();
    }
  }
  //Component initialization
  private void jbInit() throws Exception
  {
    contentPane = (JPanel) this.getContentPane();
    jRadioButton1.setText("Button One");
    jRadioButton1.addActionListener(new java.awt.event
         .ActionListener()
{
      public void actionPerformed(ActionEvent e)
{
        jRadioButton1_actionPerformed(e);
      }
    });
    contentPane.setLayout(grid1);
    this.setSize(new Dimension(400, 300));
    this.setTitle("Frame Title");
    jRadioButton2.setText("Button Two");
    jRadioButton2.addActionListener(new java.awt.event
         .ActionListener()
   {
      public void actionPerformed(ActionEvent e)
     {
        jRadioButton2_actionPerformed(e);
      }
    });
    jRadioButton3.setText("Button Three");
    jRadioButton3.addActionListener(new java.awt.event
         .ActionListener()
    {
      public void actionPerformed(ActionEvent e)
      {
        jRadioButton3_actionPerformed(e);
      }
    });
    jTextField1.setText("jTextField1");
```

```
    jButton1.setToolTipText("");
    jButton1.setText("Click Me");
    jButton1.addActionListener(new java.awt.event
         .ActionListener()
{
      public void actionPerformed(ActionEvent e)
{
        jButton1_actionPerformed(e);
      }
    });
    contentPane.add(jRadioButton1, null);
    contentPane.add(jRadioButton2, null);
    contentPane.add(jRadioButton3, null);
    contentPane.add(jTextField1, null);
    contentPane.add(jButton1, null);
    buttonGroup1.add(jRadioButton1);
    buttonGroup1.add(jRadioButton2);
    buttonGroup1.add(jRadioButton3);
  }
  //Overridden so we can exit when window is closed
  protected void processWindowEvent(WindowEvent e)
   {
    super.processWindowEvent(e);
    if (e.getID() == WindowEvent.WINDOW_CLOSING)
    {
      System.exit(0);
    }
  }
  void jRadioButton2_actionPerformed(ActionEvent e)
  {
      choice =2;
  }
  void jRadioButton1_actionPerformed(ActionEvent e)
  {
    choice = 1;
  }
  void jRadioButton3_actionPerformed(ActionEvent e)
  {
    choice = 3;
  }
  void jButton1_actionPerformed(ActionEvent e)
  {
    switch(choice)
    {
      case 1:
```

```
          jTextField1.setText("Hey, you pressed radio button 1");
          break;
        case 2:
          jTextField1.setText("You pressed radio button 2");
          break;
        case 3:
          jTextField1.setText("You have pressed radio button 3");
          break;
      }      // end of switch
      }
    }
```

This particular example may not be exciting, but it should demonstrate how to use radio buttons. You will find that the radio button is a very useful component for directing the user to make a single choice from a finite list of options.

JToggleButton

As mentioned in the previous section, the JToggleButton is the base class for the JRadioButton. As you might suspect, it has a more limited range of possibilities than the radio button and is thus less often encountered. This component should be examined for two important reasons. The first reason is that it is the basis for the JRadioButton, and therefore its methods and properties are inherited by the JRadioButton. The other reason is that it can be quite useful in a certain limited number of situations.

The JToggleButton also allows us to create it with a string for a caption, an icon, and a Boolean value determining if it is currently selected or not. The toggle button actually looks somewhat like a normal button, the difference being that when clicked it stays depressed until you click it again. This makes for a very useful visual effect when displaying Boolean values to the user. Consider the following example that uses a toggle button to indicate whether or not your application's sound is turned on or off.

Note: This application example simply shows the use of the toggle button and the setting of its properties — not the actual turning on or off of sounds.

Example 7.2

Step 1: Create a standard application as you have in all the previous applications.

Step 2: Change the layout manager for the container to a Grid-Layout and place a single toggle button on the layout.

Step 3: Add the following code to the action event of that toggle button. Remember that by double-clicking the toggle button in the Design screen, you will be taken directly to the action event.

```
if(jToggleButton1.getText()=="Sound On")
{
  jToggleButton1.setSelected(false);
  jToggleButton1.setText("Sound Off");
}
else
{
   jToggleButton1.setSelected(true);
   jToggleButton1.setText("Sound On");
}
```

Now run the application. You will see something much like the images depicted in Figures 7.5 and 7.6.

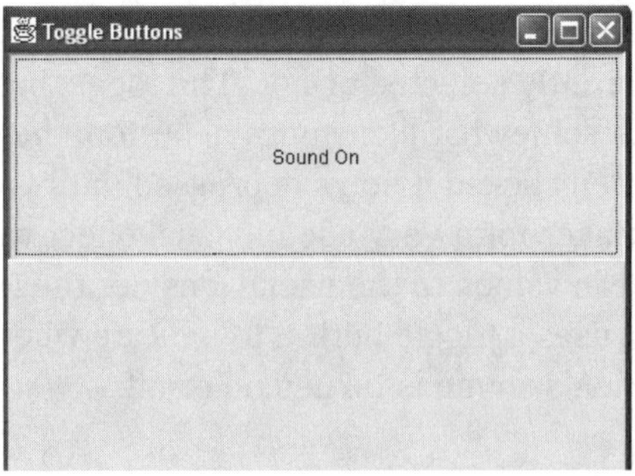

Figure 7.5 The selected toggle button

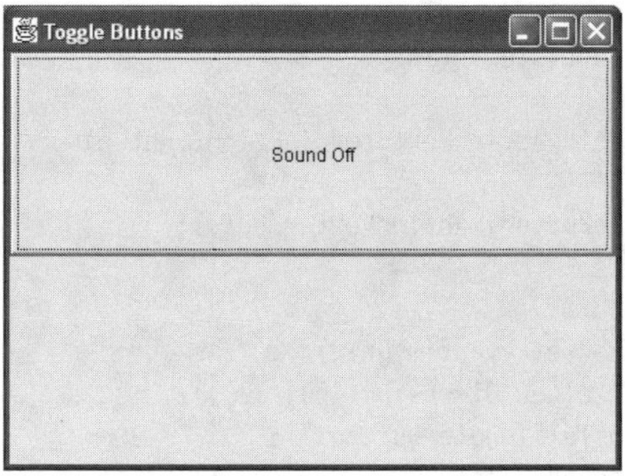

Figure 7.6 The unselected toggle button

For those readers not using JBuilder, the complete code for this example is provided here:

```
package untitled1;
import java.awt.*;
import java.awt.event.*;
import javax.swing.*;
public class Frame1 extends JFrame
{
  private JPanel contentPane;
  private GridLayout mygrid = new GridLayout(2,2,0,2);
  private JToggleButton jToggleButton1 = new JToggleButton();
  //Construct the frame
  public Frame1()
  {
    enableEvents(AWTEvent.WINDOW_EVENT_MASK);
    try
    {
      jbInit();
    }
    catch(Exception e)
    {
      e.printStackTrace();
    }
  }
  private void jbInit() throws Exception
  {
    contentPane = (JPanel) this.getContentPane();
    jToggleButton1.setSelected(true);
    jToggleButton1.setText("Sound On");
```

```
    jToggleButton1.addActionListener(new java.awt.event
         .ActionListener()
    {
      public void actionPerformed(ActionEvent e)
      {
        jToggleButton1_actionPerformed(e);
      }
    });
    contentPane.setLayout(mygrid);
    this.setSize(new Dimension(400, 300));
    this.setTitle("Toggle Buttons");
    contentPane.add(jToggleButton1, null);
  }
  //Overridden so we can exit when window is closed
  protected void processWindowEvent(WindowEvent e)
  {
    super.processWindowEvent(e);
    if (e.getID() == WindowEvent.WINDOW_CLOSING)
    {
      System.exit(0);
    }
  }
  void jToggleButton1_actionPerformed(ActionEvent e)
  {
    if(jToggleButton1.getText()=="Sound On")
    {
      jToggleButton1.setSelected(false);
      jToggleButton1.setText("Sound Off");
    }
    else
    {
       jToggleButton1.setSelected(true);
       jToggleButton1.setText("Sound On");
    }
  }
}
```

As you can see, the toggle button is a rather limited component. It is used when one wishes to allow the user to choose between two mutually exclusive options, such as on and off. Though this component is limited, it is the base class for the JRadioButton class. In the limited cases described earlier, such as on/off switches, it is the ideal component.

JCheckBox

The check box is similar to the radio button with one very important difference: The options that the user can select from are not mutually exclusive. The user can select more than one option. Interestingly, the check box also inherits from the toggle button. This is an important point for you to consider as you expand your knowledge of Java in particular and object-oriented programming in general. The entire purpose of object-oriented programming is to allow one to take existing objects and reuse or even expand upon them. This is something that Java does quite well. The toggle button has the basic functionality, but it is simply too restricted for many applications. So rather than reinvent the wheel, the makers of JFC/Swing simply took that component and expanded upon it.

As with many of the components that you have seen, the check box has a number of different constructors. Therefore, you can create a check box in one of many different ways, depending on your current needs. Table 7.3 lists the constructors for the check box.

Table 7.3 JCheckBox constructors

Constructor	Purpose
JCheckBox()	This constructor creates a check box button with no text or icon that is unselected.
JCheckBox(Action a)	This constructor creates a check box where the properties are taken from the action supplied.
JCheckBox(Icon icon)	This constructor creates a check box that is unselected and has an icon.
JCheckBox(Icon icon, boolean selected)	This constructor creates a check box with an icon and specifies whether the check box will be initially selected or not.
JCheckBox(String text)	This constructor creates an initially unselected check box with a text caption.

Constructor	Purpose
JCheckBox(String text, boolean selected)	This constructor creates a check box with text and specifies whether or not it is initially selected.
JCheckBox(String text, Icon icon)	This constructor creates a check box that is unselected but with the specified text and icon.
JCheckBox(String text, Icon icon, boolean selected)	This constructor creates a check box with text and an icon and specifies whether or not it is initially selected.

As you can see from Table 7.3, you have a number of options when it comes to creating check boxes. Your check boxes may have captions, have icons, be initially selected, or none of the above. The check box is a very versatile component.

Obviously, if the check box inherits from the toggle button, then it inherits all the methods that the toggle button has. However, the check box does have a few methods of its own that it does not share with the toggle button. Those methods are summarized in Table 7.4.

Table 7.4 JCheckBox methods

Method	Purpose
void configurePropertiesFrom-Action (Action a)	This method sets the ActionEvent source's properties according to values from the action instance.
createActionProperty-ChangeListener(Action a)	This method creates the Property-ChangeListener used to update the ActionEvent source as properties change on its action instance.
AccessibleContextget-AccessibleContext()	This method retrieves the AccessibleContext associated with this JCheckBox.
String getUIClassID()	This method will return a string that specifies the name of the class that renders this component.
Boolean isBorder-PaintedFlat()	This method returns whether or not the border is flat.
string paramString()	This method will return a string representation of this JCheckBox.
void setBorder-PaintedFlat(boolean b)	This method will set whether the border should be painted flat (it is the complementary method to isBorderFlat()).

There are a variety of methods and properties associated with the check box. Some are rather obscure and won't be used that often, while others are used all the time. The more commonly used methods and properties are illustrated in the following example.

Example 7.3

Step 1: Start a new project with a standard application object, as you have done in the previous examples. Set the layout manager to GridLayout with six rows and one column.

Step 2: Place four check boxes, one button, and one label on the screen, as shown in Figure 7.7. Notice that I have changed their captions (i.e., their text properties).

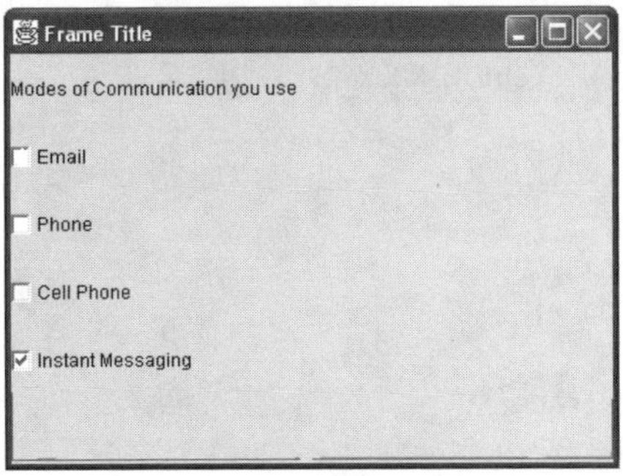

Figure 7.7 The check boxes

This example is designed to show you how to use check boxes in a practical scenario. In the example, the check boxes are used to indicate what particular modes of communication the end user utilizes. If you turn your attention to the action event of the button, you will see the properties of the check box being used. Inside the action event, we simply place a series of if statements to determine which check boxes are selected and to set some Boolean variables to reflect this fact. Those Boolean values were declared at the beginning of the class. The entire code is shown here:

```
package chkboxexample;
import java.awt.*;
import java.awt.event.*;
import javax.swing.*;
public class Frame1 extends JFrame
{
  private JPanel contentPane;
  private GridLayout mygrid = new GridLayout(6,1);
  private JCheckBox jCheckBox1 = new JCheckBox();
  private JCheckBox jCheckBox2 = new JCheckBox();
  private JCheckBox jCheckBox3 = new JCheckBox();
  private JCheckBox jCheckBox4 = new JCheckBox();
  private JLabel jLabel1 = new JLabel();
  private JButton jButton1 = new JButton();
  private boolean cell, phone, email, imessage;
  //Construct the frame
  public Frame1()
  {
    enableEvents(AWTEvent.WINDOW_EVENT_MASK);
    try
    {
      jbInit();
    }
    catch(Exception e)
    {
      e.printStackTrace();
    }
  }
  //Component initialization
  private void jbInit() throws Exception
  {
     contentPane = (JPanel) this.getContentPane();
    jCheckBox1.setText("Email");
    contentPane.setLayout(mygrid);
    this.setSize(new Dimension(400, 300));
    this.setTitle("Frame Title");
    jCheckBox2.setText("Phone");
    jCheckBox3.setText("Cell Phone");
    jCheckBox4.setText("Instant Messaging");
    jLabel1.setText("Modes of Communication you use");
    jButton1.setText("Submit");
    jButton1.addActionListener(new java.awt.event
         .ActionListener()
    {
      public void actionPerformed(ActionEvent e)
```

```
      {
        jButton1_actionPerformed(e);
      }
    });
    contentPane.add(jLabel1, null);
    contentPane.add(jCheckBox1, BorderLayout.SOUTH);
    contentPane.add(jCheckBox2, BorderLayout.NORTH);
    contentPane.add(jCheckBox3, BorderLayout.WEST);
    contentPane.add(jCheckBox4, BorderLayout.CENTER);
    contentPane.add(jButton1, null);
  }
  //Overridden so we can exit when window is closed
  protected void processWindowEvent(WindowEvent e)
  {
    super.processWindowEvent(e);
    if (e.getID() == WindowEvent.WINDOW_CLOSING)
    {
      System.exit(0);
    }
  }
  void jButton1_actionPerformed(ActionEvent e)
  {
    if (jCheckBox1.isSelected()== true)
    {
      email = true;
    }
    if (jCheckBox2.isSelected()== true)
    {
      phone = true;
    }
    if (jCheckBox3.isSelected()== true)
    {
       cell = true;
    }
    it (jCheckBox4.isSelected()== true)
    {
       imessage = true;
    }
  }
}
```

When you run this program, you will see something similar to Figure 7.8.

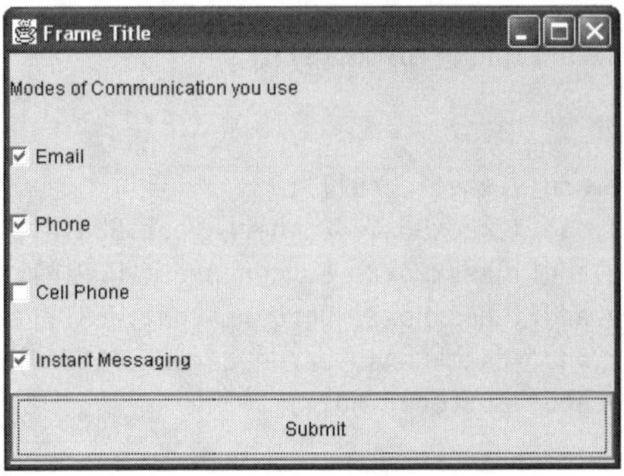

Figure 7.8 The check box example

Once you have set the Boolean values, you can do anything you wish with them. You may wish to pass them to some other function that will use the information or write the data to some database table (that is covered later in this book). This example is not too terribly complex or impressive. However, it does illustrate the essential purpose of the check box component, which is to allow the user to select multiple options from a series of choices.

JComboBox

The combo box is a favorite among programmers. It's hard to find any program that has a GUI interface that does not sport a combo box. A combo box is simply a drop-down list. It allows the user to select one choice from the list. It looks similar to a text box when it initially displays, except it has an arrow pointing down on the right side. This is shown in Figure 7.9.

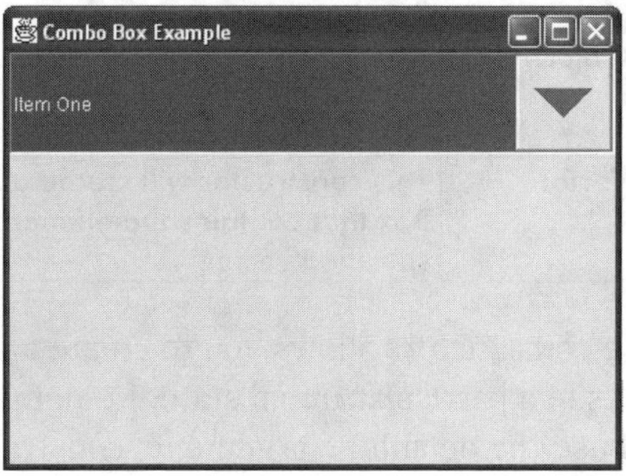

Figure 7.9 The combo box

When you click on the arrow with your mouse button, the full list drops down, showing all of your options. This is shown in Figure 7.10.

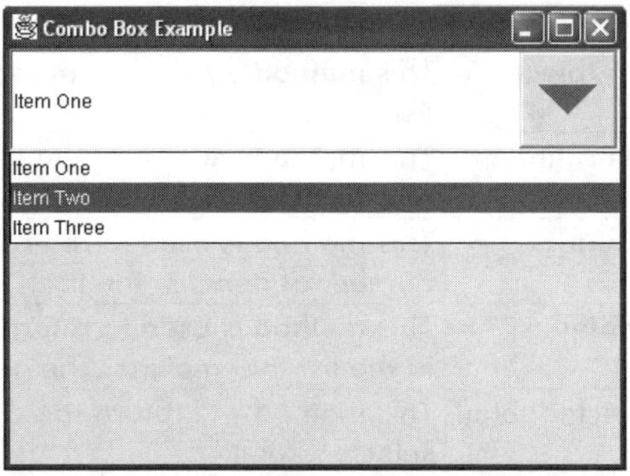

Figure 7.10 The combo box expanded

This component inherits directly from JComponent. The constructors for JComboBox are listed in Table 7.5.

Table 7.5 JComboBox constructors

Constructor	Purpose
JComboBox()	This is the default constructor, and it creates a JComboBox with a default data model.
JComboBox(Combo BoxModel aModel)	This constructor will create a JCombo-Box that takes its items from an existing ComboBoxModel.

Constructor	Purpose
JComboBox(Object[] items)	This constructor creates a JComboBox that contains the elements in the specified array.
JComboBox(Vector items)	This constructor will create a JCombo-Box that contains the elements in the specified vector.

Each of these constructors allows you to create a combo box that starts in a particular initial state. Remember that JBuilder will use the default no arguments constructor when you place a combo box on the design screen. In addition to the constructors, the combo box has a number of useful methods. The most commonly used are described in Table 7.6.

Table 7.6 JComboBox methods

Method	Purpose
void addItem(Object-anObject)	This method adds an item to the item list.
Object getItemAt(int index)	This method will return the list item at the specified index.
Int getItemCount()	This method is used to return the number of items in the list.
Int getSelectedIndex()	This method is used to return the index in the list that matches the given item.
Object getSelectedItem()	This method will return the currently selected item.
void insertItemAt(Object-anObject, int index)	This method inserts an item into the item list at a given index.
void removeAllItems()	This method clears the list by removing all items in the list.
void removeItem(Object-anObject)	This method removes a specific item from the list.
void removeItemAt(int anIndex)	This method will remove the item at a particular index. This method will only work if the JComboBox uses the default data model.
void setMaximumRow-Count(int count)	This method sets the maximum number of rows that the JComboBox displays.
void showPopup()	This method is used to force the combo box to display its pop-up window.

Each of these functions has a different purpose, and all are quite useful. However, the different permutations of the addItem method are of the most interest to us. The most common version is the one shown in Table 7.6. The add item method is used to add items to your combo box. Somewhere in the code you write, you will utilize this method to add items to your combo box. The following example illustrates this point.

Example 7.4

Step 1: Start a new project and add a new application object. Set the screen's layout manager to a grid layout, four rows by one column.

Step 2: Place a new combo box on the design screen.

Step 3: In the init section of your project (jbInit for users of JBuilder), place this code:

```
Object myobject = new Object();
myobject= "Item One";
jComboBox1.addItem(myobject);
myobject= "Item Two";
jComboBox1.addItem(myobject);
myobject= "Item Three";
jComboBox1.addItem(myobject);
contentPane.add(jComboBox1, null);
```

Step 4: On the design screen add a button and change its text property to **Combo Test**. It should look like the image you see in Figure 7.11.

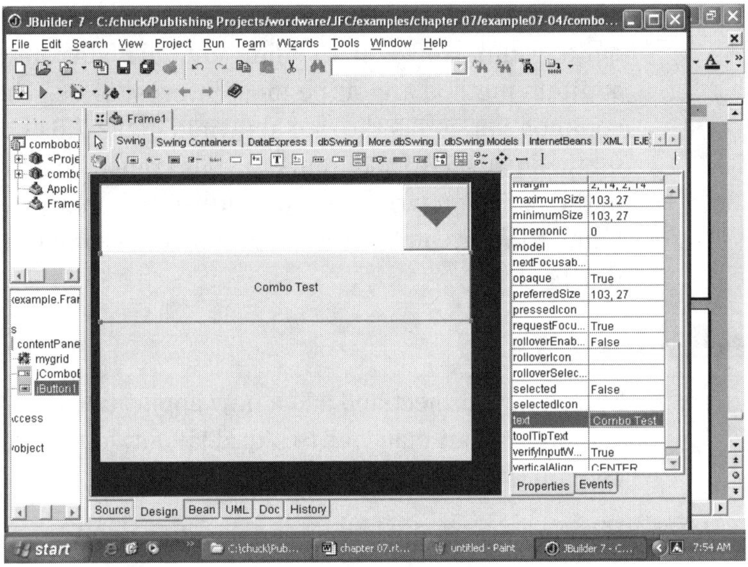

Figure 7.11 The combo box example project

Step 5: Now place the following code in the action event of the button:

```
Object cmboitem = new Object();
cmboitem = jComboBox1.getSelectedItem();
this.setTitle(cmboitem.toString());
```

When you run the example, you will see images much like the ones displayed in Figures 7.12 and 7.13.

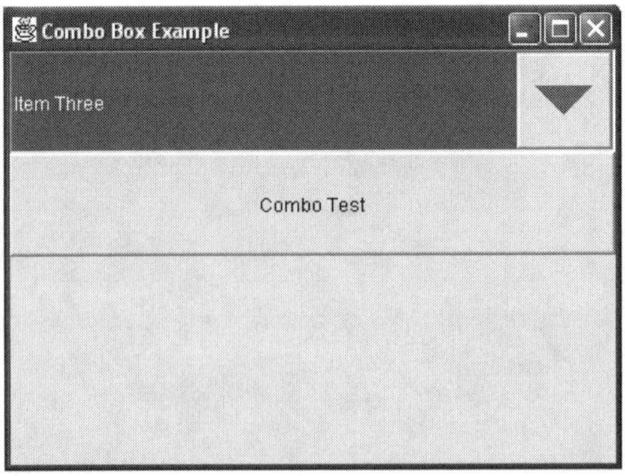

Figure 7.12 Running the combo box example

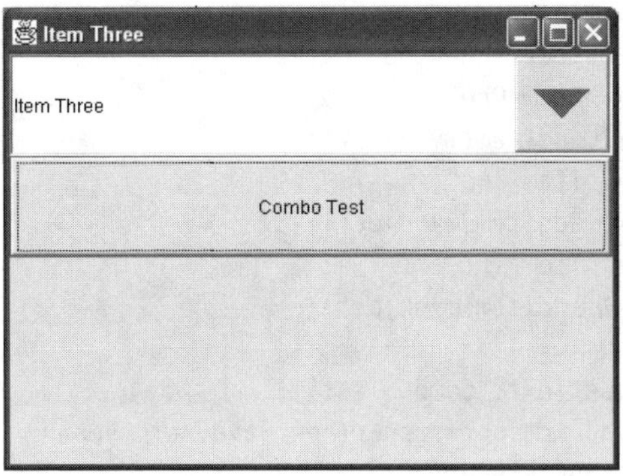

Figure 7.13 Getting the currently selected item

For those readers not using JBuilder, here is the complete code for this example:

```
package comboboxexample;
import java.awt.*;
import java.awt.event.*;
import javax.swing.*;
public class Frame1 extends JFrame
{
  private JPanel contentPane;
  private GridLayout mygrid = new GridLayout(4,1);
  private JComboBox jComboBox1 = new JComboBox();
  private JButton jButton1 = new JButton();
  //Construct the frame
  public Frame1()
  {
    enableEvents(AWTEvent.WINDOW_EVENT_MASK);
    try
    {
      jbInit();
    }
    catch(Exception e)
    {
      e.printStackTrace();
    }
  }
  private void jbInit() throws Exception
  {
    contentPane = (JPanel) this.getContentPane();
    contentPane.setLayout(mygrid);
    this.setSize(new Dimension(400, 300));
```

```
    this.setTitle("Combo Box Example");
    Object myobject = new Object();
    myobject= "Item One";
    jComboBox1.addItem(myobject);
    myobject= "Item Two";
    jComboBox1.addItem(myobject);
    myobject= "Item Three";
    jComboBox1.addItem(myobject);

    jButton1.setText("Combo Test");
    jButton1.addActionListener(new java.awt.event
         .ActionListener()
  {
      public void actionPerformed(ActionEvent e)
     {
        jButton1_actionPerformed(e);
      }
    });
    contentPane.add(jComboBox1, null);
    contentPane.add(jButton1, null);
  }
  protected void processWindowEvent(WindowEvent e)
  {
    super.processWindowEvent(e);
    if (e.getID() == WindowEvent.WINDOW_CLOSING)
    {
      System.exit(0);
    }
  }
  void jButton1_actionPerformed(ActionEvent e)
  {
    Object cmboitem = new Object();
    cmboitem = jComboBox1.getSelectedItem();
    this.setTitle(cmboitem.toString());
  }
}
```

This example illustrates the essential elements of the combo box component. In the init function, we load the combo box with a series of strings, using an object variable and the addItem method. Then in the action event of the button, we retrieve the item that the user has selected and change our example's title to match that item. While this example may not seem like a stunning display of programming acumen, it does show you how to add items to a combo box and retrieve the item the user has selected.

JList

The next component that we need to explore is the list. A list is quite similar to a combo box except that rather than drop down, its items are always on display. Also, like the combo box, it inherits directly from JComponent. Unlike a combo box, the user may select more than one item from a list. You can either create a list with data already in it, or you can create the list and then add the data. The latter method is shown here:

```
String[] mystring = {"one", "two", "three", "four"};
JList someList = new JList(mystring);
```

The list, like all components, has a variety of different constructors that allow you to create a list with a range of different initial options. Table 7.7 summarizes these constructor options.

Table 7.7 JList constructors

Constructor	Purpose
JList()	This constructor will create a JList with an empty model.
JList(ListModel dataModel)	This constructor will create a JList that displays the elements in the specified model.
JList(Object[] listData)	This method is used to construct a JList that displays the elements in the specified array.
JList(Vector listData)	This method constructs a JList that displays the elements in the specified vector.

Notice the term "model" in the descriptions of some of the constructors. This term simply refers to how the JList is handling data and what model of operation it is using. You saw the second constructor used at the beginning of this section.

In addition to these constructors, there are a number of methods the list has that you will need to become familiar with. The most commonly used methods are summarized in Table 7.8.

Table 7.8 JList methods

Method	Purpose
void clearSelection()	This method is used to clear the selection.
ListModel getModel()	This method will return the data model that holds the list of items displayed by the JList component.
Int getSelectedIndex()	This method returns the first selected index. It will return a –1 if there is no index selected.
Object[] getSelected-Values()	This method returns an array of the values for the selected cells.
void setListData (Object[] listData)	This method builds a ListModel from an array of objects and then applies setModel to it.
void setListData (Vector listData)	This method builds a ListModel from a vector and then applies setModel.
void setModel(List-Model model)	This method sets the model that represents the contents or "value" of the list and clears the list selection after notifying PropertyChangeListeners.
void setSelectedIndex (int index)	This method simply retrieves a single item from the list.
void setSelectedIndices (int[] indices)	This method selects a set of items.

As you can see, there are a variety of methods associated with the list component. Of particular interest should be those methods that allow you to select more than one item and the related methods that allow you to retrieve multiple selections. This is the primary advantage of a list over a combo box — the ability to select multiple items. If you wish to draw parallels with other components, one could say that the combo box has essentially the same purpose as the radio button (i.e., to allow the selection of one choice from many options), whereas the list has the same purpose as the check box (i.e., to allow multiple options to be selected). An example of how to select and retrieve a single option from a list might be useful.

Example 7.5

Step 1: Start a new project and add a new application object. In this case you can leave the layout manager as the default BorderLayout.

Step 2: Add a list to the Center of the BorderLayout, a text field to the North section, and a button to the South section of the BorderLayout. It should look like Figure 7.14.

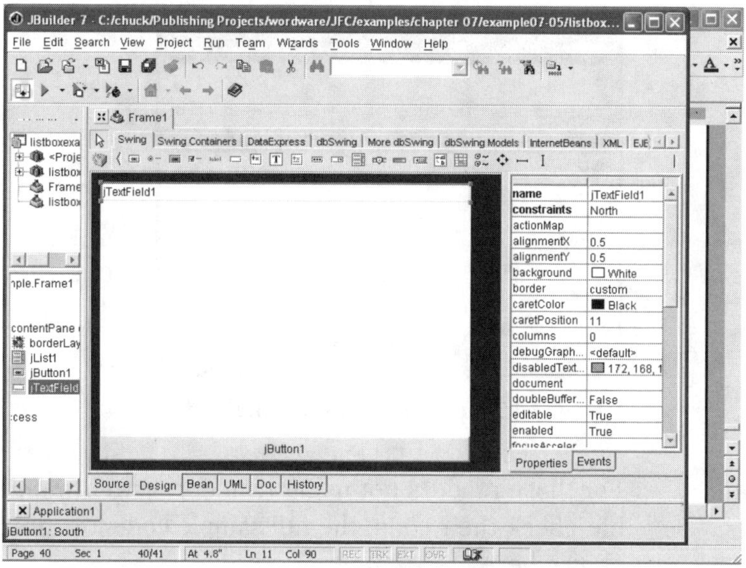

Figure 7.14 List example component layout

Step 3: You will need to go into the code for this projcct and change the way the list is constructed. JBuilder uses the default no arguments constructor for all components. Open the source code and find where an instance of the JList component is created. Then replace that single line of code with these two lines:

```
private String[] mystring = {"Java", "JBuilder",
      "JFC", "Swing"};
private JList jList1 = new JList(mystring);
```

Step 4: In the action event of the button, place this code:

```
Object contents= new Object();
contents = jList1.getSelectedValue();
jTextField1.setText(contents.toString());
```

When you run this application and select any single item from the list, you can then click the button and have that item display in the text field. While this example is rather simplistic, it does demonstrate the basics of how to use a list and shows its use in conjunction with other components. You should be able to run the application and see an image much like the one shown in Figure 7.15.

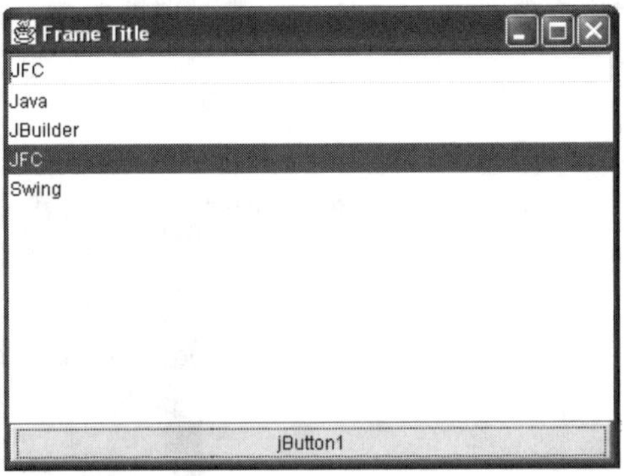

Figure 7.15 Running the list example

For those readers not using JBuilder or who want to double-check their code, the full sample code for this project is shown here:

```
package listboxexample;
import java.awt.*;
import java.awt.event.*;
import javax.swing.*;
public class Frame1 extends JFrame
{
  private JPanel contentPane;
  private BorderLayout borderLayout1 = new BorderLayout();
  private String[] mystring = {"Java", "JBuilder",
       "JFC", "Swing"};
  private JList jList1 = new JList(mystring);
  private JButton jButton1 = new JButton();
  private JTextField jTextField1 = new JTextField();
```

```
  public Frame1()
  {
    enableEvents(AWTEvent.WINDOW_EVENT_MASK);
    try
    {
      jbInit();
    }
    catch(Exception e)
    {
      e.printStackTrace();
    }
  }
  private void jbInit() throws Exception
  {
    contentPane = (JPanel) this.getContentPane();
    contentPane.setLayout(borderLayout1);
    this.setSize(new Dimension(400, 300));
    this.setTitle("Frame Title");
    jButton1.setText("jButton1");
    jButton1.addActionListener(new java.awt.event
         .ActionListener() {
      public void actionPerformed(ActionEvent e) {
        jButton1_actionPerformed(e);
      }
    });
    jTextField1.setText("jTextField1");
    contentPane.add(jList1, BorderLayout.CENTER);
    contentPane.add(jButton1, BorderLayout.SOUTH);
    contentPane.add(jTextField1, BorderLayout.NORTH);
  }
  protected void processWindowEvent(WindowEvent e)
  {
    super.processWindowEvent(e);
    if (e.getID() == WindowEvent.WINDOW_CLOSING)
    {
      System.exit(0);
    }
  }
  void jButton1_actionPerformed(ActionEvent e)
  {
    Object contents= new Object();
    contents = jList1.getSelectedValue();
     jTextField1.setText(contents.toString());
  }
}
```

The list is a versatile and useful component. It is well worth your time to become acquainted with its various methods. Hopefully, this section and this example gave you an adequate understanding of the list to allow you to use it in your own programs.

JSlider

The last component that we examine in this chapter is the slider. The slider allows the user to select from a set of values, usually numeric values, along a preset continuum. For example, if you have an application that allows booking agents to book passengers on a flight and they can have from 1 to 100 passengers, then a slider might be the best component to facilitate this.

Like many of the components that we have examined in this chapter, the slider inherits directly from JComponent, and it has a variety of constructor options. Those options are listed in Table 7.9.

Table 7.9 JSlider constructors

Constructor	Purpose
JSlider()	This constructor will create a horizontal slider with a range of 0 to 100 and an initial value of 50.
JSlider(Bounded-RangeModel brm)	This constructor creates a horizontal slider using the specified BoundedRangeModel.
JSlider(int orientation)	This creates a slider using the specified orientation with a range of 0 to 100 and an initial value of 50. Note: Horizontal is the default orientation for all sliders.
JSlider(int min, int max)	This constructor creates a horizontal slider using the specified minimum and maximum values and an initial value of 50.
JSlider(int min, int max, int value)	This constructor creates a horizontal slider using the specified minimum, maximum, and initial values.
JSlider(int orientation, int min, int max, int value)	This constructor is used to create a slider with the specified orientation and the specified minimum, maximum, and initial values.

Each of these constructor options allows you to construct a slider with various initial starting settings. Of course, like all the components in Swing, the slider component has a host of useful methods that you should familiarize yourself with. These methods are summarized in Table 7.10.

Table 7.10 JSlider methods

Method	Purpose
Int getExtent()	This method returns the range of values in the slider.
Int getMaximum()	This method returns the maximum value supported by the slider.
Int getMinimum()	This method returns the minimum value supported by the slider.
Int getMinorTick-Spacing()	This method returns the minor tick spacing.
Boolean getSnapToTicks()	This method will return true if the slider resolved to the closest tick mark next to where the user positioned the slider knob.
Int getValue()	This method returns the slider's current value.
void setMaximum(int maximum)	This method will set the slider's maxi-mum property.
void setMinimum(int minimum)	This method sets the slider's minimum property.
void setOrientation(int orientation)	This method sets the scroll bar's orientation to either vertical or horizontal.
void setValue(int n)	This method sets the slider's current value.

Each of these methods are quite useful, and they are fairly self-explanatory. However, an example using some of these methods might be in order.

Example 7.6

Step 1: As with all the preceding examples, you will need to start a new project with a new Application object. You should change the layout manager to a grid layout that is four rows by two columns.

Step 2: Place a slider, a button, and a text field on the design screen; it should look like what you see in Figure 7.16.

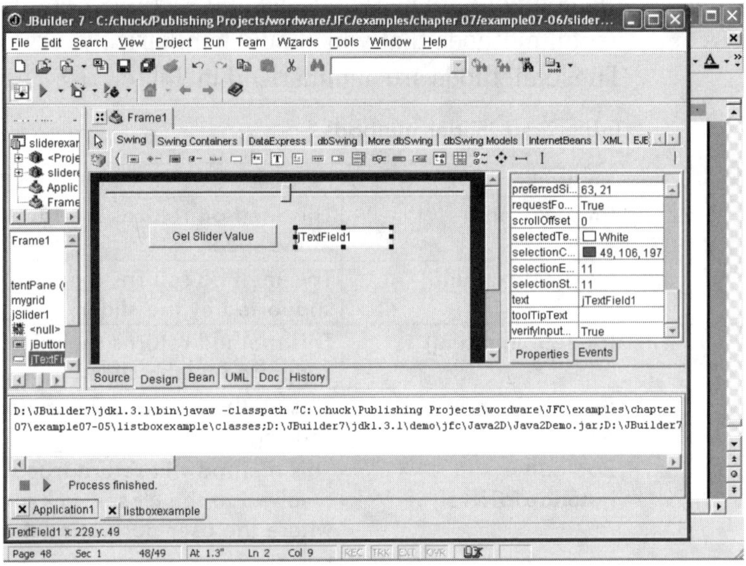

Figure 7.16 The slider example component layout

Step 3: Now set several of the slider's properties. We accomplish this by locating where the slider is added to the content pane and replacing that single line of code with these lines:

```
jSlider1.setMajorTickSpacing(5);
jSlider1.setSnapToTicks(true);
jSlider1.setToolTipText("Sliders are cool");
contentPane.add(jSlider1, null);
```

Step 4: Now in the action event of the button, place this code:

```
int value = jSlider1.getValue();
String mystring = new String();
mystring = mystring.valueOf(value);
jTextField1.setText(mystring);
```

When you run this application, it should work much like what is shown in Figure 7.17.

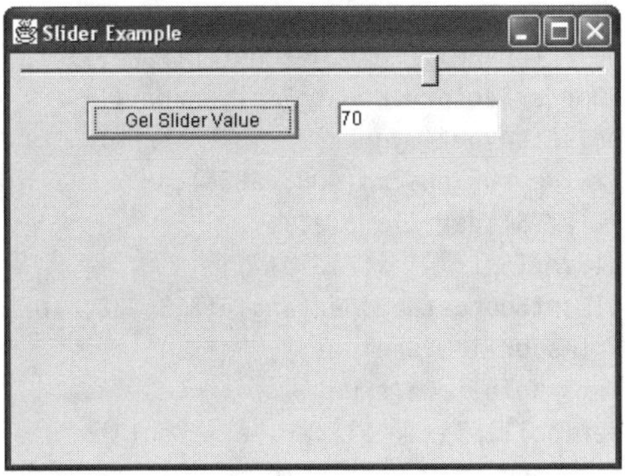

Figure 7.17 Running the slider example

For those readers who need to see the full code for this example, it is provided here:

```
package sliderexample;
import java.awt.*;
import java.awt.event.*;
import javax.swing.*;
import javax.swing.border.*;

public class Frame1 extends JFrame
{
  private JPanel contentPane;
  private GridLayout mygrid = new GridLayout(4,2);
  private JSlider jSlider1 = new JSlider(0,100,50);
  private JTextField jTextField1 = new JTextField();
  private Border border1;
  private JButton jButton1 = new JButton();
  //Construct the frame
  public Frame1()
  {
    enableEvents(AWTEvent.WINDOW_EVENT_MASK);
    try
    {
      jbInit();
    }
    catch(Exception e)
    {
      e.printStackTrace();
    }
  }
  private void jbInit() throws Exception
```

```
    {
      contentPane = (JPanel) this.getContentPane();
      border1 = BorderFactory.createEmptyBorder();
      contentPane.setLayout(mygrid);
      this.setSize(new Dimension(400, 300));
      this.setTitle("Slider Example");
      jTextField1.setText("jTextField1");
      jTextField1.setBounds(new Rectangle(213, 32, 105, 22));
      jSlider1.setMajorTickSpacing(5);
      jSlider1.setSnapToTicks(true);
      jSlider1.setToolTipText("Sliders are cool");
      jButton1.setBounds(new Rectangle(50, 31, 138, 25));
      jButton1.setText("Get Slider Value");
      jButton1.addActionListener(new java.awt.event
           .ActionListener()
      {
        public void actionPerformed(ActionEvent e)
        {
          jButton1_actionPerformed(e);
        }
      });
      contentPane.add(jSlider1, null);
      jSlider1.add(jButton1, null);
      jSlider1.add(jTextField1, null);
    }
    protected void processWindowEvent(WindowEvent e)
    {
      super.processWindowEvent(e);
      if (e.getID() == WindowEvent.WINDOW_CLOSING)
      {
        System.exit(0);
      }
    }
    void jButton1_actionPerformed(ActionEvent e)
    {
      int value = jSlider1.getValue();
      String mystring = new String();
      mystring = mystring.valueOf(value);
      jTextField1.setText(mystring);
    }
  }
```

As you can see, the slider is very easy to use, perhaps even the easiest component that we have worked with in this chapter. The only real issue that needed to be overcome in this project was converting the integer value of the slider into a string so that it could be displayed in the text field. The actual use of the slider and the retrieval of its value were quite easy. However, like the toggle button, its usefulness is limited to a specific genre of programming situations.

Summary

Throughout this chapter, you have been introduced to a variety of Swing components. Each of these components has been designed to help the user make individual selections from a group of choices. The differences between the components lie in how many choices a user can select and in how the choices are presented. In this chapter you have seen the radio button, toggle button, check box, combo box, list, and slider all used in example programs. The usage and the structure of each of these has been explained in some detail. At this point, you should be comfortable using any of these components in your own programs.

The knowledge that you have gained in this chapter, coupled with the information presented in the previous chapters, should make you ready to produce fairly sophisticated graphical user interfaces using Swing components. It is important that you, as a programmer, keep in mind that modern computer users are accustomed to interacting with responsive and intuitive graphical user interfaces. If your GUI is not responsive or intuitive enough, your application will not gain widespread user acceptance.

Review Questions

1. What component does the JComboBox inherit from?
2. Which components in this chapter allow the user to select multiple options?
3. What method do you use with a combo box to insert an item at a specific place in the combo box?
4. When is a slider the ideal component?

5. In what situation is a toggle button the appropriate component?
6. What is the primary difference between a check box and a radio button?
7. What is the main advantage of a list over a combo box?
8. What method do you use to retrieve multiple selections from a list?
9. What does that method return?

Chapter 8

Menus and Toolbars

This chapter covers the following:

- Menus
- Toolbars
- A practical example

Introduction

In this chapter, we expand upon the previous chapters. We add the use of various drop-down menus and toolbars to our repertoire of graphical user interface components and techniques. Also in this chapter, we begin working with some practical examples that tie together the techniques we have been developing in the preceding seven chapters. Now that we have laid the foundation of how to utilize these various components, it is a good time to start combining them to produce practical applications.

Menus and toolbars are prevalent in any GUI that you might encounter. Most Windows programs use them, as do Macintosh programs and KDE or GNOME programs. Users have grown accustomed to the use of drop-down menus and toolbars in applications. In fact, the IDE provided by JBuilder has an extensive set of drop-down menus as well as several toolbars. This chapter explores the use of these components.

Menus

Drop-down menus are enormously popular simply because they allow you to provide a wide array of choices to your application's user without cluttering up the screen. Each option is contained in logically grouped drop-down menus that are virtually out of sight until the user selects them. This allows you to have an uncluttered, clean-looking user interface and still offer a rich set of user options.

Creating a menu is a little more complex than creating most other components. That is one reason why it was not discussed until Chapter 8. You will need to combine the use of the JMenuBar class with JPopupMenu classes. JMenuBar creates the basic menu bar, and JPopupMenu creates the individual menu items.

To create a drop-down menu, start with the JMenuBar class. After you have created an instance of JMenuBar, simply add JMenu objects to the menu bar to construct a menu. When the user selects a JMenu object, its associated JPopupMenu is displayed, allowing the user to select a JMenuItem on it. Like the other components that we have dealt with, the JMenuBar component has several methods. The most important methods are summarized in Table 8.1.

Table 8.1 JMenuBar methods

Method	Purpose
JMenu add(JMenu c)	This function will append the specified menu to the end of the menu bar.
component getComponent()	This method returns a specific component.
component get-ComponentAtIndex(int i)	This is an old method that has been deprecated, but you still might see it rather frequently. It has been replaced by getComponent(int i).
int getComponent-Index(Component c)	This function will return the index of the specified component.
insets getMargin()	This function returns the margin between the menu bar's border and its menus.
int getMenuCount()	This function is used to retrieve the number of items in the menu bar.

Method	Purpose
MenuElement[] getSubElements()	This function returns the menus in a particular menu bar.
Boolean isSelected()	This function will return a value of true if the menu bar currently has a component selected.
void setHelpMenu (JMenu menu)	This function is used to set the help menu that appears when the user selects the Help option in the menu bar.
void setMargin(Insets m)	This function will set the margin between the menu bar's border and its menus.
void setSelected (Component sel)	This function is used to select a given component.

These methods are the most important and widely used for the JMenuBar class. Unlike the other components you have examined in the preceding seven chapters, JMenuBar only has one basic, no arguments constructor. So there is no need to summarize the constructor options.

As already mentioned, JMenuBar does not work alone. It works in conjunction with JMenu and JMenuItem. Each of these three components is used to successfully create a menu. Here is a standard, rather generic example of the three working in conjunction to create a menu:

```
// Create an instance of the menu bar
JMenuBar mymenuBar = new JMenuBar();
// Create a menu
JMenu menu = new JMenu("This is a menu");
mymenuBar.add(menu);
// Create an instance of the menu item
JMenuItem myitem = new JMenuItem("This is an item");
myitem.addActionListener(actionListener);
menu.add(item);
// Install the menu bar in the frame
frame.setJMenuBar(menuBar);
```

As you can see, all three components are needed for a menu. The JMenuBar creates the bar that will contain the other menus. The JMenu provides a top-level drop-down menu (such as File or Help). The JMenuItem provides individual items under that menu. If you select the Add Menu Bar option when using the wizard to add an Application object to your project, the following code will be generated:

```
package example08_01;
import java.awt.*;
import java.awt.event.*;
import javax.swing.*;
public class jMenuExample extends JFrame
{
  private JPanel contentPane;
  private JMenuBar jMenuBar1 = new JMenuBar();
  private JMenu jMenuFile = new JMenu();
  private JMenuItem jMenuFileExit = new JMenuItem();
  private JMenu jMenuHelp = new JMenu();
  private JMenuItem jMenuHelpAbout = new JMenuItem();
  private BorderLayout borderLayout1 = new BorderLayout();
  //Construct the frame
  public jMenuExample()
{
    enableEvents(AWTEvent.WINDOW_EVENT_MASK);
    try {
      jbInit();
    }
    catch(Exception e)
{
      e.printStackTrace();
    }
  }
  //Component initialization
  private void jbInit() throws Exception
 {
    contentPane = (JPanel) this.getContentPane();
    contentPane.setLayout(borderLayout1);
    this.setSize(new Dimension(400, 300));
    this.setTitle("Menu Example");
    jMenuFile.setText("File");
    jMenuFileExit.setText("Exit");
    jMenuFileExit.addActionListener(new ActionListener()
   {
      public void actionPerformed(ActionEvent e)
    {
        jMenuFileExit_actionPerformed(e);
      }
    });
    jMenuHelp.setText("Help");
```

```
    jMenuHelpAbout.setText("About");
    jMenuHelpAbout.addActionListener(new ActionListener()  {
      public void actionPerformed(ActionEvent e) {
        jMenuHelpAbout_actionPerformed(e);
      }
    });
    jMenuFile.add(jMenuFileExit);
    jMenuHelp.add(jMenuHelpAbout);
    jMenuBar1.add(jMenuFile);
    jMenuBar1.add(jMenuHelp);
    this.setJMenuBar(jMenuBar1);
  }
  //File | Exit action performed
  public void jMenuFileExit_actionPerformed(ActionEvent e)
{
    System.exit(0);
  }
  //Help | About action performed
  public void jMenuHelpAbout_actionPerformed(ActionEvent e)
  {
  }
  //Overridden so we can exit when window is closed
  protected void processWindowEvent(WindowEvent e)
  {
    super.processWindowEvent(e);
    if (e.getID() == WindowEvent.WINDOW_CLOSING)
 {
      jMenuFileExit_actionPerformed(null);
    }
  }
}
```

By examining this code, generated by the JBuilder wizard, we can see exactly how menus work. First, direct your attention to the beginning of the class. Note that a JMenuBar is instantiated. Remember that this is the actual starting point, or base, to which all of the drop-down menus will connect. Then instances of JMenu and JMenuItem are created. The JMenu is the top-level drop-down that you see. The JMenu is essentially what is displayed in Figure 8.1.

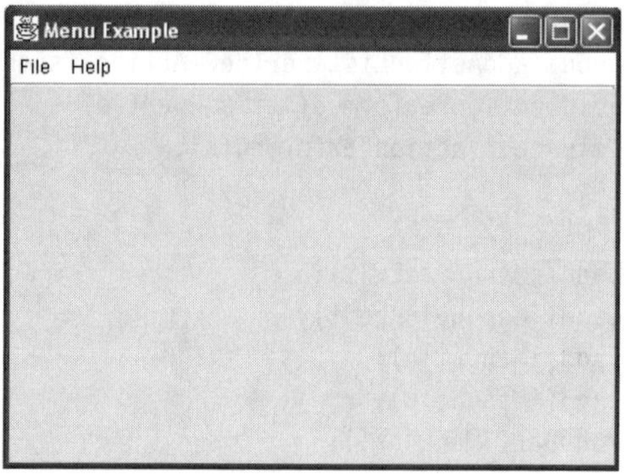

Figure 8.1 JMenu

Notice the captions File and Help. These are displayed via the text property of the JMenu class. If you click on one of these, a menu drops down, displaying the individual JMenuItem objects, as you can see in Figure 8.2.

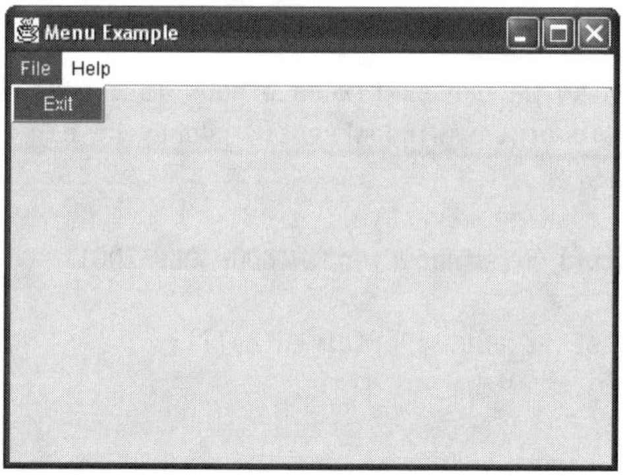

Figure 8.2 JMenuItem

You can see that creating the menu bar, top-level menus, and drop-down menus is really just a matter of instantiating the proper JFC classes and connecting them using the add method. The real trick is what to do when a user clicks on an item. When a top-level menu (an instantiation of the JMenu class) is selected, the action taken is simply to drop down and display the menu items beneath it. But what do you do when one of those menu items is selected? The answer is that an action listener is added during the jbInit operation (simply init() for those readers not using JBuilder).

```
jMenuFileExit.addActionListener(new ActionListener()
{
  public void actionPerformed(ActionEvent e)
  {
    jMenuFileExit_actionPerformed(e);
  }
});
```

This code creates a new instance of an ActionListener class and assigns it to a particular JMenuItem. This causes that menu item to listen for and respond to events. Then all you need is a simple function to respond to some action:

```
public void jMenuFileExit_actionPerformed(ActionEvent e)
{
  System.exit(0);
}
```

In this case, the action chosen is to exit.

The next obvious step is to demonstrate how to add more menu items and make them respond to the user. The process is really fairly simple. However, before we delve into that, it would be a good idea to give you an overview of the JMenu and JMenuItem classes.

Table 8.2 JMenu and JMenuItem methods

Method	Purpose
JMenuItem add(Action a)	This function adds a new menu item attached to the specified Action object and appends it to the end of this menu.
Component add (Component c)	This function adds a component to the end of this menu.
JMenuItem add(JMenu-Item menuItem)	This function will add a menu item to the end of this menu.
void addSeparator()	This function inserts a new separator at the end of the menu.
void addMenuListener (MenuListener l)	This function is used to add a listener for menu events.

Method	Purpose
void doClick(int pressTime)	This function causes a "click" to occur. It essentially simulates a user clicking on the menu.
Component get Component()	This function will return the java.awt.Component used to paint this MenuElement.
JMenuItem getItem (int pos)	This will return the JMenuItem at the specified position.
Int getItemCount()	This function returns the number of items on the menu, including separators.
JMenuItem insert (Action a, int pos)	This function is used to insert a new menu item attached to the specified Action object at a given position.
JMenuItem insert(JMenu Item mi, int pos)	This function inserts the specified JMenuItem at a given position.
Boolean isTopLevelMenu()	This function will return a value of true if the menu is a top-level menu (that is, if it is the direct child of a menu bar).
Boolean isSelected()	This function returns a value of true if the menu is currently selected.
void remove(int pos)	This function will remove the menu item at the specified index from this menu.
void remove(JMenuItem item)	This function will remove the specified menu item from this menu.
void removeAll()	This function will remove all menu items from this menu.
void setSelected (boolean b)	This function sets the selection status of the menu.

As you can see, there are a number of very useful methods in this class. Table 8.2 is not an exhaustive listing either; it's merely a summary of the most commonly encountered and widely used methods.

Note: In the author's opinion, the menu is one of the many strong points that Java has. The options you have with a menu in Java far outstrip your options in either C++ or Visual Basic.

As with almost all the component classes we have examined, this one has a few different options for its constructor. Those options are summarized in Table 8.3.

Table 8.3 JMenu constructors

Constructor	Purpose
JMenu()	This is the default no arguments constructor, and it creates a JMenu with no text.
JMenu(Action a)	This constructor will create a menu whose properties are taken from the action supplied.
JMenu(String s)	This constructor is used to create a JMenu with the supplied string as its text.
JMenu(String s, boolean b)	This constructor is used to create a JMenu with the supplied string as its text and is specified as a tear-off menu or not.

As important and versatile as the JMenu class is, it is not of much use without individual menu items. Thus, the next thing for us to examine would be the methods and constructors available for the JMenuItem class. Before we delve into those specific methods, you should note that JMenuItem inherits from JAbstractButton, which in turn inherits from JComponent. This is really logical if you give it some thought. A menu item serves essentially the same purpose as a button; it is simply displayed to the user a bit differently.

Table 8.4 JMenuItem methods

Method	Purpose
protected void getComponent()	This method returns the java.awt.Component used to paint the menu.
protected void init (String text, Icon icon)	This method will initialize the menu item with the specified text and icon.
Void setEnabled (boolean b)	This method is used to enable or disable the menu item.

While this table is by no means exhaustive, it should be noted that there are fewer methods for JMenuItem than for the menu. This makes perfect sense, as a JMenu may need to manage several JMenuItems that are beneath it in the menu hierarchy.

Table 8.5 JMenuItem constructors

Constructor	Purpose
JMenuItem()	This constructor is used to create a JMenuItem with no set text or icon.
JMenuItem(Action a)	This constructor is used to create a JMenuItem whose properties are taken from the action supplied.
JMenuItem(Icon icon)	This function creates a JMenuItem with an icon.
JMenuItem(String text)	This function will create a JMenuItem with text.

Adding other menu items is really quite simple. In the following example we add a few items to the default menu.

Example 8.1

Step 1: Create a new project and add a new Application object. From the Application object's wizard, select **Add JMenuBar**. The default code we just examined will be generated.

Step 2: At the beginning of the class just prior to creating the JMenuExit, add this code:

```
private JMenuItem jmenuclick = new JMenuItem("Click me");
```

This will create yet another JMenuItem, with a caption that says "Click me."

Step 3: We will need to add another action listener for our new menu item. So in the jbInit() function, either immediately before or after the action listener is added to the Exit menu item, we will put in almost identical code to add an action listener for our new menu item.

```
jmenuclick.addActionListener(new ActionListener()
 {
      public void actionPerformed(ActionEvent e)
      {
            jmenuclick_actionPerformed(e);
       }
});
```

Step 4: At the end of the jbInit function, just prior to adding the JMenuExit item to JMenuFile, add our menu item:

```
jMenuFile.add(jmenuclick);
```

Step 5: At this point, our menu item is listening for events, but what will it do when it gets one? Right now, nothing. We need to go into the code just past or just before the JMenuFileExit code (shown below) and then add in our own.


```
public void jMenuFileExit_actionPerformed(ActionEvent e)
{
  System.exit(0);
}
```

Either just before this function or just after, we need to create an actionPerformed function. You can take any action you wish here. You can instantiate new classes, call functions, launch new screens, etc. However, what we will do is simply change the title of the application.

```
public void jmenuclick_actionPerformed(ActionEvent e)
 {
   this.setTitle("Ahhhh, much better");
}
```

When you run this, you will see two images. Figure 8.3 shows the application before our menu is selected, while Figure 8.4 shows it after clicking on our menu option.

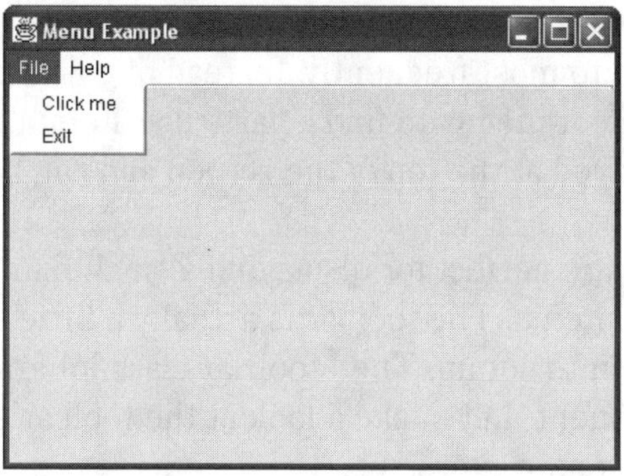

Figure 8.3 Before clicking the menu item

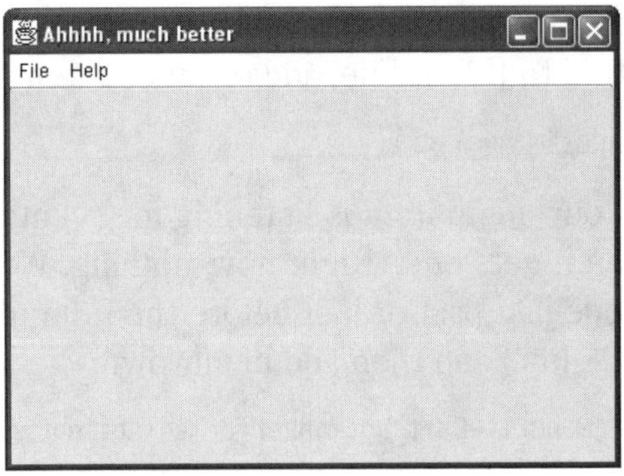

Figure 8.4 After clicking the menu item

You can see that adding your own menu items is really not particularly difficult. Even having those menu items respond to user interaction is not hard. While the preceding example was actually quite simple, it did illustrate all the steps needed to create menus and menu items.

Toolbars

Using menus, as described in the preceding section, is a wonderful way to give the user multiple options without cluttering up the screen, but it is only one technique for giving the user the opportunity to interact with your application. The toolbar provides another option. The toolbar is particularly suited for displaying those items that the user needs access to most frequently. Instead of going through several different menus to find a particular item, that item is always displayed at the top of the screen and can be selected at any time.

Toolbars are perfect for displaying a small number of frequently used items. The toolbar is actually a little simpler than the menu to set up. The JToolBar class inherits directly from JComponent. Let's take a look at the toolbar's methods and then its constructors.

Table 8.6 JToolBar methods

Method	Purpose
JButton add(Action a)	This method is used to add a new JButton that dispatches the action.
void addSeparator()	This method will add a toolbar separator of default size to the end of the toolbar.
void addSeparator (Dimension size)	This method will add a toolbar separator of a specified size to the end of the toolbar.
component getComponent-AtIndex(int i)	This function returns the component at the specified index.
insets getMargin()	This function returns the margin between the toolbar's border and its buttons.
int getOrientation()	This function is used to return the current orientation of the toolbar.
Boolean isFloatable()	This function returns a value of true if JToolBar can be dragged out by the user.
void setFloatable (boolean b)	This function is used to set whether the toolbar can be made to float.
void setMargin(Insets m)	This function sets the margin between the toolbar's border and its buttons.
void setOrientation(int o)	This function is used to set the orientation of the toolbar.

Table 8.7 JToolBar constructors

Constructor	Purpose
JToolBar()	This constructor will create a new toolbar; the orientation defaults to horizontal.
JToolBar(int orientation)	This constructor is used to create a new toolbar with the specified orientation.
JToolBar(String name)	This constructor will create a new toolbar with the specified name.
JToolBar(String name, int orientation)	This constructor will create a new toolbar with a specified name and orientation.

Example 8.2

If you use JBuilder's wizard to set up your application, you can have it set up a basic toolbar for you (just as you previously used it to set up a basic menu). If you choose to do this, JBuilder will generate the following code:

```
package example8_02;
import java.awt.*;
import java.awt.event.*;
import javax.swing.*;
public class toolbarexample extends JFrame
{
  private JPanel contentPane;
  private JToolBar jToolBar = new JToolBar();
  private JButton jButton1 = new JButton();
  private JButton jButton2 = new JButton();
  private JButton jButton3 = new JButton();
  private ImageIcon image1;
  private ImageIcon image2;
  private ImageIcon image3;
  private BorderLayout borderLayout1 = new BorderLayout();
  //Construct the frame
  public toolbarexample()
{
    enableEvents(AWTEvent.WINDOW_EVENT_MASK);
    try
   {
      jbInit();
    }
    catch(Exception e)
  {
      e.printStackTrace();
    }
  }
  //Component initialization
  private void jbInit() throws Exception
 {
    image1 = new ImageIcon(example8_02.toolbarexample.class
         .getResource("openFile.gif"));
    image2 = new ImageIcon(example8_02.toolbarexample.class
         .getResource("closeFile.gif"));
    image3 = new ImageIcon(example8_02.toolbarexample.class
         .getResource("help.gif"));
    contentPane = (JPanel) this.getContentPane();
```

```
    contentPane.setLayout(borderLayout1);
    this.setSize(new Dimension(400, 300));
    this.setTitle("Toolbar Example");
    jButton1.setIcon(image1);
    jButton1.setToolTipText("Open File");
    jButton2.setIcon(image2);
    jButton2.setToolTipText("Close File");
    jButton3.setIcon(image3);
    jButton3.setToolTipText("Help");
    jToolBar.add(jButton1);
    jToolBar.add(jButton2);
    jToolBar.add(jButton3);
    contentPane.add(jToolBar, BorderLayout.NORTH);
  }
  //File | Exit action performed
  public void jMenuFileExit_actionPerformed(ActionEvent e)
{
    System.exit(0);
  }
  //Help | About action performed
  public void jMenuHelpAbout_actionPerformed(ActionEvent e)
{
  }
  protected void processWindowEvent(WindowEvent e)
{
    super.processWindowEvent(e);
    if (e.getID() == WindowEvent.WINDOW_CLOSING)
{
      System.exit(0);
    }
  }
}
```

If you run this, you will see something much like what is shown in Figure 8.5 on the following page.

Let's take a close look at this code, line by line. First, let's see the initial creation of the toolbar. At the beginning of the class, you have a toolbar and some buttons being created:

```
private JToolBar jToolBar = new JToolBar();
private JButton jButton1 = new JButton();
private JButton jButton2 = new JButton();
private JButton jButton3 = new JButton();
```

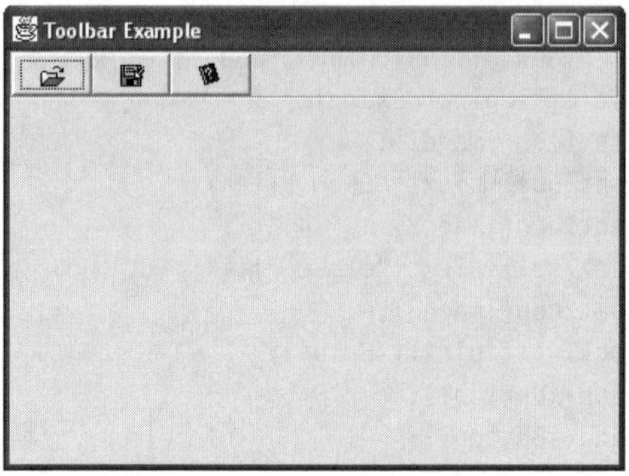

Figure 8.5 The default toolbar

It is important to realize that a toolbar is essentially just a group of buttons that act in concert. This becomes clear in our example because you literally create individual buttons that you place on the toolbar. Next you should note that most toolbars use icons. For this reason, JBuilder has created some icon objects:

```
private ImageIcon image1;
private ImageIcon image2;
private ImageIcon image3;
```

In the jbInit() function, these images and buttons are all brought together on the toolbar. First, the icon objects are set to specific images located on the hard drive:

```
image1 = new ImageIcon(example8_02.toolbarexample.class
     .getResource("openFile.gif"));
image2 = new ImageIcon(example8_02.toolbarexample.class
     .getResource("closeFile.gif"));
image3 = new ImageIcon(example8_02.toolbarexample.class
     .getResource("help.gif"));
```

Next, each button is given an image and tooltip text:

```
jButton1.setIcon(image1);
jButton1.setToolTipText("Open File");
jButton2.setIcon(image2);
jButton2.setToolTipText("Close File");
jButton3.setIcon(image3);
jButton3.setToolTipText("Help");
```

Finally, the buttons are added to the toolbar:

```
jToolBar.add(jButton1);
jToolBar.add(jButton2);
jToolBar.add(jButton3);
```

We can summarize this into a four-step process for creating a toolbar with images:

1. Create instances of JToolBar, JButton, and Icon.
2. Set the icons equal to some image on your hard drive.
3. Use the setIcon method of the buttons to add the icons to the buttons.
4. Add the buttons to the toolbar.

That's it. If you wish to add more buttons, simply follow the steps outlined (of course, you only need one JToolBar).

One of the coolest things that you can do with any toolbar is make it floatable. This means that the user can drag the toolbar to a different part of the screen if desired. With JFC, this is amazingly easy. Simply add one little line of code to the jbInit function:

```
jToolBar.setFloatable(true);
```

When you do this, you will be able to drag and drop the toolbar to other parts of the application screen. This is clearly shown in Figures 8.6 and 8.7.

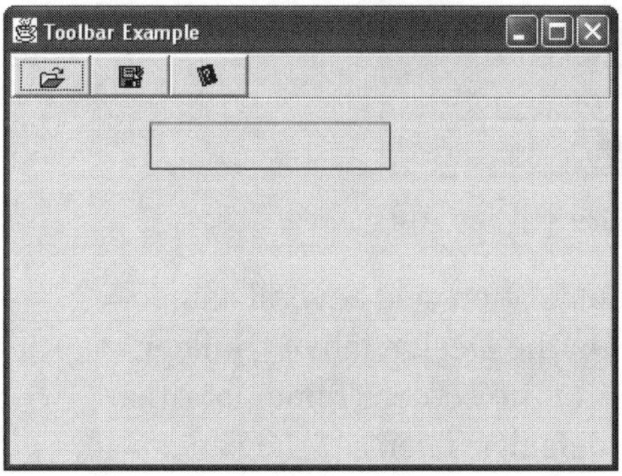

Figure 8.6 Dragging the toolbar

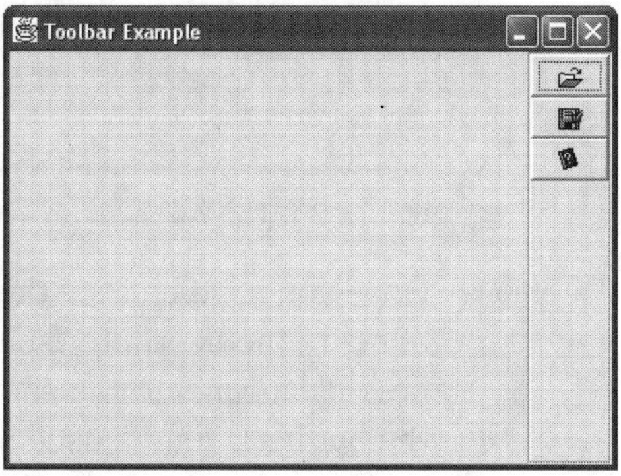

Figure 8.7 Dropping the toolbar

Many applications now provide toolbars that can be moved around. You should probably consider making any toolbar you put in your application movable.

A Practical Example

Throughout this chapter and the preceding chapters, you have seen rather simple examples. These examples were intended to demonstrate the functionality of a given JFC component, not necessarily to show practical applications of those components. This example will tie together many of the components you have seen up to this point in this book to create a practical, albeit rather simple, application.

Example 8.3

Step 1: Start a new project with a new Application object. When using the Application Wizard, choose to generate a toolbar, menu bar, and About dialog. This is shown in Figure 8.8.

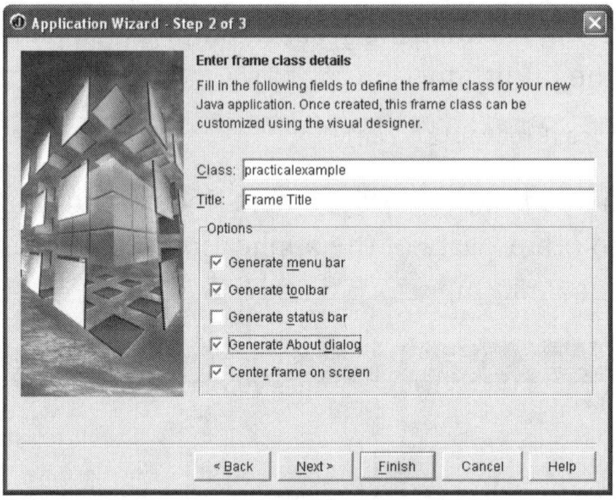

Figure 8.8 The Application Wizard

Step 2: Once you have created the application, add several components to the user interface. On the Design tab of JBuilder, first add a panel to the center of the screen (remember that the border layout is used by default). Then set the panel's layout to three rows by three columns. If you have any trouble doing this on the Design tab, you can go to the source code and add three simple lines of code to accomplish this:

```
private JPanel innerpanel = new JPanel();
innerpanel.setLayout(new GridLayout(3,3));
contentPane.add(innerpanel,BorderLayout.CENTER);
```


Step 3: Now add two text fields, two labels, one combo box, and one button. All of these components should be added to the panel that is now in the center of the application's interface. It should look much like what you see in Figure 8.9.

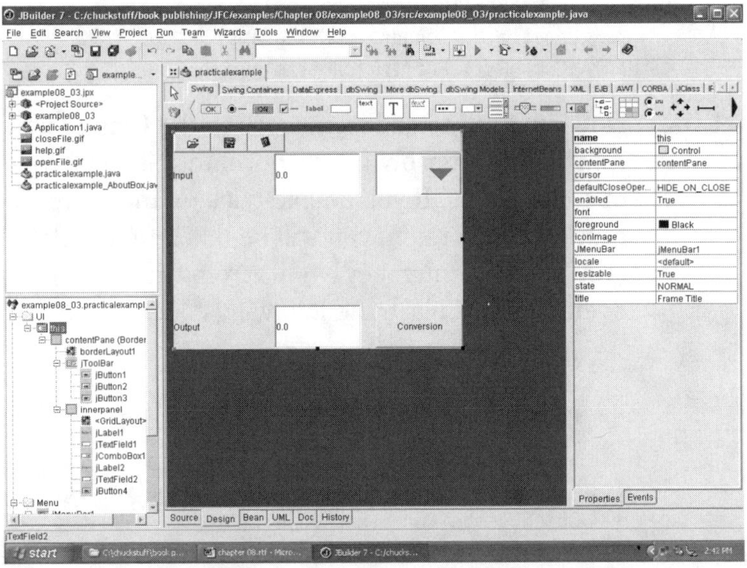

Figure 8.9 The GUI layout

Note: In order to space the components like you see in Figure 8.9, you will need to set the inner panel to a grid layout and alter the parameters of the grid layout constructor. Instead of just writing:

```
innerpanel.setLayout(new GridLayout(2,3)
```

You will need to use:

```
innerpanel.setLayout(new GridLayout(2,3,20,150)
```

The last two parameters designate horizontal and vertical spacing.

Step 4: We need to place our various conversion options into the combo box. Recall how we used object variables and the addItem method in Chapter 7 to add items to a combo box. Somewhere in the jbInit() function, prior to adding the combo box to the panel, you need to add this code:

```
Object cboitem = new Object();
cboitem = "Centimeters to Inches";
jComboBox1.addItem(cboitem);
cboitem = "Inches to Centimeters";
jComboBox1.addItem(cboitem);
cboitem = "Kilograms to Pounds";
jComboBox1.addItem(cboitem);
cboitem = "Pounds to Kilograms";
jComboBox1.addItem(cboitem);
```

Step 5: Now we need to add some code to the Conversion button. As you can probably guess, our intent is to provide a series of conversions. If you double-click on the button with the caption Conversion, you will be taken to its action event (you should remember events from Chapter 6). Inside this event, we will place the following code:

```
float finputval=0, foutputval=0;
int itemp;
String stemp = new String();
stemp = jTextField1.getText();
finputval = Float.valueOf(stemp).floatValue();
Object cmboitem = new Object();
cmboitem = jComboBox1.getSelectedItem();
stemp = cmboitem.toString();
jTextField2.setText(stemp);
if(stemp == "Centimeters to Inches")
    foutputval = finputval/2.54f;
if(stemp == "Inches to Centimeters")
   foutputval =finputval * 2.54f;
if(stemp == "Kilograms to Pounds")
   foutputval = finputval * 2.2f;
if(stemp == "Pounds to Kilograms")
   foutputval = finputval/2.2f;
stemp = String.valueOf(foutputval);
jTextField2.setText(stemp);
```

Step 6: Now for a few cosmetic touches. You should change the title of the frame to Metric/English conversions. Then change the inner panel border property as you see in Figure 8.10.

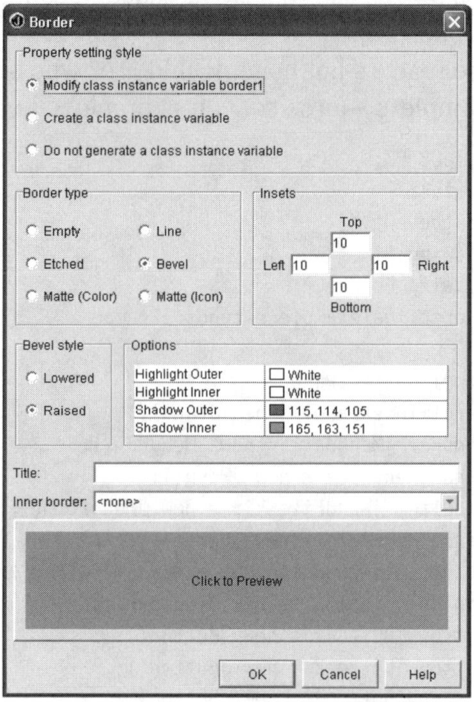

Figure 8.10 Inner panel border property

Now run your application. You should see something like what is displayed in Figure 8.11.

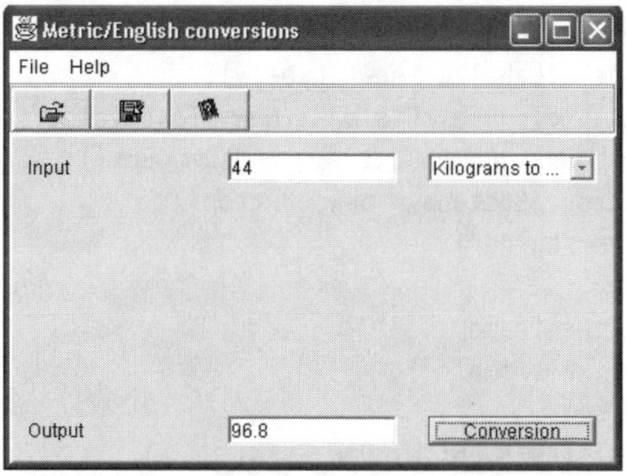

Figure 8.11 The conversion application

This application is not particularly earth shattering; however, it does bring together the techniques that you have seen thus far in this book. You have buttons, text fields, labels, combo boxes, and toolbars all used in conjunction to make this application.

For those readers not using JBuilder or who simply wish to see the complete source code, it is provided here:

```
package example08_03;
import java.awt.*;
import java.awt.event.*;
import javax.swing.*;
import javax.swing.border.*;
public class practicalexample extends JFrame
 {
  private JPanel contentPane;
  private JPanel innerpanel = new JPanel();
  private JMenuBar jMenuBar1 = new JMenuBar();
  private JMenu jMenuFile = new JMenu();
  private JMenuItem jMenuFileExit = new JMenuItem();
  private JMenu jMenuHelp = new JMenu();
  private JMenuItem jMenuHelpAbout = new JMenuItem();
  private JToolBar jToolBar = new JToolBar();
  private JButton jButton1 = new JButton();
  private JButton jButton2 = new JButton();
  private JButton jButton3 = new JButton();
  private ImageIcon image1;
  private ImageIcon image2;
  private ImageIcon image3;
  private BorderLayout borderLayout1 = new BorderLayout();
  private JLabel jLabel1 = new JLabel();
  private JTextField jTextField1 = new JTextField();
  private JLabel jLabel2 = new JLabel();
  private JTextField jTextField2 = new JTextField();
  private JComboBox jComboBox1 = new JComboBox();
  private JButton jButton4 = new JButton();
  private Border border1;

  //Construct the frame
  public practicalexample()
 {
    enableEvents(AWTEvent.WINDOW_EVENT_MASK);
    try
    {
```

```
    jbInit();
  }
  catch(Exception e)
  {
    e.printStackTrace();
  }
}
//Component initialization
private void jbInit() throws Exception  {

  border1 = BorderFactory.createCompoundBorder
       (BorderFactory.createBevelBorder
       (BevelBorder.RAISED,Color.white,Color
       .white,new Color(115, 114, 105),
       new Color(165, 163, 151)),BorderFactory
       .createEmptyBorder(10,10,10,10));
  innerpanel.setLayout(new GridLayout(2,3,20,150));
  image1 = new ImageIcon(example08_03.practicalexample
       .class.getResource("openFile.gif"));
  image2 = new ImageIcon(example08_03.practicalexample
       .class.getResource("closeFile.gif"));
  image3 = new ImageIcon(example08_03.practicalexample
       .class.getResource("help.gif"));

  contentPane = (JPanel) this.getContentPane();
  contentPane.setLayout(borderLayout1);
  this.setSize(new Dimension(400, 300));
  this.setTitle("Metric/English conversions");
  jMenuFile.setText("File");
  jMenuFileExit.setText("Exit");
  jMenuFileExit.addActionListener(new ActionListener()
   {
    public void actionPerformed(ActionEvent e)
    {
      jMenuFileExit_actionPerformed(e);
    }
  });
  jMenuHelp.setText("Help");
  jMenuHelpAbout.setText("About");
  jMenuHelpAbout.addActionListener(new ActionListener()
 {
    public void actionPerformed(ActionEvent e)
    {
      jMenuHelpAbout_actionPerformed(e);
    }
```

```
    });
    jButton1.setIcon(image1);
    jButton1.setToolTipText("Open File");
    jButton2.setIcon(image2);
    jButton2.setToolTipText("Close File");
    jButton3.setIcon(image3);
    jButton3.setToolTipText("Help");
    jLabel1.setText("Input");
    jTextField1.setText("0.0");
    jLabel2.setText("Output");
    jTextField2.setText("0.0");
    jButton4.setMaximumSize(new Dimension(27, 27));
    jButton4.setMinimumSize(new Dimension(27, 27));
    jButton4.setPreferredSize(new Dimension(27, 27));
    jButton4.setToolTipText("This will execute the
         conversion");
    jButton4.setMnemonic('O');
    jButton4.setText("Conversion");
    jButton4.addActionListener(new java.awt.event
         .ActionListener()
{
      public void actionPerformed(ActionEvent e) {
        jButton4_actionPerformed(e);
      }
    });
    innerpanel.setBorder(border1);
    jToolBar.add(jButton1);
    jToolBar.add(jButton2);
    jToolBar.add(jButton3);
    jMenuFile.add(jMenuFileExit);
    jMenuHelp.add(jMenuHelpAbout);
    jMenuBar1.add(jMenuFile);
    jMenuBar1.add(jMenuHelp);
    this.setJMenuBar(jMenuBar1);
    contentPane.add(innerpanel,BorderLayout.CENTER);
    Object cboitem = new Object();
    cboitem = "Centimeters to Inches";
    jComboBox1.addItem(cboitem);
    cboitem = "Inches to Centimeters";
    jComboBox1.addItem(cboitem);
    cboitem = "Kilograms to Pounds";
    jComboBox1.addItem(cboitem);
    cboitem = "Pounds to Kilograms";
    jComboBox1.addItem(cboitem);
    innerpanel.add(jLabel1, null);
```

```
  innerpanel.add(jTextField1, null);
  innerpanel.add(jComboBox1, null);
  innerpanel.add(jLabel2, null);
  innerpanel.add(jTextField2, null);
  innerpanel.add(jButton4, null);
  contentPane.add(jToolBar, BorderLayout.NORTH);
}
//File | Exit action performed
public void jMenuFileExit_actionPerformed(ActionEvent e) {
  System.exit(0);
}
//Help | About action performed
public void jMenuHelpAbout_actionPerformed(ActionEvent e) {
  practicalexample_AboutBox dlg = new practicalexample_
       AboutBox(this);
  Dimension dlgSize = dlg.getPreferredSize();
  Dimension frmSize = getSize();
  Point loc = getLocation();
  dlg.setLocation((frmSize.width - dlgSize.width) / 2 +
       loc.x, (frmSize.height - dlgSize.height) / 2 + loc.y);
  dlg.setModal(true);
  dlg.pack();
  dlg.show();
}
//Overridden so we can exit when window is closed
protected void processWindowEvent(WindowEvent e) {
  super.processWindowEvent(e);
  if (e.getID() == WindowEvent.WINDOW_CLOSING) {
    jMenuFileExit_actionPerformed(null);
  }
}
void jButton4_actionPerformed(ActionEvent e)
{
  float finputval=0, foutputval=0;
  int itemp;
  String stemp = new String();
  stemp = jTextField1.getText();
  finputval = Float.valueOf(stemp).floatValue();
  Object cmboitem = new Object();
  cmboitem = jComboBox1.getSelectedItem();
  stemp = cmboitem.toString();
  jTextField2.setText(stemp);

  if(stemp == "Centimeters to Inches")
      foutputval = finputval/2.54f;
```

```
        if(stemp == "Inches to Centimeters")
           foutputval =finputval * 2.54f;
        if(stemp == "Kilograms to Pounds")
           foutputval = finputval * 2.2f;
        if(stemp == "Pounds to Kilograms")
           foutputval = finputval/2.2f;
        stemp = String.valueOf(foutputval);
        jTextField2.setText(stemp);
     }
   }
```

Summary

This chapter has introduced you to two very important components used in most modern graphical interfaces. The menu is most appropriate when you have large numbers of options and you do not wish to clutter the screen. You can group the options by function, and then the user only sees individual menu items when he or she selects a top-level menu.

The toolbar is more appropriately used to keep a small number of frequently used functions constantly at the user's disposal. Each function is available simply by clicking one of the buttons on the toolbar, and that toolbar is constantly visible. Most modern applications have drop-down menus and toolbars.

Review Questions

1. What classes are needed to create a complete drop-down menu?
2. What is the purpose of the JMenuBar class?
3. How would you add a line separating menu items?
4. How would you clear a menu?
5. Can JToolBars be made floatable?
6. How would you make a toolbar initially display as vertical rather than horizontal?
7. Can you simulate a user clicking a menu item?
8. Must new menu items be added at the end of the current list of menu items?

Chapter 9

Dialogs

This chapter covers the following:

- Dialogs
- Using dialogs
- Creating custom dialogs
- Using the color chooser
- Using the file chooser

Introduction

As has already been mentioned, the ultimate goal of the Java Foundation Classes is user interaction. Dialogs provide a common method for complex interaction. There are times when simply clicking a button or drop-down menu is just inadequate for proper user interaction. When a user needs to open a file, save a file to a specific location, or choose a color from a palette, a dialog is the most appropriate method for providing user interaction. This chapter introduces you to dialogs and how to create and use them.

What Is a Dialog?

Before we delve too deeply into the details of a dialog, it would probably be a good idea to define exactly what a dialog is. A technical definition might be that a *dialog* is a top-level window with a title and a border that is typically used to take some form of input from the user. A less technical definition might be that a dialog is a pop-up window that allows the user to make some complex selection.

The size of the dialog includes any area designated for the border. You can retrieve the dimensions of the border area using the getInsets method. Since the border area is included in the overall size of the dialog, the border effectively obscures a portion of the dialog, constraining the area available for displaying subcomponents to the rectangle, which has an upper-left corner location of (insets.left, insets.top) and a size of width – (insets.left + insets.right) by height – (insets.top + insets.bottom). The dialog's default layout is the BorderLayout. It is important to keep in mind that a dialog is not a standalone item; it must be created within the context of some container. A dialog must have either a frame or another dialog defined as its owner/container. When the owner window of a visible dialog is hidden or minimized, the dialog will automatically be hidden from the user. Should the owner window be reopened, the dialog will, of course, also become visible again.

A dialog can be either modeless or modal. A modal dialog is one that blocks input to all other top-level windows within the application's context. This means that you must respond to the dialog before you can use any other portion of the application. If you have seen operating system error messages pop up in any graphical interface (Windows, Macintosh, Gnome, or KDE), they were probably modal dialogs. The default for dialogs, however, is modeless. Dialogs are capable of generating the following window events (you should recall events from Chapter 6):

- WindowOpened
- WindowClosing
- WindowClosed
- WindowActivated
- WindowDeactivated

Dialogs have a number of methods that you might use. These are summarized in Table 9.1.

Table 9.1 Dialog methods

Method	Purpose
void addNotify()	This function will cause the dialog to be displayable by connecting it to a native screen resource.
void dispose()	This function is used to dispose of the dialog.
AccessibleContext getAccessibleContext()	This function retrieves the AccessibleContext associated with this dialog.
String getTitle()	This function will return the title of the dialog.
void hide()	This function is used to hide the dialog.
Boolean isModal()	This function indicates whether or not the dialog is modal.
Boolean isResizable()	This function will indicate whether or not this dialog is resizable by the user.
void setModal(boolean b)	This function is used to specify whether or not this dialog should be modal.
void setResizable(boolean resizable)	This function is used to specify whether or not this dialog is resizable by the user.
void setTitle(String title)	This function is used to specify the title of the dialog.
void show()	This function is used to make the dialog visible.

In addition to these methods, the Dialog class has a number of constructor options. These options are summarized in Table 9.2.

Table 9.2 Dialog constructors

Constructor	Purpose
Dialog(Dialog owner)	This constructor will create a dialog that is initially invisible and non-modal and has an empty title and the specified owner dialog.
Dialog(Dialog owner, String title)	This constructor will create a dialog that is initially invisible and non-modal, with the specified owner dialog and title.

Constructor	Purpose
Dialog(Dialog owner, String title, boolean modal)	This constructor will create a dialog that is initially invisible with the specified owner dialog, title, and modality.
Dialog(Frame owner)	This constructor is used to create a dialog that is initially invisible and non-modal, with an empty title and the specified owner frame.
Dialog(Frame owner, boolean modal)	This constructor will create a dialog that is initially invisible, with an empty title and the specified owner frame and modality.
Dialog(Frame owner, String title)	This constructor is used to create a dialog that is initially invisible and non-modal, with the specified owner frame and title.
Dialog(Frame owner, String title, boolean modal)	This constructor is used to create a dialog that is initially invisible, with the specified owner frame, title, and modality.

You can see that you have a number of choices for dialog constructors. This plethora of choices is indicative of how flexible this component really is. In addition to these constructors, you can see that the Dialog class has several methods that you can utilize. Having a basic familiarity with the constructors and methods will be essential before we move forward into using the Dialog class.

Using Dialogs

As informative as the preceding tables might be, they do not get to the real heart of the issue, and that is simply how does one go about adding a dialog to a project and using it?

You actually have two options for adding dialogs to any given project. The first option is to add an existing one from the component palette. The second option is to create a custom dialog using the Dialog Wizard in the Object Gallery. Let's begin by examining the first option since it is much simpler. If you wish to add an existing dialog, you simply select one of the dialog components, such as JFileChooser, on the component palette. You'll find them on the Swing Containers tab, as shown in Figure 9.1.

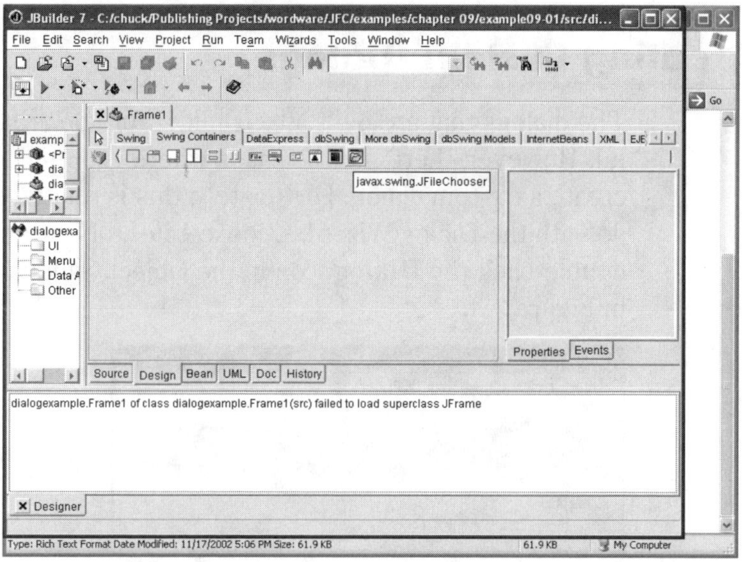

Figure 9.1 Dialogs on the component palette

If you have the Enterprise edition of JBuilder, you can find more dialogs located on the More dbSwing tab, as shown in Figure 9.2.

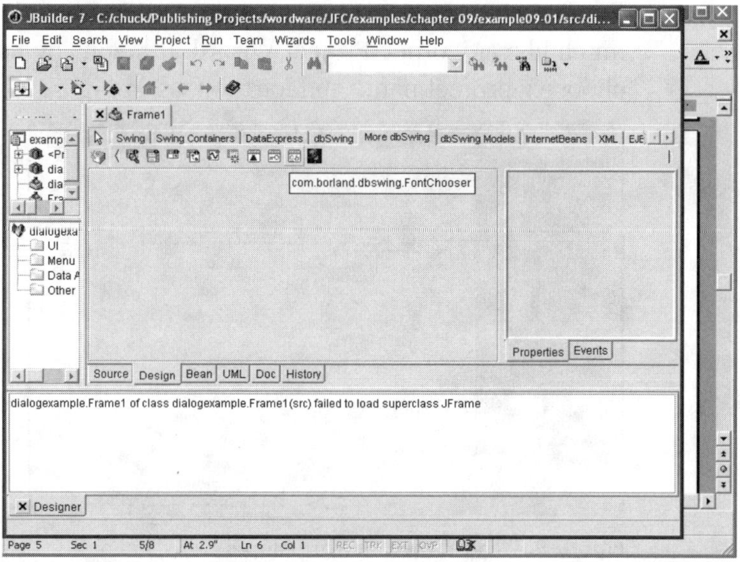

Figure 9.2 Dialogs on the dbSwing palette

These preexisting dialogs are quite useful, and we experiment with them later in this chapter.

Creating Custom Dialogs

The dialogs that are built into JBuilder for you are quite useful. However, there may be cases where you might want to create a custom dialog. Fortunately, this is relatively easy to do with the Dialog Wizard. Choose **File** > **New** and then double-click the **Dialog** icon in the Object Gallery, as shown in Figure 9.3.

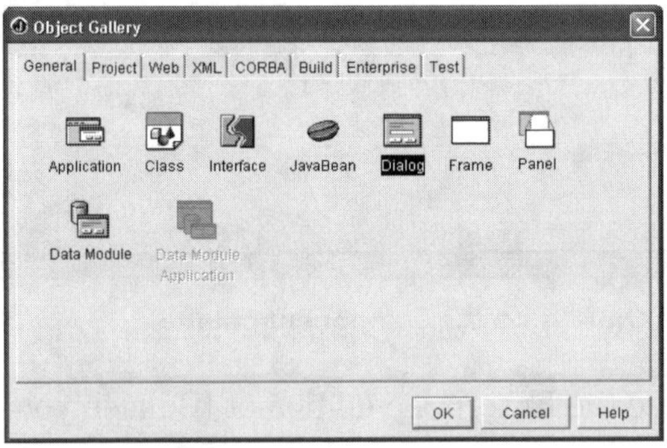

Figure 9.3 New dialogs

By selecting this, you will start the Dialog Wizard. It is much like any other Project Wizard. It begins by having you choose a project name and location, as in Figure 9.4.

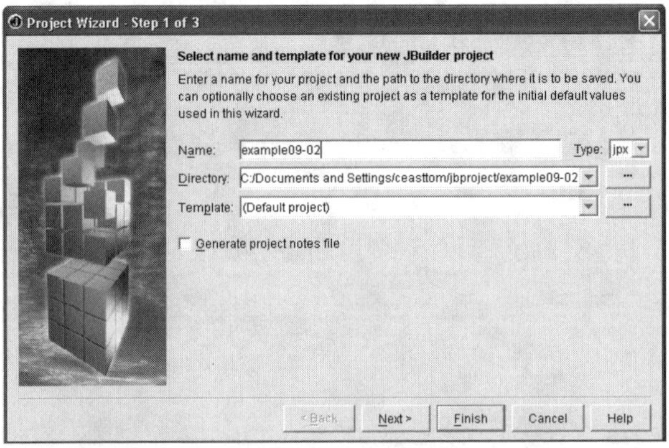

Figure 9.4 The Project Wizard step 1

The process is relatively straightforward, but let's walk through an example to make sure you are comfortable with it.

Example 9.1

Let's create a dialog that will allow users to select what base number system they wish to use. The Project Wizard proceeds much like any of the other wizards that you have seen in this book.

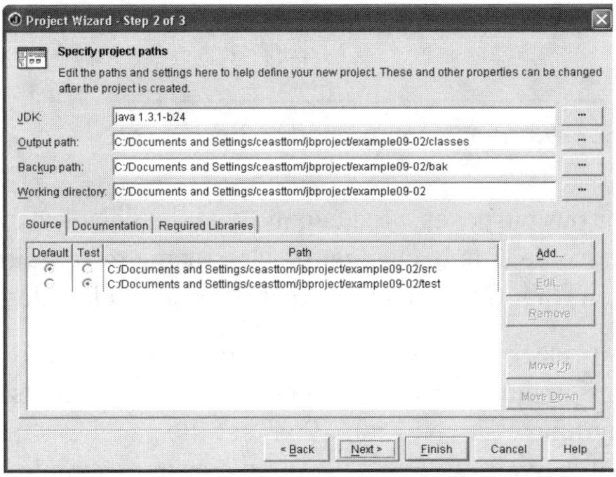

Figure 9.5 The Project Wizard step 2

However, after you have clicked the Finish button in Step 3, you will be taken to some screens specific to dialog applications. This is where our example really begins.

Step 1: Name your dialog class and choose the base class from which you want the class to inherit: javax.swing.JDialog or java.awt.Dialog.

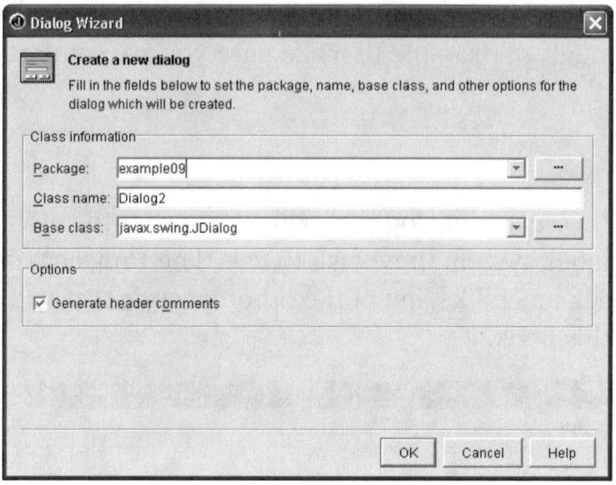

Figure 9.6 The Dialog Wizard

Step 2: For our purposes, we keep most of the default dialog settings. We simply change the class name to **testdialog** and then click **OK**. This will create a basic shell dialog project.

Step 3: Now place whatever visual components you need on the Design tab. These components may be text fields, labels, or anything else you wish. First, set the panel to a grid layout that is five rows by one column. For our example, we have a dialog box that lets the user choose what base number system to use, so our dialog components will look much like what you see in Figure 9.7.

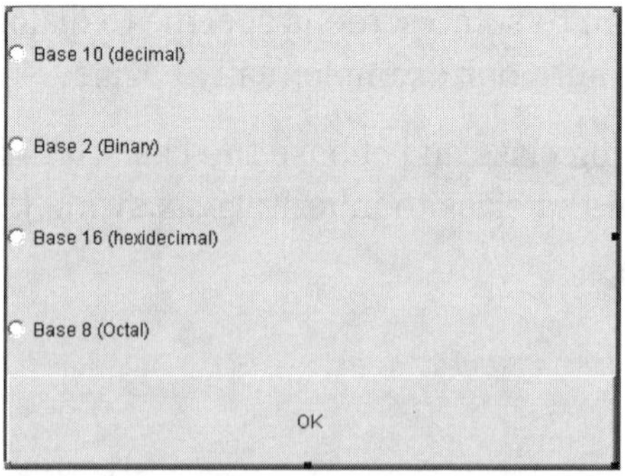

Figure 9.7 The dialog components

Step 4: At the beginning of your class, place the following variable declaration:

```
public int numsys;
```

Then in the action event of each of the radio buttons, set it to the appropriate value; for example, for base 10 decimal, you would put:

```
numsys = 10;
```

Step 5: Now for the OK button at the bottom of the screen. This is where the action will take place. In the action event (remember you get there by double-clicking on the button itself), place the following code:

```
this.hide();
```

Now you have a dialog with a public property called numsys that represents the number system the user chose. Congratulations, you have created your own custom dialog.

Note: To use any dialog that is not a bean, you must instantiate that Dialog class from somewhere in your code where you have access to a frame that can serve as the parent or container component.

If you want your dialog to be modal, you will need to use a form of the constructor that has the Boolean modal parameter set to true, such as in the following example:

```
Dialog1 dialog1=new Dialog1(this, true);
```

Remember that the Java keyword "this" refers to the class that you are in, so you are saying that this class should be modal. You will probably want to place this line as an instance variable at the top of the class (in which case the dialog box will be instantiated during the construction of your frame and be reusable). This line of code instantiates the dialog but does not make it visible yet. Before making a dialog box visible, you will probably want to set up any default values that the dialog fields should display.

When the user presses the OK button (or the Apply button on a modeless dialog box), the code that is using the dialog box will need to call the dialog's properties and methods to read the user-entered information from the dialog and then do something with that information. For a modal dialog box, you can do this right after the show() method call because show() doesn't return until the modal dialog is dismissed. You can use a result property to determine whether the OK or Cancel button was pressed. For a modeless dialog, show() returns immediately. Because of this, the Dialog class itself will need to expose events for each of the button presses. When using the dialog box, you will need to register listeners to the dialog's events and place code in the event-handling methods to use property getters to get the information out of the dialog box.

At this point, you may feel a bit overwhelmed by the plethora of constructors and events. You may be ready to forget about dialogs altogether! Not to worry — JBuilder makes creating and using dialogs quite easy. But if you still feel that creating a dialog is simply too much work, JBuilder provides you with several standard dialogs that will work for you in a variety of situations. In the following sections we examine these in some detail.

Using the Color Chooser

JColorChooser is a component that is new in Swing. There was no similar component in AWT. It lets the user select a color from a palette. The default behavior is to present a dialog box containing a tabbed pane that lets the user choose colors.

It is not at all uncommon for a user to require some particular color setting. If you have used any of the popular graphics programs, such as Adobe Photoshop, CorelDRAW, or GIMP, you have definitely seen dialogs where the user chooses a particular color from a palette. If you allow the user of your program to customize any color in your application, you are well advised to utilize the built-in color chooser dialog.

The JColorChooser class inherits from the JComponent class and thus inherits methods and properties from that class. JColorChooser provides a pane of controls designed to allow a user to select a specific color. The methods of this class are summarized in Table 9.3.

Table 9.3 JColorChooser methods

Method	Purpose
void addChooserPanel (AbstractColorChooserPanel panel)	Adds a color chooser panel to the color chooser.
static JDialogcreateDialog (Component c, String title, boolean modal, JColorChooser chooserPane, ActionListener okListener, ActionListener cancelListener)	Creates and returns a new dialog containing the specified ColorChooser pane along with OK, Cancel, and Reset buttons.
AbstractColor ChooserPanel[] getChooserPanels()	Returns the specified color panels.
ColorgetColor()	Gets the current color value from the color chooser.
JComponentgetPreviewPanel()	Returns the preview panel that shows a chosen color.
void setChooserPanels (AbstractColorChooserPanel[] panels)	Specifies the color panels used to choose a color value.
void setColor(Color color)	Sets the current color of the color chooser to the specified color.
void setColor(int c)	Sets the current color of the color chooser to the specified color.
void setColor(int r, int g, int b)	Sets the current color of the color chooser to the specified RGB color.
static ColorshowDialog (Component component, String title, Color initialColor)	Shows a modal color chooser dialog and blocks until the dialog is hidden.

In addition to these methods, there are several possible constructors that you can use with JColorChooser. Those are summarized in Table 9.4.

Table 9.4 JColorChooser constructors

Constructor	Purpose
JColorChooser()	Creates a color chooser pane with an initial color of white.
JColorChooser(Color initialColor)	Creates a color chooser pane with the specified initial color.
JColorChooser (ColorSelectionModel model)	Creates a color chooser pane with the specified ColorSelectionModel.

Obviously, each of these constructors has a different purpose. The first constructor is relatively obvious in its purpose. The second constructor, when called, is passed as an instance of the Color object. Since some readers may not be familiar with this, the various color class methods are summarized in Table 9.5.

Table 9.5 Color class methods

Method	Purpose
static Color getColor (String nm)	Finds a color in the system properties.
static Color getColor (String nm, Color v)	Finds a color in the system properties.
Color darker()	Creates a new color that is a darker version of this color.
Color brighter()	Creates a new color that is a brighter version of this color.

Of course, before you can use these methods, you will need to create an instance of the Color class. Which constructor you use is of paramount importance. Table 9.6 summarizes the most commonly used constructors.

Table 9.6 Color class constructors

Constructor	Purpose
Color(int rgb)	Creates an opaque sRGB color with the specified combined RGB value consisting of the red component in bits 16 to 23, the green component in bits 8 to 15, and the blue component in bits 0 to 7.
Color(float r, float g, float b)	Creates an opaque sRGB color with the specified red, green, and blue values in the range 0.0 to 1.0.

Constructor	Purpose
Color(int r, int g, int b)	Creates an opaque sRGB color with the specified red, green, and blue values in the range 0 to 255.

The last one is the easiest to understand and therefore the one we use for examples in this section. The following code shows how the color chooser is implemented in Java:

```
import java.awt.*;
import java.awt.event.*;
import javax.swing.*;
public class JColorChooserExample extends JFrame implements
      ActionListener
{
  public static void main(String[] args)
   {
    new JColorChooserExample ();
  }
  public JColorChooserExample ()
 {
    super("Using  the JColorChooser");
    WindowUtilities.setNativeLookAndFeel();
    addWindowListener(new ExitListener());
    Container content = getContentPane();
    content.setBackground(Color.white);
    content.setLayout(new FlowLayout());
    JButton btncolor  = new JButton("Choose Color");
    btncolor.addActionListener(this);
    content.add(btncolor);
    setSize(300, 100);
    setVisible(true);
  }
  public void actionPerformed(ActionEvent e)
{
    Color backcolor = new Color();
     backcolor= JColorChooser.showDialog(this,
          "Choose Background Color", getBackground());
    if (bgColor != null)
      getContentPane().setBackground(backcolor);
  }
}
```

There are several things worth noting in this code, which is rather straightforward and simply involves the creation of standard components to display. However, this line:

```
backcolor= JColorChooser.showDialog(this,
     "Choose Background Color", getBackground());
```

...is new code. Basically this shows how you display a JColorChooser using the showDialog method. That method takes three arguments: the component that you want the dialog to be associated with, the caption, and the initial color. In our generic example, the component is a reference to the class you are in; this is the usual way to do this. The color is, in our example, the current background color; however, you may have it default to any color you wish.

Example 9.2

Step 1: Create a new project with an Application object as you have done in all the previous examples.

Step 2: Change the layout to a grid that is five rows by one column. You will place three text fields, one button, and one color chooser. It should look much like what you see in Figure 9.8.

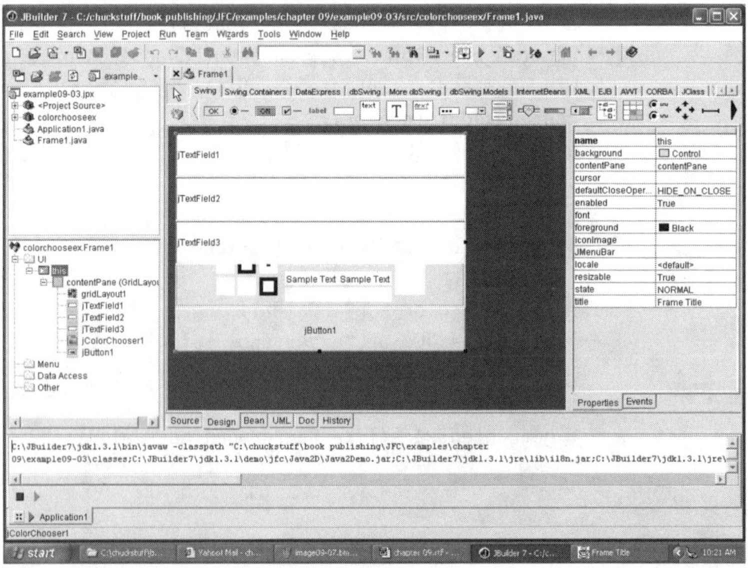

Figure 9.8 The color chooser example component layout

Step 3: Now we merely need to add a little code to the command button.

```
Color cred = new Color(255,0,0);
Color fcolor = jColorChooser1.showDialog(this,
     "Pick Font Color",cred);
jTextField1.setForeground(fcolor);
jTextField2.setForeground(fcolor);
jTextField3.setForeground(fcolor);
```

This code displays the color chooser with a default color of red. It then takes whatever color you choose and changes the foreground of the various text fields to match that color. When you run the application and click on the button, you will see something much like what is displayed in Figures 9.9 and 9.10.

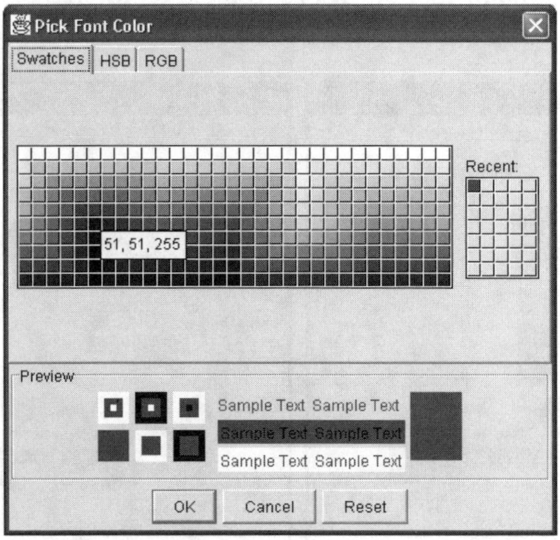

Figure 9.9 Selecting a color

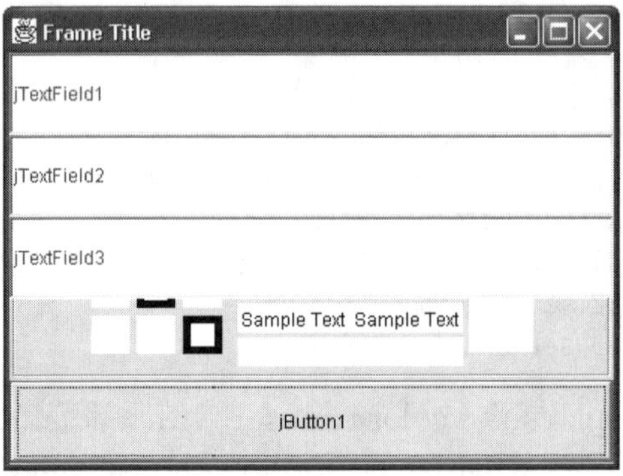

Figure 9.10 After your color is selected

When you selected a color, you may have noticed that there were other tabs on the color chooser. These tabs allow you to set the color manually. Figures 9.11 and 9.12 show these tabs.

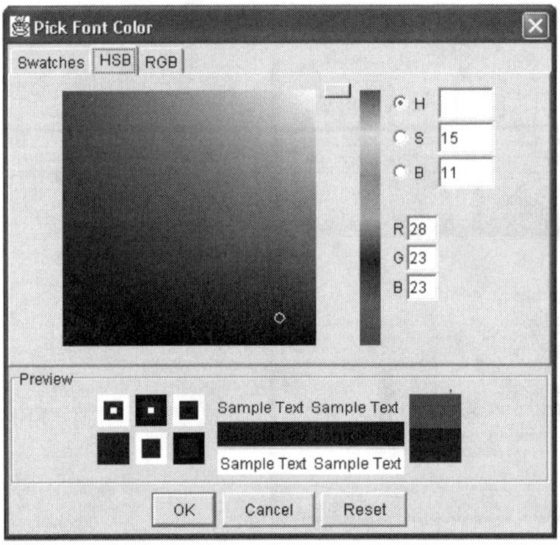

Figure 9.11 HSB color choices

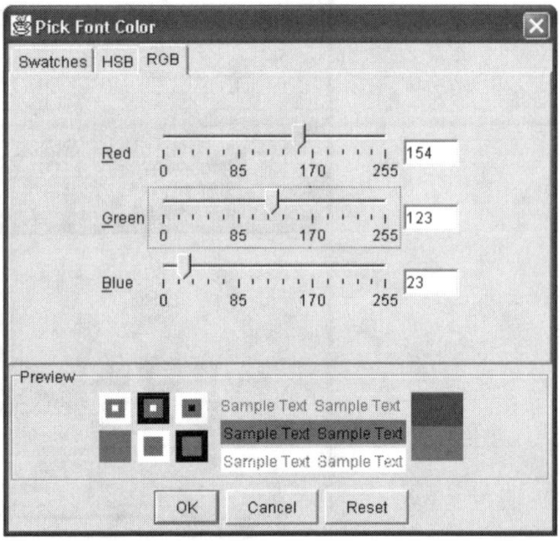

Figure 9.12 RGB color choices

As you can see, the color chooser gives you several options for picking colors. You can use the color swatches, HSB colors, or RGB colors. This makes for a very versatile component. For those users who either do not have JBuilder or simply wish to see the complete source code, here it is:

```
package colorchooseex;
import java.awt.*;
import java.awt.event.*;
import javax.swing.*;
public class Frame1 extends JFrame
 {
  private JPanel contentPane;
  private GridLayout gridLayout1 = new GridLayout(5,1);
  private JTextField jTextField1 = new JTextField();
  private JTextField jTextField2 = new JTextField();
  private JTextField jTextField3 = new JTextField();
  private JColorChooser jColorChooser1 = new JColorChooser();
  private JButton jButton1 = new JButton();
  //Construct the frame
  public Frame1()
    {
    enableEvents(AWTEvent.WINDOW_EVENT_MASK);
    try
     {
      jbInit();
    }
    catch(Exception e)
      {
      e.printStackTrace();
    }
  }
  //Component initialization
  private void jbInit() throws Exception
{
    contentPane = (JPanel) this.getContentPane();
    jTextField1.setText("jTextField1");
    contentPane.setLayout(gridLayout1);
    this.setSize(new Dimension(400, 300));
    this.setTitle("Frame Title");
    jTextField2.setText("jTextField2");

    jTextField3.setText("jTextField3");
    jButton1.setText("jButton1");
    jButton1.addActionListener(new java.awt.event
         .ActionListener()
     {
      public void actionPerformed(ActionEvent e)
      {
        jButton1_actionPerformed(e);
      }
```

```
    });
    contentPane.add(jTextField1, null);
    contentPane.add(jTextField2, null);
    contentPane.add(jTextField3, null);
    contentPane.add(jColorChooser1, null);
    contentPane.add(jButton1, null);
  }
  //Overridden so we can exit when window is closed
  protected void processWindowEvent(WindowEvent e)
   {
    super.processWindowEvent(e);
    if (e.getID() == WindowEvent.WINDOW_CLOSING)
     {
      System.exit(0);
    }
  }
  void jButton1_actionPerformed(ActionEvent e)
  {
    Color cred = new Color(255,0,0);
    Color fcolor = jColorChooser1.showDialog(this,
         "Pick Font Color", cred);
    jTextField1.setForeground(fcolor);
    jTextField2.setForeground(fcolor);
    jTextField3.setForeground(fcolor);
  }
}
```

Using the File Chooser

The file chooser is even more commonly used. Frequently, users will need to open a given file, and to do this, they must select that file. This is a perfect place to use the JFile-Chooser class. This class, like most classes in Java, has a number of useful methods. The most important and commonly used methods are summarized in Table 9.7.

Table 9.7 JFileChooser methods

Method	Purpose
boolean accept(File f)	This function will return a value of true if the file should be displayed.
void approveSelection()	This function is called by the user interface when the user hits the approve button (labeled Open or Save).
void cancelSelection()	This function is called by the user interface when the user chooses the Cancel button.
void ensureFileIsVisible (File f)	This function is used to make sure that the specified file is viewable and not hidden.
File getCurrentDirectory()	This method will return the current directory.
String getDescription(File f)	This method will return a description of the currently selected file.
String getDialogTitle()	This function retrieves the string that goes in the JFileChooser's title bar.
Icon getIcon(File f)	This method will return the icon for this file or type of file, depending on the system.
String getName(File f)	This function returns the name of the file.
File getSelectedFile()	This function actually returns the file itself.
boolean isFileSelection-Enabled()	This method determines if files are selectable based on the current file selection mode.
void setCurrentDirectory (File dir)	This method will set the current directory.
void setDialogTitle(String dialogTitle)	This method will set the string that goes in the JFileChooser window's title bar.
void setSelectedFile(File file)	This method sets the selected file.
int showDialog(Component parent, String approveButtonText)	This method will display a custom file chooser dialog with a custom approve button.
int showOpenDialog (Component parent)	This method will display an Open File file chooser dialog.
int showSaveDialog (Component parent)	This method will display a Save File file chooser dialog.

As you probably suspect from the previous examples throughout this book, this class has a number of options for a constructor. These are summarized in Table 9.8.

Table 9.8 JFileChooser constructors

Constructor	Purpose
JFileChooser()	This constructor will build a JFileChooser pointing to the user's home directory.
JFileChooser(File currentDirectory)	This constructor will build a JFileChooser using the given file as the path.
JFileChooser(File currentDirectory, FileSystemView fsv)	This constructor will build a JFileChooser using the given current directory and FileSystemView.
JFileChooser (FileSystemView fsv)	This constructor will create a JFileChooser using the given FileSystemView.
JFileChooser(String currentDirectoryPath)	This constructor will create a JFileChooser using the given path.
JFileChooser(String currentDirectoryPath, FileSystemView fsv)	This constructor will create a JFileChooser using the given current directory path and FileSystemView.

Example 9.3

Step 1: Start a new project and add an Application object, as you have done in all previous examples.

Step 2: Change your layout manager to a grid that is three rows by one column, and then place one text field, one button, and one file chooser, as you can see in Figure 9.13.

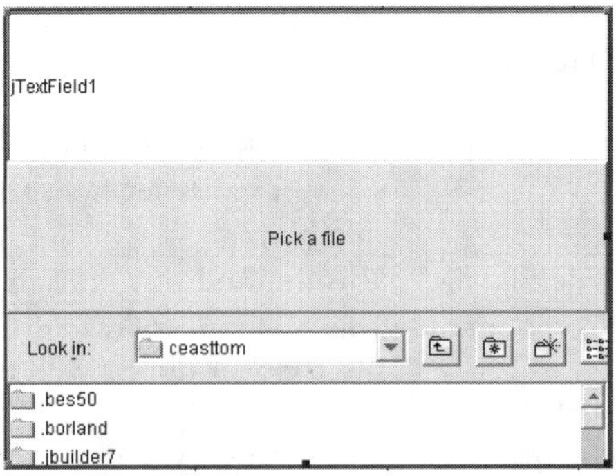

Figure 9.13 The file chooser example component layout

Step 3: In the action event of the button, place this code:

```
String filename;
int retval;
retval = jFileChooser1.showDialog(this, "Save");
filename = jFileChooser1.getName();
jTextField1.setText(filename);
```

Now when you run this and click on the button, you should see something much like the sequence displayed in Figure 9.14.

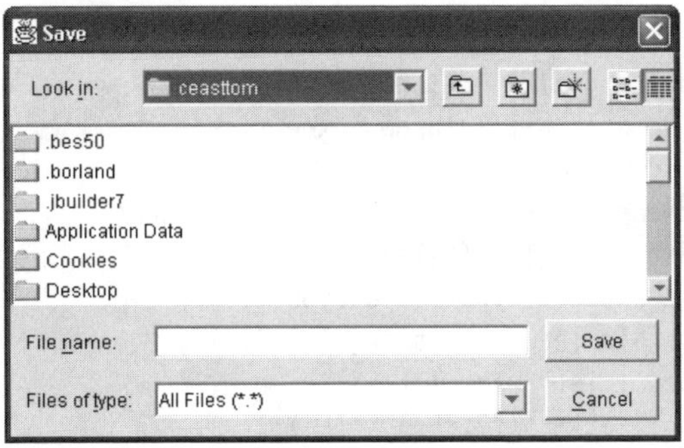

Figure 9.14 The file chooser

This simple example should illustrate the basics of using the JFileChooser, finding files, and using the methods of the JFileChooser. You should note that after you have pointed the file chooser at a particular file, it represents that file. You can then use methods such as getName() to find information about that file. For those users either not using JBuilder or who just like to see the full source code, here it is:

```
package filechooserexample;

import java.awt.*;
import java.awt.event.*;
import javax.swing.*;
public class Frame1 extends JFrame
{
  private JPanel contentPane;
  private GridLayout gridLayout1 = new GridLayout(3,1);
  private JTextField jTextField1 = new JTextField();
  private JButton jButton1 = new JButton();
  private JFileChooser jFileChooser1 = new JFileChooser();
```

```
//Construct the frame
public Frame1()
{
  enableEvents(AWTEvent.WINDOW_EVENT_MASK);
  try
  {
    jbInit();
  }
  catch(Exception e)
  {
    e.printStackTrace();
  }
}
//Component initialization
private void jbInit() throws Exception
{
 contentPane = (JPanel) this.getContentPane();
  jTextField1.setText("jTextField1");
  contentPane.setLayout(gridLayout1);
  this.setSize(new Dimension(400, 300));
  this.setTitle("Frame Title");
  jButton1.setText("Pick a file");
  jButton1.addActionListener(new java.awt.event
       .ActionListener()
  {
    public void actionPerformed(ActionEvent e)
    {
      jButton1_actionPerformed(e);
    }
  });
  contentPane.add(jTextField1, null);
  contentPane.add(jButton1, null);
  contentPane.add(jFileChooser1, null);
}
//Overridden so we can exit when window is closed
protected void processWindowEvent(WindowEvent e)
{
  super.processWindowEvent(e);
  if (e.getID() == WindowEvent.WINDOW_CLOSING)
   {
    System.exit(0);
  }
}
void jButton1_actionPerformed(ActionEvent e)
{
```

```
    String filename;
    int retval;
    retval = jFileChooser1.showDialog(this, "Save");
    filename = jFileChooser1.getName();
    jTextField1.setText(filename);
  }
}
```

Summary

In this chapter you were introduced to dialogs. You were shown their methods and constructors and how to create and use them. This chapter also explored specialized dialogs such as the color chooser and the file chooser. With this information, you should be able to add significant functionality to your programs.

Review Questions

1. By default are dialogs modal or modeless?
2. What does it mean to say that a given dialog is modal?
3. What does the "this" argument in showDialog represent?
4. What are three ways you can choose colors in JColorChooser?
5. What method will get you the name of the file you have selected with JFileChooser?
6. In JFileChooser, what method is called if the user selects the Cancel button?
7. What methods would you use to change the intensity of a color you had selected with the JColorChooser?

Chapter 10

The Graphics Class

This chapter covers the following:

- Graphics class essentials
- Details of the Graphics class
- A practical example

Introduction

The Graphics class is perhaps one of the most flexible classes in JFC. It existed previously in the Abstract Windowing Toolkit and has been enhanced and expanded in Java Foundation Classes. This class provides a rich set of methods that allow you to perform a variety of graphics renderings, including drawings. This chapter explores this class and its various methods in some detail.

Graphics Class Essentials

The Graphics class inherits directly from the Object class. This means that it is relatively high in Java's object hierarchy. The Graphics class is the abstract base class for all graphics contexts that allow an application to draw on components. The fact that the Graphics class is abstract means that you cannot directly instantiate it. However, most components have a getGraphics method that returns an instance of the graphics method with which you can use to draw on that component. A Graphics object encapsulates all the state information needed for the basic rendering operations that

Java supports. This state information includes several properties:

- The component object on which to draw
- The current color
- The current font
- The current clip
- A translation origin for rendering and clipping coordinates
- The current logical pixel operation function (XOR or Paint)
- The current XOR alternative color (see setXORMode (java.awt.Color))

Graphics Class Details

There are a few details of the Graphics class that, while not essential for using the class, can be useful for readers who want an in-depth understanding of how the class actually renders images. These details are summarized in this section.

The various rendering operations work by treating the pixels as an infinitely thin set of coordinates. Operations that draw the outline of a figure operate by traversing an infinitely thin path between pixels with a pixel-sized pen that hangs down and to the right of the anchor point on the path. Operations that fill a figure do so by filling the interior of that same infinitely thin path. The graphics pen hangs down and to the right from the path that it traverses. This means that if you draw a figure that covers a particular rectangle, that figure occupies one extra row of pixels on the right and bottom than the picture does. It also means that if you draw a horizontal line along the same y coordinate as the baseline of a line of text, that line is actually drawn below the text.

Many methods of the Graphics class take coordinates as arguments. Usually, there are four numbers. The first two define the starting point, and the second two define the ending point. The point of origin for this graphics system (0,0) is the upper left-hand corner. It is *not* the center of the screen, as it is with Cartesian coordinate systems. All coordinates that appear as arguments to the methods of this Graphics object are considered relative to the translation origin of this Graphics object prior to the invocation of the method. All rendering operations modify only pixels that lie within the area bounded by the current clip, which is specified by a shape in user space and controlled by the program using the Graphics object. This user clip is transformed into device space and combined with the device clip, which is defined by the visibility of windows and device extents. The combination of the user clip and device clip defines the composite clip, which determines the final clipping region. The user clip cannot be modified by the rendering system to reflect the resulting composite clip. The user clip can only be changed through the setClip or clipRect methods. All drawing or writing is done in the current color using the current paint mode and in the current font.

This class has a number of exciting methods that we explore in this chapter. Table 10.1 summarizes the most commonly used methods.

Table 10.1 Graphics class methods

Method	Purpose
abstract void clearRect(int x, int y, int width, int height)	This method will clear the specified rectangle by filling it with the background color of the current drawing surface.
abstract void copyArea(int x, int y, int width, int height, int dx, int dy)	This method is used to copy an area of the component by a distance specified by dx and dy.
abstract Graphics create()	This method will create a new Graphics object that is a copy of the current Graphics object.
abstract void dispose()	This method will dispose of the current Graphics context and release any system resources that it is using.
void draw3DRect(int x, int y, int width, int height, boolean raised)	This method is used to draw a 3D highlighted outline of the specified rectangle.

Method	Purpose
abstract void drawArc(int x, int y, int width, int height, int startAngle, int arcAngle)	This method will draw the outline of a circular or elliptical arc covering the specified rectangle.
abstract Boolean drawImage(Image img, int x, int y, Color bgcolor, ImageObserver observer)	This method will draw as much of the specified image as is currently available.
abstract void drawLine(int x1, int y1, int x2, int y2)	This method will draw a line between the points (x1, y1) and (x2, y2) in this graphics context's coordinate system.
abstract void drawOval (int x, int y, int width, int height)	This method is used to draw the outline of an oval.
abstract void drawPolygon(int[] xPoints, int[] yPoints, int nPoints)	This method will draw a closed polygon defined by arrays of x and y coordinates.
void drawRect(int x, int y, int width, int height)	This method is used to draw the outline of a rectangle.
abstract void drawRoundRect(int x, int y, int width, int height, int arcWidth, int arcHeight)	This method is used to draw an outlined round-cornered rectangle.
abstract void drawString(String str, int x, int y)	This method is used to draw the text given by the specified string, using this graphics context's current font and color.
void fill3DRect(int x, int y, int width, int height, boolean raised)	This method will paint a 3D highlighted rectangle filled with the current color.
abstract void fillArc(int x, int y, int width, int height, int startAngle, int arcAngle)	This method will fill a circular or elliptical arc covering the specified rectangle.
abstract void fillOval(int x, int y, int width, int height)	This method is used to fill an oval bounded by the specified rectangle with the current color.
abstract void fillPolygon(int[] xPoints, int[] yPoints, int nPoints)	This method is used to fill a closed polygon defined by arrays of x and y coordinates.
abstract void fillRect(int x, int y, int width, int height)	This method is used to fill a specified rectangle.

Method	Purpose
abstract void fillRoundRect(int x, int y, int width, int height, int arcWidth, int arcHeight)	This method is used to fill the specified round-cornered rectangle with the current color.
abstract Color getColor()	This method will return this graphics context's current color.
abstract void setColor(Color c)	This method will set this graphics context's current color to the specified color.

Unlike many of the other classes that we have seen throughout this text, this class has only one no arguments constructor. But that's enough theory; let's look at an example.

Example 10.1

Step 1: Create a new project with a standard Application object, as with previous examples throughout this book.

Step 2: Place one panel in the West part of the layout named **pnlbuttons** and one panel in the Center named **pnldraw**. Change the color of pnldraw to white, as shown in Figure 10.1.

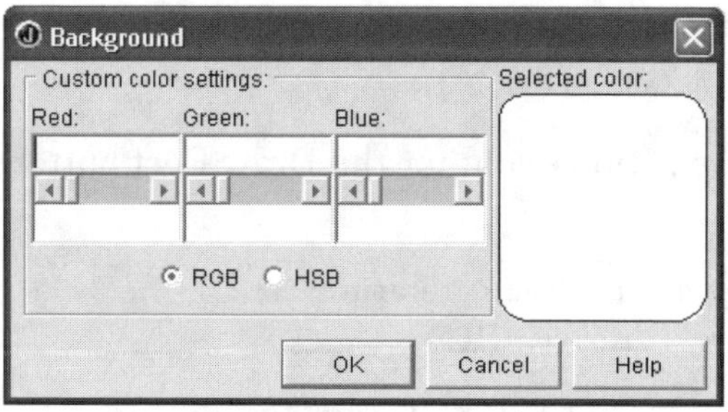

Figure 10.1 Background color for panel draw

Step 3: The panel on the West side, pnlbuttons, should have a grid layout that is four rows by one column. You will then place four buttons on it. When you're done, your design screen should look much like what you see in Figure 10.2.

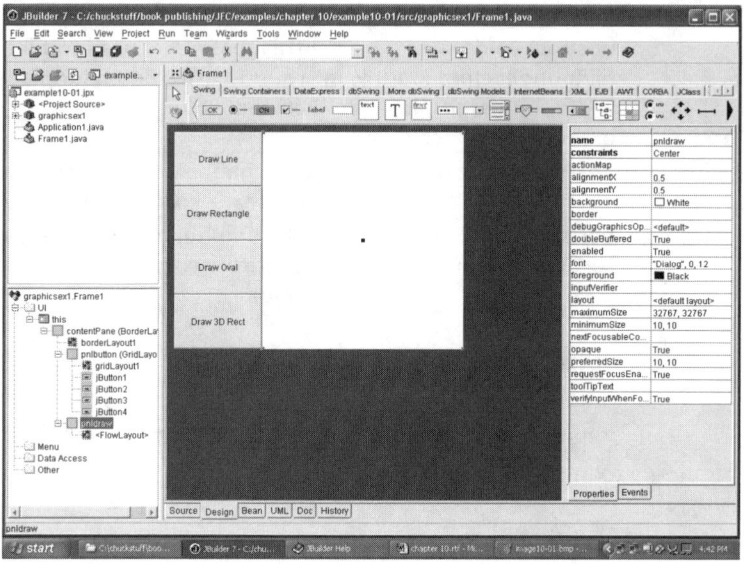

Figure 10.2 The example component layout

Step 4: Remember that the Graphics class is abstract. This means that you cannot directly instantiate it. However, most components support a getGraphics() method that returns an instance of the Graphics class. That is what we will use to do the drawing. In the button for Draw Line, place this code:

```
Graphics g = pnldraw.getGraphics();
g.drawLine(50,50,200,200);
```

Then in the action event for the Draw Rect button, place this code:

```
Graphics g = pnldraw.getGraphics();
g.drawRect(55,55,100,100);
```

In the action event for the Draw Oval button, place this code:

```
Graphics g = pnldraw.getGraphics();
g.drawOval(25,25,75,75);
```

Finally, in the action event for the Draw 3D Rect button, place this code:

```
Graphics g = pnldraw.getGraphics();
g.draw3DRect(60,60,120,120,true);
```

When you click each of these buttons, you will see the image for that button displayed. This is shown in Figures 10.3 through 10.6.

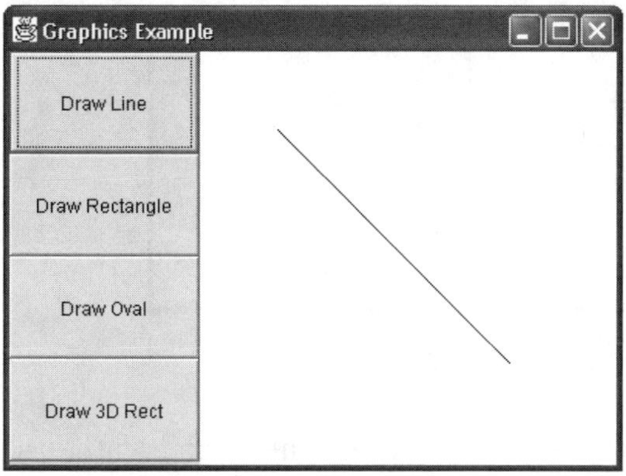

Figure 10.3 The drawLine method

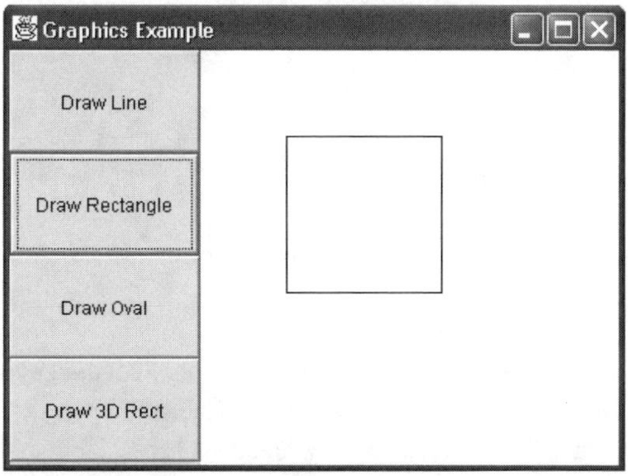

Figure 10.4 The drawRect method

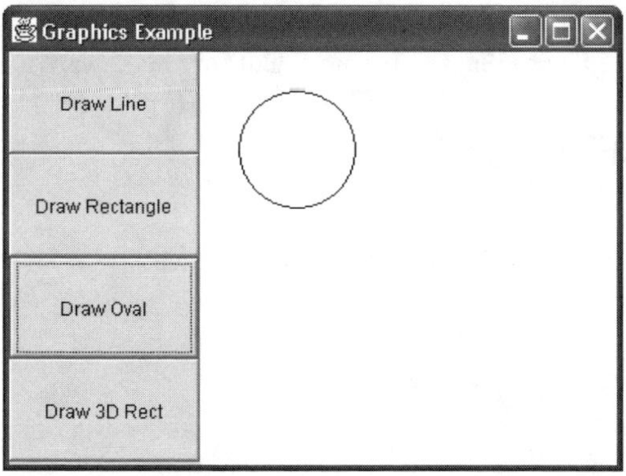

Figure 10.5 The drawOval method

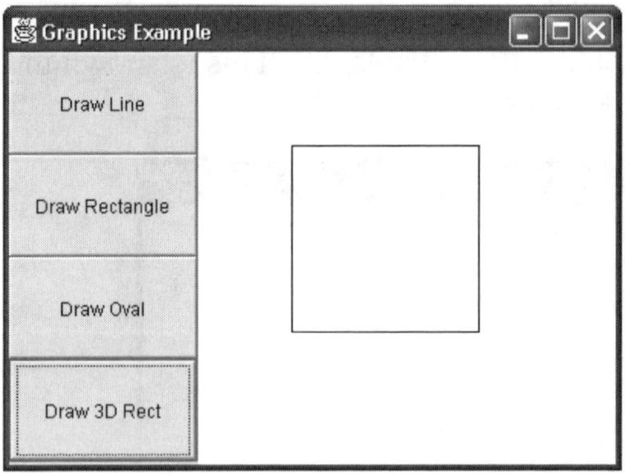

Figure 10.6 The draw3DRect method

As you can see, each of these methods is rather simple to use. Drawing basic lines, shapes, etc. is very easy with the Graphics class. For those readers not using JBuilder or who just like to see the entire code, it is provided here:

```
package graphicsex1;
import java.awt.*;
import java.awt.event.*;
import javax.swing.*;
public class Frame1 extends JFrame
{
  private JPanel contentPane;
  private BorderLayout borderLayout1 = new BorderLayout();
  private JPanel pnldraw = new JPanel();
  private JPanel pnlbutton = new JPanel();
  private GridLayout gridLayout1 = new GridLayout(4,1);
  private JButton jButton1 = new JButton();
  private JButton jButton2 = new JButton();
  private JButton jButton3 = new JButton();
  private JButton jButton4 = new JButton();
  //Construct the frame
  public Frame1()
  {
    enableEvents(AWTEvent.WINDOW_EVENT_MASK);
    try
    {
      jbInit();
    }
    catch(Exception e)
    {
```

```
    e.printStackTrace();
  }
}
//Component initialization
private void jbInit() throws Exception
{
  contentPane = (JPanel) this.getContentPane();
  contentPane.setLayout(borderLayout1);
  this.setSize(new Dimension(400, 300));
  this.setTitle("Graphics Example");
  pnldraw.setBackground(Color.white);
  pnlbutton.setLayout(gridLayout1);
  jButton1.setText("Draw Line");
  jButton1.addActionListener(new java.awt.event
       .ActionListener()
  {
    public void actionPerformed(ActionEvent e)
    {
      jButton1_actionPerformed(e);
    }
  });
  jButton2.setText("Draw Rectangle");
  jButton2.addActionListener(new java.awt.event
       .ActionListener()
  {
    public void actionPerformed(ActionEvent e)
    {
      jButton2_actionPerformed(e);
    }
  });
  jButton3.setText("Draw Oval");
  jButton3.addActionListener(new java.awt.event
       .ActionListener()
 {
    public void actionPerformed(ActionEvent e)
    {
      jButton3_actionPerformed(e);
    }
  });
  jButton4.setText("Draw 3D Rect");
  jButton4.addActionListener(new java.awt.event
       .ActionListener()
  {
    public void actionPerformed(ActionEvent e) {
      jButton4_actionPerformed(e);
```

```
      }
    });
    pnlbutton.add(jButton1, null);
    pnlbutton.add(jButton2, null);
    pnlbutton.add(jButton3, null);
    pnlbutton.add(jButton4, null);
    contentPane.add(pnlbutton, BorderLayout.WEST);
    contentPane.add(pnldraw, BorderLayout.CENTER);
  }
  //Overridden so we can exit when window is closed
  protected void processWindowEvent(WindowEvent e)
  {
    super.processWindowEvent(e);
    if (e.getID() == WindowEvent.WINDOW_CLOSING)
    {
      System.exit(0);
    }
  }
  void jButton1_actionPerformed(ActionEvent e)
  {
   Graphics g = pnldraw.getGraphics();
    g.drawLine(50,50,200,200);
  }
  void jButton2_actionPerformed(ActionEvent e)
  {
   Graphics g = pnldraw.getGraphics();
   g.drawRect(55,55,100,100);
  }
  void jButton3_actionPerformed(ActionEvent e)
  {
   Graphics g = pnldraw.getGraphics();
   g.drawOval(25,25,75,75);
  }
  void jButton4_actionPerformed(ActionEvent e)
  {
   Graphics g = pnldraw.getGraphics();
   g.draw3DRect(60,60,120,120,true);
  }
}
```

This example should illustrate for you just how flexible and useful the Graphics class can be.

A Practical Example

The previous examples of how to draw circles, lines, and rectangles is interesting, but it's not terribly practical. In this section we explore a very practical method for using these same graphics methods to create useful graphs on the fly with live data. That is definitely a useful application of the Graphics class.

Example 10.2

Step 1: Start a new project with a new Application object, as you have with all the other examples in this book.

Step 2: Leave the application frame with the default border layout. Place a panel in the Center. Name that panel **pnldraw** and set its background color to white. Place another panel on the West side and name it **pnlstart**. Set pnlstart's layout to **VerticalFlow**.

Step 3: Place three labels, three text fields, and one button on the pnlstart panel. Lay them out as you see in Figure 10.7.

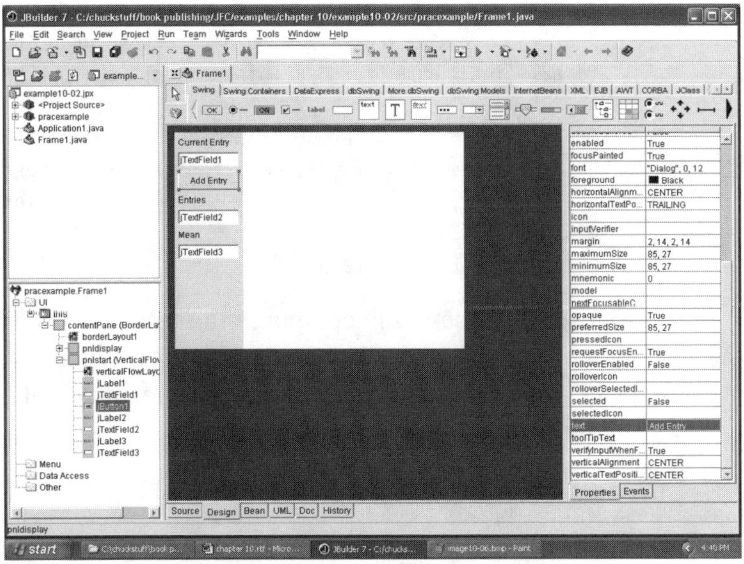

Figure 10.7 Practical example layout

Step 4: Add these declarations to the beginning of the class:

```
private float currentry, totentry = 0, meanentry;
private String stemp;
 private int numenteries;
```

Step 5: Now place the following code in the action event of the button:

```
 stemp = jTextField1.getText();
 currentry = Float.valueOf(stemp).floatValue();
 totentry = totentry + currentry;  // total of all entries
 numentries++;              // how many items have been entered
 meanentry = totentry/numentries;  // compute the mean
 stemp = Float.toString(totentry);
 jTextField2.setText(stemp);
 stemp = Float.toString(meanentry);
 jTextField3.setText(stemp);


//now we draw a line graph for each line added
//Color c = new Color(0,0,255);
//g.setColor(c);

int temp1, temp2;        //temp variables to draw graph
temp1 = numentries *15; // this will be used for the y
                        // coordinate when graphing
temp2 =(int)currentry;  // This converts the current entry
                        // to an integer for use in the graph
Graphics g = pnldisplay.getGraphics();
Color c = new Color(temp1,temp1,temp2); //this makes a unique
g.setColor(c);                          //color for each line
g.drawRect(10,temp1,temp2,10);
g.fillRect(10,temp1,temp2,10);
```

This code essentially computes the total and the mean for your entries and draws a bar graph for each one. When you run it, you should see a series of images much like what is depicted in Figures 10.8, 10.9, and 10.10.

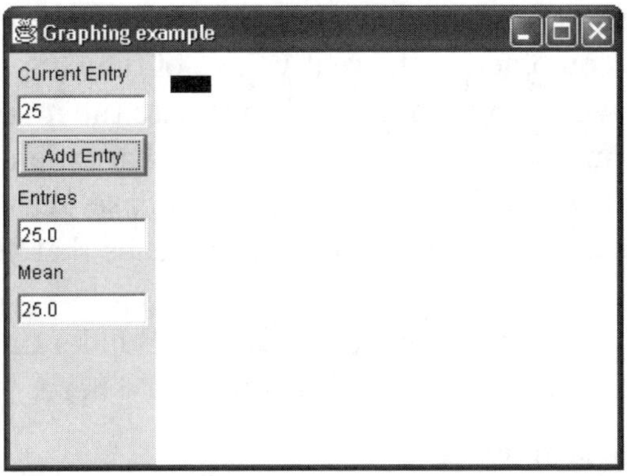

Figure 10.8 Bar graph example screen 1

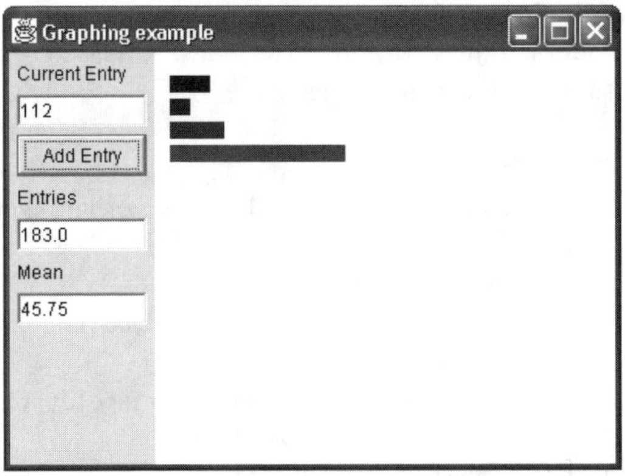

Figure 10.9 Bar graph example screen 2

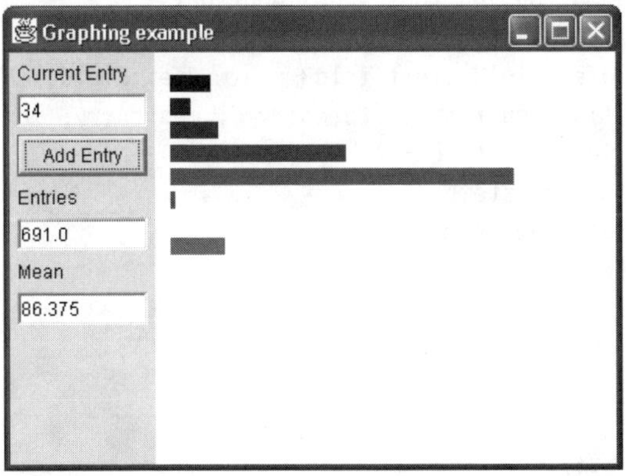

Figure 10.10 Bar graph example screen 3

By using some very basic techniques that you have seen in this book, combined with creative use of the Graphics class, we now have a program that will calculate the mean of any set of floating-point values and display a bar graph of the various entries. This is a program that is useful as is and can easily be expanded to suit any special needs that you might have.

For those readers who do not have JBuilder or who just want to see the entire code, it is presented here:

```
package pracexample;
import java.awt.*;
import java.awt.event.*;
import javax.swing.*;
import com.borland.jbcl.layout.*;
public class Frame1 extends JFrame
{
  private JPanel contentPane;
  private BorderLayout borderLayout1 = new BorderLayout();
  private JPanel pnldisplay = new JPanel();
  private JPanel pnlstart = new JPanel();
  private VerticalFlowLayout verticalFlowLayout1 =
       new VerticalFlowLayout();
  private JTextField jTextField1 = new JTextField();
  private JLabel jLabel1 = new JLabel();
  private JLabel jLabel2 = new JLabel();
  private JTextField jTextField2 = new JTextField();
  private JButton jButton1 = new JButton();
  private JLabel jLabel3 = new JLabel();
  private JTextField jTextField3 = new JTextField();
  private float currentry, totentry=0, meanentry;
  private int numentries;
  private String stemp;
  //Construct the frame
  public Frame1()
  {
    enableEvents(AWTEvent.WINDOW_EVENT_MASK);
    try
    {
      jbInit();
    }
    catch(Exception e)
    {
      e.printStackTrace();
```

```
    }
  }
  //Component initialization
  private void jbInit() throws Exception
  {
    contentPane = (JPanel) this.getContentPane();
    contentPane.setLayout(borderLayout1);
    this.setSize(new Dimension(400, 300));
    this.setTitle("Frame Title");
    pnldisplay.setBackground(Color.white);
    pnlstart.setLayout(verticalFlowLayout1);
    jTextField1.setText("0");
    jLabel1.setText("Current Entry");
    jLabel2.setText("Entries");
    jTextField2.setText("0");
    jButton1.setText("Add Entry");
    jButton1.addActionListener(new java.awt.event
         .ActionListener() {
      public void actionPerformed(ActionEvent e) {
        jButton1_actionPerformed(e);
      }
    });
    jLabel3.setText("Mean");
    jTextField3.setText("0");
    contentPane.add(pnldisplay, BorderLayout.CENTER);
    contentPane.add(pnlstart, BorderLayout.WEST);
    pnlstart.add(jLabel1, null);
    pnlstart.add(jTextField1, null);
    pnlstart.add(jButton1, null);
    pnlstart.add(jLabel2, null);
    pnlstart.add(jTextField2, null);
    pnlstart.add(jLabel3, null);
    pnlstart.add(jTextField3, null);
  }
  //Overridden so we can exit whcn window is closed
  protected void processWindowEvent(WindowEvent e)
  {
    super.processWindowEvent(e);
    if (e.getID() == WindowEvent.WINDOW_CLOSING)
    {
      System.exit(0);
    }
  }
  void jButton1_actionPerformed(ActionEvent e)
  {
```

```
        stemp = jTextField1.getText();
        currentry = Float.valueOf(stemp).floatValue();
        totentry = totentry + currentry;   // total of all entries
        numentries++;                     // how many items have been
                                          // entered
        meanentry = totentry/numentries;   // compute the mean
        stemp = Float.toString(totentry);
        jTextField2.setText(stemp);
        stemp = Float.toString(meanentry);
        jTextField3.setText(stemp);
      //now we draw a line graph for each line added.
      //Color c = new Color(0,0,255);
      //g.setColor(c);
      int temp1, temp2;          //temp variables to draw graph
      temp1 = numentries *15;    // this will be used for the y
                                 // coordinate when graphing
      temp2 =(int)currentry; // This converts the current entry
                             // to an integer for use in the graph
      Graphics g = pnldisplay.getGraphics();
      Color c = new Color(temp1,temp1,temp2);//this makes a unique
      g.setColor(c);                         //color for each line
      g.drawRect(10,temp1,temp2,10);
      g.fillRect(10,temp1,temp2,10);
    }
  }
```

Summary

In this chapter you were introduced to the Graphics class. This class has a number of very useful and interesting methods. With these methods, you can draw any basic shape, line, or arc. You can set the color of the lines, change the fill color, or erase the entire image altogether. More artistically inclined programmers might wish to spend even more time carefully exploring this exciting class. With a bit of creativity, which might be beyond this author, you could do some interesting graphics work.

It is also important that you realize that, in addition to artwork, you can use the Graphics class to generate business graphics, including charts and diagrams. This makes this class very useful and robust.

Review Questions

1. How do you create an instance of the Graphics class?
2. List any four methods of the Graphics class.
3. What class does the Graphics class inherit from?
4. How would you fill a rectangle that you have drawn with the Graphics class?
5. What do the numbers passed to graphics methods represent?
6. How would you clear all the drawing done by an instance of the Graphics class?
7. What does the point 0,0 represent in the Graphics class coordinate system?
8. How would you change the color that the instance of the Graphics class is using?

Chapter 11

JFC Databases

This chapter covers the following:

- Swing
- dbSwing

Introduction

The preceding chapters have taken you through almost every aspect of the graphical elements available to you with JFC and Swing. Java Foundation Classes are renowned for their graphical features. However, graphics are not the only thing that JFC has to offer a programmer — quite the contrary. In fact, you have a great many database classes available to you. Some of these were available in AWT but have been enhanced and expanded upon in JFC. JBuilder takes this a step further and makes database programming very easy. This chapter explores the various options available for creating database applications with JFC and specifically by using JBuilder. This chapter assumes that you have some basic knowledge of how a database works and at least a passing familiarity with Structured Query Language. However, if you lack this knowledge, don't panic. Appendix D provides a tutorial for using the Microsoft Access database, as well as the basics of Structured Query Language.

As you have already seen throughout this book, JBuilder frequently makes Java programming much easier. Database programming is no exception. JBuilder offers you a choice between the standard Swing components and dbSwing. The former are simply the standard JFC database classes found in Java. The latter, dbSwing, offers significant advantages over Swing with increased functionality and data-aware capabilities. The beauty of JBuilder is that you can use either option.

Swing

Let's first take a look at the standard JFC database classes. These are a group of classes that are part of the Java specification and work with any Java compiler. As with all aspects of Java, database connectivity is handled via a set of classes found in a given package. In this case the package is java.sql. The most important classes and interfaces are summarized in Table 11.1.

Table 11.1 Java.sql classes

Class/Interface	Description
Connection	This class represents the actual connection to the database in question. It allows you to open and close connections to databases.
Statement	This class is used to represent SQL statements that are transmitted to the underlying database.
ResultSet	This class represents the actual results of a given SQL query.

As you can readily see, there are classes for all of the basic functions one might need to connect to a database and execute various SQL statements. Each of these classes, of course, has a variety of methods. The most important methods of each class are summarized in the following tables.

Table 11.2 Connection interface methods

Method	Purpose
void close()	This method releases a connection's database and JDBC resources immediately instead of waiting for them to be automatically released.
String nativeSQL (String sql)	This method converts the given SQL statement into the system's native SQL grammar.

Method	Purpose
void commit()	This method makes permanent all changes made since the previous commit/rollback and releases any database locks currently held by the connection.
Statement createStatement()	This method will create a Statement object for sending SQL statements to the database.
Boolean isClosed()	This method checks to see if a connection is closed.

This interface is obviously fundamental to database operations using Java. It is the class that allows you to connect to a given data source. Without the Connection object, you can have no database programming, at least not with Java.

Table 11.3 Statement interface methods

Method	Purpose
void cancel()	This method will cancel this Statement object if both the DBMS and driver support aborting an SQL statement.
boolean execute (String sql)	This method will execute an SQL statement that may return multiple records.
void close()	This method releases this Statement object's database and JDBC resources immediately instead of waiting for this to happen when it is automatically closed.
Int getMaxRows()	This method will return the maximum number of rows that a ResultSet object can contain.
ResultSet getResultSet()	This method will return the current result as a ResultSet object.
void setMaxRows(int max)	This method will set the limit for the maximum number of rows that any ResultSet object can contain to the given number.

The Statement interface is the real workhorse of the java.sql package. This is where SQL queries are passed to the database and results returned. Ultimately, all database operations are merely a sequence of SQL statements executed against some database table(s).

Table 11.4 ResultSet interface methods

Method	Purpose
void deleteRow()	This method will delete the current row from this ResultSet object and the underlying database.
utovoid close()	This method will release this ResultSet object's database and JDBC resources immediately.
Boolean first()	This method will move the cursor to the first row in this ResultSet object.
Array getArray(String colName)	This method returns the value of the designated column in the current row of this ResultSet object as an Array object in the Java programming language.
Int getRow()	This method retrieves the current row number.
void insertRow()	This method will insert the contents of the insert row into this ResultSet and the database.
void moveToCurrentRow()	This method will move the cursor to the remembered cursor position, usually the current row.
Boolean last()	This method will move the cursor to the last row in this ResultSet object.
Boolean next()	This method will move the cursor down one row from its current position.
Boolean previous()	This method will move the cursor to the previous row in this ResultSet object.

Connecting to a database and executing SQL queries is usually done for the purpose of obtaining some records from that database. The ResultSet interface is used to deal with the resulting records. It allows you to navigate through that result set, insert or delete rows, and retrieve the data in a variety of formats.

This is all fine, but you would probably like to see an example using these classes and interfaces to actually connect to some database and retrieve some value. The following is an example using the java.sql package to connect to a database and return specific data. This example can be done in any text editor and compiled. I am providing it here to show you how database connectivity can be accomplished sans JBuilder.

Example 11.1

Step 1: Write the following code in your favorite text editor:

```
import java.sql.*;
class sql
{
// The URL is the location of the data source
static String url = "jdbc:odbc:mysource";
// Connection objects represent the actual connection to
// some data source.
static Connection connection;
public static void main(String args[])
{
String sz_field;   // This will hold a single field/column
// returned from a database
String sqlquery;  // This will hold any valid SQL Query
try
{
// These statements make the initial connection to
// The data source
Class.forName("sun.jdbc.odbc.JdbcOdbcDriver");
connection = DriverManager.getConnection(url);
// Build an sql query that will be passed to the data source
sqlquery = "SELECT * FROM bank";
// The statement object represents any valid sql statement
Statement statement = connection.createStatement();
// Execute the sql and get back the recordset
ResultSet rs = statement.executeQuery(sqlquery);
// move to the first record
rs.next();
// retrieve and display the first field
sz_field= rs.getString(1);
System.out.println("The account number " + sz_field);
// retrieve and display the second field
sz_field= rs.getString(2);
System.out.println("The checking balance is " + sz_field);
// retrieve and display the third field
sz_field= rs.getString(3);
System.out.println("The savings balance is " + sz_field);
// close the connection
connection.close();
```

```
}
catch(Exception e)
{
System.out.println("Error! " + e.toString());
}
}
}
```

Step 2: Compile the code with any Java compiler.

Step 3: Ensure that you have an MS Access database with the appropriate table created (the table must have the same fields as in our code). Also create a data source for it. If you do not know how to do this, refer to Appendix D.

Step 4: Execute the code from a command line.

This example illustrates a simple and direct way to connect to a database table, retrieve certain fields, and display them in a console application. The first thing that should come to your attention is the URL object. This represents the data source. In our case it represents a data source or DSN on a Windows PC. However, it could represent virtually any data source on any machine that is accessible from the client PC.

The two strings sz_field and sqlquery have rather singular purposes. The first holds the data contained in a single field of the database. The second holds any valid SQL query that you may wish to send to the underlying database table. You can also see in this code the creation of a Statement object and a ResultSet object. SQL queries can only be passed to the underlying database via a Statement object. The ResultSet object contains the records that result from the execution of a given SQL query.

Note: Before attempting to access any records, notice the rs.next command. The result set begins pointing to a null record. Calling the next method of the result set will point it to the first record in the result set.

This method of connecting to a database is actually rather simple. As you can see, simply using a handful of SQL objects such as the Statement, ResultSet, and Connection, you can connect to a data source and retrieve data. Let's look at another example, which is a little more complex, with a complete JFC Swing graphical user interface.

Example 11.2

Step 1: Start a standard project, as you have done in all the preceding examples.

Step 2: We are going to place a few components on the interface. This layout is a little more complicated than some of the others we have seen, so let's examine it step by step.

1. Leave the default border layout for the content pane, but place a panel in the North section and one in the Center.
2. The North panel will have a grid layout one row by three columns.
3. The Center panel will have a grid layout three rows by two columns.
4. You can then place the buttons, text fields, and labels on those panels, as you see in Figure 11.1.

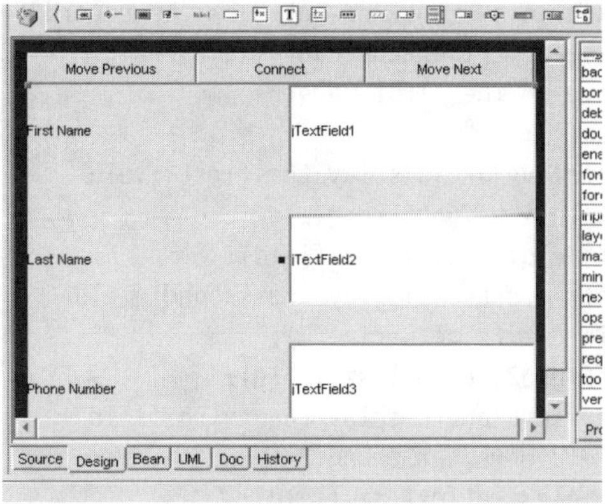

Figure 11.1 Illustration of Example 11.2 layout

Before we continue, notice that we used containers (i.e., panels) inside of other containers to get the layout exactly the way we wanted. This is a common trick used by Java programmers.

Step 3: Add the import.sql*; statement to your import statements at the beginning of the code.

Step 4: At the beginning of your class module where you declare variables, add the declarations for these database-related variables:

```
// The URL is the location of the data source
static String url = "jdbc:odbc:mysource";
// Connection objects represent the actual connection to
// some data source.
 static Connection connection;
String sz_field; // This will hold a single field/column
 // returned from a database
String sqlquery; // This will hold any valid SQL query
ResultSet rs;
```

Step 5: In the jbInit function, add this code:

```
connection = DriverManager.getConnection(url);
// Build an SQL query that will be passed to the data source
 sqlquery = "SELECT * FROM names";
 // The Statement object represents any valid SQL statement
 Statement statement = connection.createStatement();
 // Execute the SQL and get back the record set
 rs = statement.executeQuery(sqlquery);
 // move to the first record
 rs.next();
 // retrieve and display the first field
 sz_field = rs.getString(1);
 jTextField1.setText(sz_field);
 // retrieve and display the second field
 sz_field = rs.getString(2);
 jTextField2.setText(sz_field);
 // retrieve and display the third field
 sz_field = rs.getString(3);
jTextField3.setText(sz_field);
```

Step 6: Now in the Move Previous button, we will add this code:

```
try
 {
     rs.previous();
     // retrieve and display the first field
     sz_field = rs.getString(1);
     jTextField1.setText(sz_field);
     // retrieve and display the second field
     sz_field = rs.getString(2);
     jTextField2.setText(sz_field);
     // retrieve and display the third field
     sz_field = rs.getString(3);
     jTextField3.setText(sz_field);
 }
 catch(Exception be)
 {
 }
```

Step 7: Finally, in the Move Next button, we will add this code:

```
try
 {
     rs.next();
     // retrieve and display the first field
     sz_field = rs.getString(1);
     jTextField1.setText(sz_field);
     // retrieve and display the second field
     sz_field = rs.getString(2);
     jTextField2.setText(sz_field);
     // retrieve and display the third field
     sz_field = rs.getString(3);
     jTextField3.setText(sz_field);
 }
 catch(Exception be)
 {
 }
```

When you run this, you should be able to see something very much like what is shown in Figures 11.2 and 11.3.

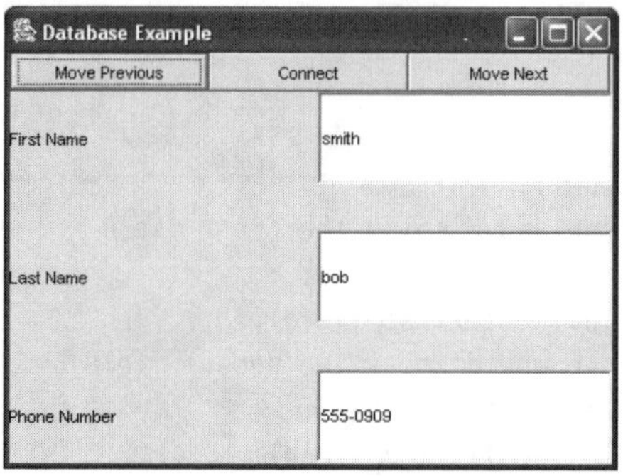

Figure 11.2 The database example

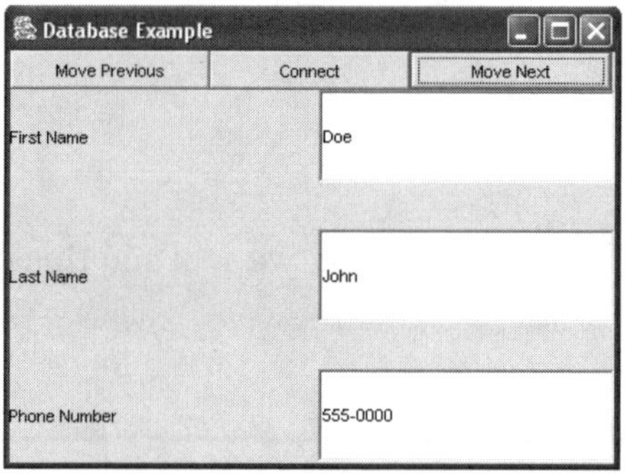

Figure 11.3 The database example part 2

What has happened in this example is really quite simple. We took the code from the console-based example shown in Example 11.1 and placed it within a JFC interface. This gives the end user a nice graphical way to maneuver through the database. You might wonder why we use the try/catch blocks in the Move Next and Move Previous buttons. The answer is simple: Many classes in the java.sql package must be inside a try/catch block in order to execute. This is a safeguard built into Java. Given that so many things can go wrong when doing database programming, the creators of Java thought it prudent to put in this safeguard.

Note: The database used for this is included with the sample code in the downloadable companion files (www.wordware.com/files/jbuilder). If you use a different database, you will have to change the name

of the table used in the code. You will also need to create a data source for this. If you don't know how to do this, refer to Appendix D.

For those readers who are either not using JBuilder or just wish to see the entire source code, it is presented here. This is a rather long code sample.

```
package example11_02;
import java.awt.*;
import java.awt.event.*;
import javax.swing.*;
import java.sql.*;

public class dbframe extends JFrame
{
  JPanel contentPane;
  BorderLayout borderLayout1 = new BorderLayout();
  JPanel jPanel1 = new JPanel();
  GridLayout gridLayout1 = new GridLayout(1, 3);
  JPanel jPanel2 = new JPanel();
  GridLayout gridLayout2 = new GridLayout(3, 2, 10, 30);
  JButton jButton1 = new JButton();
  JButton jButton2 = new JButton();
  JButton jButton3 = new JButton();
  JLabel jLabel1 = new JLabel();
  JTextField jTextField1 = new JTextField();
  JLabel jLabel2 = new JLabel();
  JTextField jTextField2 = new JTextField();
  JLabel jLabel3 = new JLabel();
  JTextField jTextField3 = new JTextField();
  // database variables/objects
  // The URL is the location of the data source
  static String url = "jdbc:odbc:mysource";
  // Connection objects represent the actual connection to
  // some data source.
  static Connection connection;
  String sz_field;   // This will hold a single field/column
                     // returned from a database
  String sqlquery;   // This will hold any valid SQL query
  ResultSet rs;
  //Construct the frame
  public dbframe()
  {
    enableEvents(AWTEvent.WINDOW_EVENT_MASK);
```

```
    try
  {
      jbInit();
    }
    catch (Exception e)
  {
      e.printStackTrace();
    }
  }
  //Component initialization
  private void jbInit() throws Exception
{
    contentPane = (JPanel)this.getContentPane();
    contentPane.setLayout(borderLayout1);
    this.setSize(new Dimension(400, 300));
    this.setTitle("Database Example");
    jPanel1.setLayout(gridLayout1);
    jPanel2.setLayout(gridLayout2);
    jButton1.setActionCommand("jButton1");
    jButton1.setText("Move Previous");
    jButton1.addActionListener(new dbframe_jButton1_
         actionAdapter(this));
    jButton2.setToolTipText("Connect or disconnect from the
         database");
    jButton2.setText("Connect");
    jButton2.addActionListener(new dbframe_jButton2_
         actionAdapter(this));
    jButton3.setText("Move Next");
    jButton3.addActionListener(new dbframe_jButton3_
         actionAdapter(this));
    jLabel1.setText("First Name");
    jTextField1.setText("jTextField1");
    jLabel2.setText("Last Name");
    jTextField2.setText("jTextField2");
    jLabel3.setText("Phone Number");
    jTextField3.setText("jTextField3");
    contentPane.add(jPanel1, BorderLayout.NORTH);
    contentPane.add(jPanel2, BorderLayout.CENTER);
    jPanel2.add(jLabel1, null);
    jPanel2.add(jTextField1, null);
    jPanel2.add(jLabel2, null);
    jPanel2.add(jTextField2, null);
    jPanel2.add(jLabel3, null);
    jPanel2.add(jTextField3, null);
    jPanel1.add(jButton1, null);
```

```
    jPanel1.add(jButton2, null);
    jPanel1.add(jButton3, null);
    Class.forName("sun.jdbc.odbc.JdbcOdbcDriver");

    connection = DriverManager.getConnection(url);
  // Build an SQL query that will be passed to the data source
    sqlquery = "SELECT * FROM names";
    // The Statement object represents any valid SQL statement
    Statement statement = connection.createStatement();
    // Execute the SQL and get back the record set
    rs = statement.executeQuery(sqlquery);
    // move to the first record
    rs.next();
    // retrieve and display the first field
    sz_field = rs.getString(1);
    jTextField1.setText(sz_field);
    // retrieve and display the second field
    sz_field = rs.getString(2);
    jTextField2.setText(sz_field);
    // retrieve and display the third field
    sz_field = rs.getString(3);
    jTextField3.setText(sz_field);
  }
  //Overridden so we can exit when window is closed
  protected void processWindowEvent(WindowEvent e)
  {
    super.processWindowEvent(e);
    if (e.getID() == WindowEvent.WINDOW_CLOSING)
    {
      System.exit(0);
    }
  }
  void jButton2_actionPerformed(ActionEvent e)
  {
  }
  class dbframe_jButton2_actionAdapter
      implements java.awt.event.ActionListener
  {
    dbframe adaptee;
    dbframe_jButton2_actionAdapter(dbframe adaptee)
    {
      this.adaptee = adaptee;
    }
    public void actionPerformed(ActionEvent e)
   {
```

```
      adaptee.jButton2_actionPerformed(e);
    }
  }

  void jButton1_actionPerformed(ActionEvent e)
  {
    try
    {
        rs.previous();
        // retrieve and display the first field
        sz_field = rs.getString(1);
        jTextField1.setText(sz_field);
        // retrieve and display the second field
        sz_field = rs.getString(2);
        jTextField2.setText(sz_field);
        // retrieve and display the third field
        sz_field = rs.getString(3);
        jTextField3.setText(sz_field);
    }
    catch(Exception be)
    {
    }
    }
  void jButton3_actionPerformed(ActionEvent e)
  {
    try
    {
        rs.next();
        // retrieve and display the first field
        sz_field = rs.getString(1);
        jTextField1.setText(sz_field);
        // retrieve and display the second field
        sz_field = rs.getString(2);
        jTextField2.setText(sz_field);
        // retrieve and display the third field
        sz_field = rs.getString(3);
        jTextField3.setText(sz_field);
    }
    catch(Exception be)
    {

    }
  }
  }
    class dbframe_jButton1_actionAdapter
```

```
    implements java.awt.event.ActionListener
    {
      dbframe adaptee;
      dbframe_jButton1_actionAdapter(dbframe adaptee)
    {
      this.adaptee = adaptee;
     }
     public void actionPerformed(ActionEvent e)
     {
       adaptee.jButton1_actionPerformed(e);
     }
    }
class dbframe_jButton3_actionAdapter implements java.awt.event
     .ActionListener
    {
  dbframe adaptee;

  dbframe_jButton3_actionAdapter(dbframe adaptee)
  {
    this.adaptee = adaptee;
  }
  public void actionPerformed(ActionEvent e)
  {
    adaptee.jButton3_actionPerformed(e);
  }
}
```

Obviously, you can add even more functionality to this by adding New, Delete, and Save buttons. You might also consider adding a table that would display all the records simultaneously. However, this example, and the preceding one, should give you enough information to allow you to create whatever database applications you might require.

dbSwing

As was previously mentioned in this chapter, JBuilder provides some additional ways to operate with a database. In addition to the standard objects that you saw in the previous section, you can also use the dbSwing objects. The dbSwing package contains all the classes you will need.

Note: dbSwing is only available with JBuilder Enterprise editions. If you do not have the Enterprise edition, you will not be able to use these components.

You probably also noticed that JBuilder has an entire tab just for dbSwing components. The dbSwing package allows you to build database applications that use the Java Swing component architecture. In addition to these data-aware subclasses of most Swing components, dbSwing also includes several utility components designed specifically for use in developing DataExpress and JDataStore-based applications. DataExpress and JDataStore are utilities that come with JBuilder. If you are unfamiliar with these essential JBuilder components, I suggest you read *Charlie Calvert's Learn JBuilder*, available from Wordware Publishing, Inc. It is truly an outstanding book; after reading it, you will have a very thorough understanding of the essentials of JBuilder.

The real point to the dbSwing classes is that they are data aware. That means that you can have them automatically synchronize with an underlying database. For those readers who have a background in Microsoft's Visual Basic, this should sound very much like data bound components. The point is that once you have created a tie between a component and an underlying data source, the component will automatically synchronize itself with that data source. The major classes used in dbSwing are summarized in Table 11.5.

Table 11.5 dbSwing classes

Class	Purpose
JdbTable	This is a data-aware extension of JTable.
JdbTextField	This is a data-aware extension of JTextField.
JdbList	This is a data-aware extension of JList.
JdbTextArea	This is a data-aware extension of the JTextArea class.

Table 11.5 is not comprehensive. In fact, most of the standard Swing components have data-aware dbSwing subclasses. This list just shows the most commonly

encountered dbSwing classes. The JBuilder help files contain several tutorials that walk you through how to create an application using dbSwing. Since this option is only available to users of the Enterprise edition of JBuilder, we do not devote an inordinate amount of time to it here.

Summary

This chapter showed you how to use Java to connect to a database and retrieve data. First you saw how to do this with a simple console application and then with a JFC graphical user interface. Finally, you were shown how to accomplish this task with dbSwing classes. As you can see, Java and JBuilder provide a rich set of options when it comes to database programming.

Review Questions

1. What is a result set?
2. What is dbSwing?
3. What is the purpose of the Connection class?
4. Why must you use the next method of the ResultSet class when you first connect to the data source?
5. What is the purpose of the execute method of the Statement class?
6. List any three methods of the ResultSet class.
7. Can you use the classes from java.sql without specific error handling?
8. What package do you import in order to use classes such as Connection, ResultSet, and Statement?

Chapter 12

JFC Applets

This chapter covers the following:

- Applet basics
- Creating applets in JBuilder
- Creating applets with parameters
- Creating dual-purpose applets

Introduction

Working with JFC applets is really not much different than working with JFC applications. The classes and methods all work in much the same manner. However, the general environment is different, necessitating that we spend some time covering this topic. This chapter walks you through the basics of applets. Since applets are embedded into HTML, it is imperative that you have at least some basic grasp of HTML. I am certain that most readers have that knowledge. However, if you do not, refer to Appendix E for a brief HTML primer before proceeding.

Applet Basics

Before we can jump into how to create applets using Borland's JBuilder and the Java Foundation Classes, we need to establish exactly what an applet is and how it differs from a standard application. An *applet* is a program written in the Java programming language that can be embedded directly into an HTML page. When you use a Java-enabled browser to view a page that contains an applet, the applet's code is transferred to your system and executed by the browser's Java Virtual Machine (JVM). Fortunately, virtually all browsers will support Java, so it is highly unlikely that you would find a browser that does not properly display your applet. Since applets run in the browser, the browser is really their environment, not the host machine.

Java has a base class called Applet. This class is abstract; it cannot be directly instantiated. It is used as the base class for all applets. Every applet is implemented by creating a subclass of the Applet class.

There is a specific life cycle to every applet. This life cycle is demonstrated by the four life cycle related functions in every applet: init, start, stop, and destroy. Table 12.1 summarizes the purpose of each of these.

Table 12.1 Life cycle functions in applets

Function	Purpose
init	This function will initialize the applet each time it's loaded or reloaded.
start	This function is used to start the applet's execution, such as when the applet is loaded or the user revisits a page that contains the applet.
stop	This function is used to stop the applet's execution, such as when the user leaves the applet's page or quits the browser.
destroy	This function is used to perform a final cleanup in preparation for unloading.

An applet that requires code in one of these functions will simply override that function. Not every applet needs to override every one of these methods. It is even possible for an applet to not override any of them. Most applets will, however, override at least the init method.

The init method is useful for one-time initialization that is not particularly time consuming. You can think of the init method as serving a similar purpose to a constructor in a standard application. Applets don't actually have constructors, but whatever code you put into a constructor can be put into the init method.

Every applet that does something after initialization, other than in direct response to user actions, will need to override the start method. What do I mean by "does something other than in direct response to user actions"? It's really quite simple. If your applet will take any actions other than those generated by user events after the init function, then that code will go in the start function.

The stop method is, of course, used when your applet is ceasing its normal operations. A good rule of thumb is that any applet that overrides the start method should also override the stop method. The stop method should suspend the applet's execution so that it doesn't take up system resources when the user isn't viewing the applet's page.

The destroy method is probably the least-used method of the four. Many applets don't need to override the destroy method, since their stop method does everything necessary to shut down the applet's execution. However, destroy is available for applets that need to release additional resources.

You can, of course, create applets without JBuilder. Use any text editor to create your applet code and compile it with any Java compiler (such as the Sun Java SDK). Then create an HTML document, again using your favorite text editor, and place the code in the HTML document to include your applet. The following is the source code for a very simple applet:

```
import java.awt.*;
import java.applet.*;
// create controls on the screen and respond to //events on
those // controls.
// This class inherits the Java Applet class. All applets must
do this.
class button extends Applet
{
// create an instance of the Button class
Button hiButton;
// applets use an init instead of a main function.
public void init()
```

```
{
// create a button component with a caption
hiButton = new Button("Click Me!");
// Add that button to the browser window
add(hiButton);
}// close init
// The action function handles the various events the //applet
// can potentially respond to.
public boolean action(Event evt, Object objme)
{
// see if the event was on our hi button
if(evt.target == hiButton)
{
// change that button's caption
hiButton.setLabel("Ahhhh!");
return true;
}// close if statement
else
return false;
}// close action
}// close class button
```

This applet doesn't do much. The code is provided for educational purposes. You can see that applets have a few significant differences from standard applications. To begin with, you should notice that the components are not placed on a container control first. This is because the browser itself is the container. You do not have to place components on a panel or other container before you can display them. The next thing you should notice is the use of the init function that we discussed earlier. It is in this function that components are actually displayed to the user.

Creating Applets in JBuilder

By now you should be used to the fact that most things are much easier in JBuilder than doing them by hand in a text editor. Applets are no different. To create an applet you will start a standard project; however, when you are ready to add an object, you will need to add an Applet object from the Web tab. This is shown in Figure 12.1.

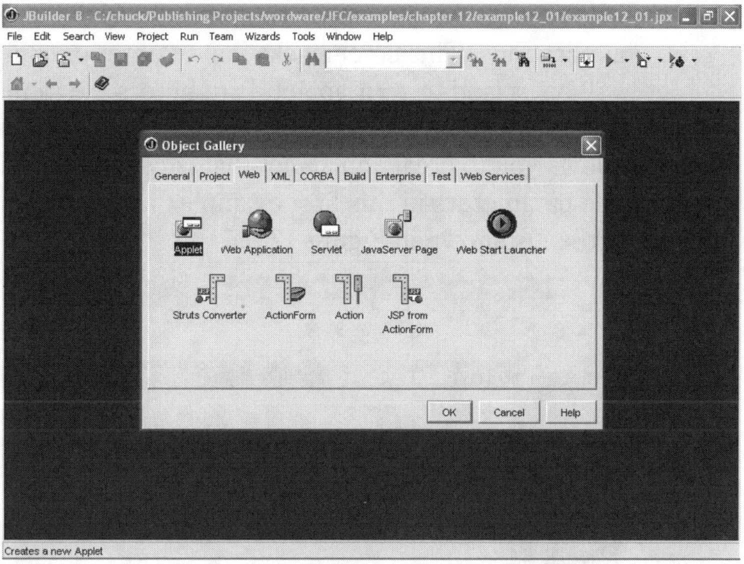

Figure 12.1 Starting an applet project

Once you have done this, the course of action will be slightly different than it is in a traditional application. The first screen of the wizard simply asks you to choose the names for your class and package. This is shown in Figure 12.2.

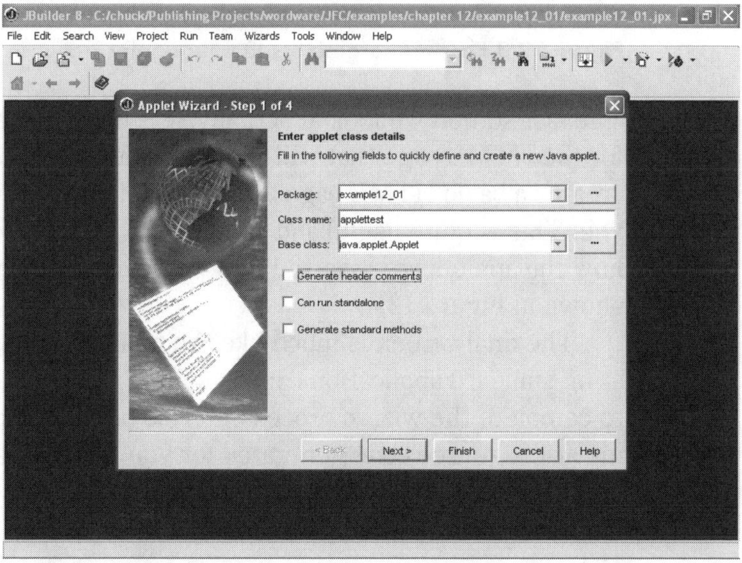

Figure 12.2 Step 1 of 4 in the Applet Wizard

The next screen is really quite different from traditional applications. This screen asks you to enter parameters that will be passed to your applet. Parameters are items written into the HTML code that get passed to your applet. This allows you to create an applet that is customizable. We don't use parameters in this first example, but we will later. This screen is shown in Figure 12.3.

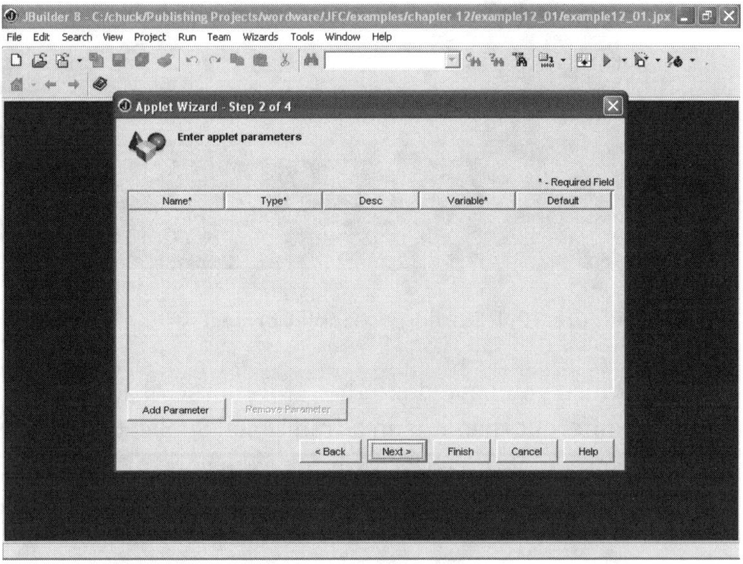

Figure 12.3 Passing parameters to your applet

The last screen we look at actually sets up the parameters for the HTML page that will contain your applet. JBuilder creates a basic HTML page that will contain your applet for you. This is quite useful and should help you to understand how the applets are inserted into web pages. This screen is shown in Figure 12.4.

The final screen is much like the final screen when creating standard applications and is simply there to allow you to complete the wizard process. At this point, you are looking at the source code generated for you by JBuilder. In fact, you have the same design screen and all the same tools you had access to in Java applications. This is depicted in Figure 12.5.

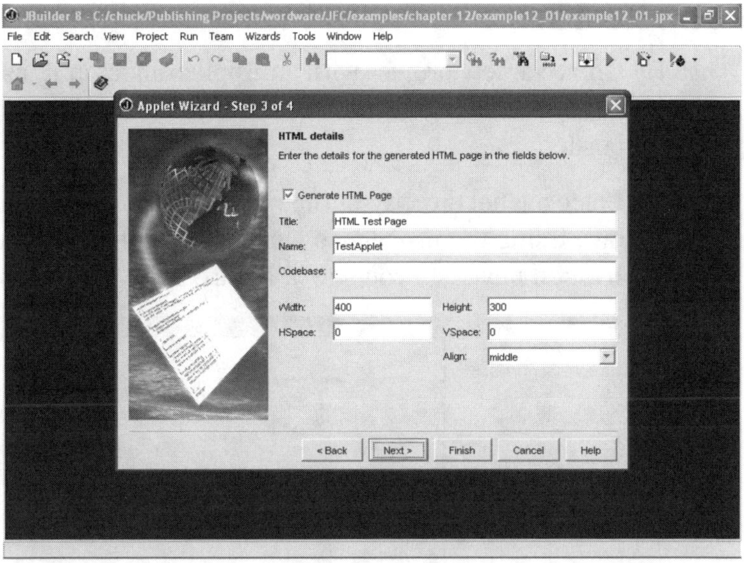

Figure 12.4 Setting the HTML parameters with the Applet Wizard

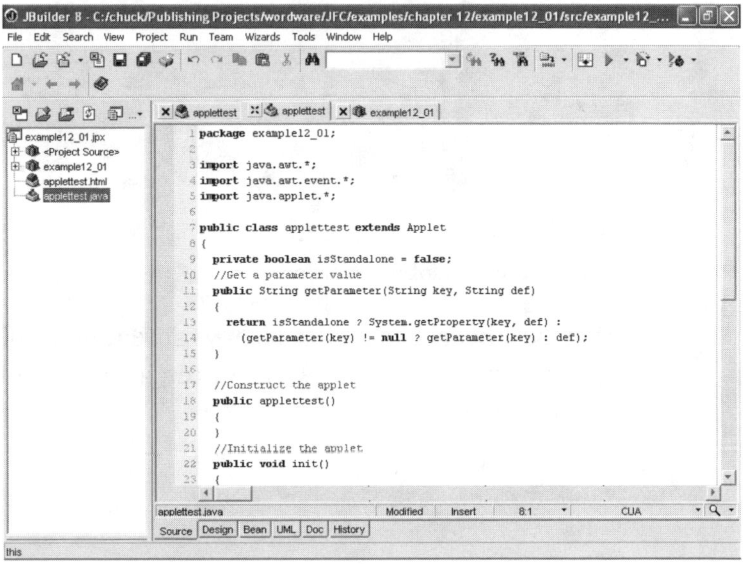

Figure 12.5 The applet IDE

Now you can design any type of Java applet you wish. In fact, you can design applets that do pretty much anything that a standard application can do. Why don't we just create a simple JFC/Swing applet right now?

Example 12.1

Step 1: Create a new project with an Applet object in it, as you saw in the preceding section. Set the background layout to border.

Step 2: Place a label directly in the center portion of the border layout. Using the properties window, set the label's border to a **Raised** bevel, as you see in Figure 12.6.

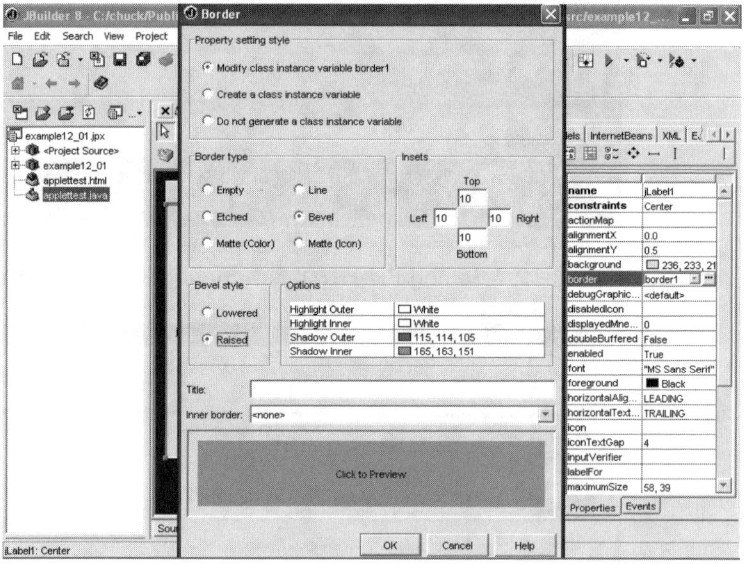

Figure 12.6 The labels' border

Then set the label's font to size **24**, foreground color to **blue**, horizontal alignment to **Center**, and its text to **00:00**, as you see in Figure 12.7.

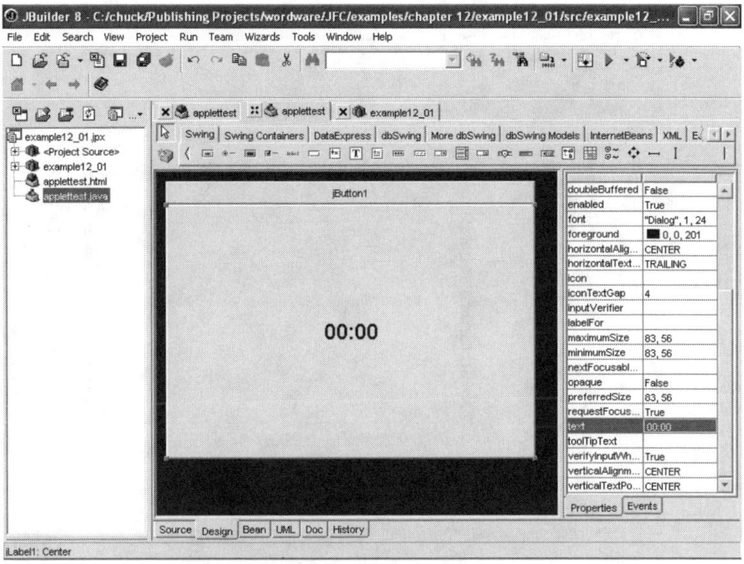

Figure 12.7 The label's properties

We are going to use this label to display time information to the user. Essentially, we are creating a clock applet.

Step 3: In the import statements at the beginning of your source code, add the java.util package:

```
import java.util.*;
```

Step 4: Then place a panel in the North section of the border layout. Give the panel a grid layout of three columns by one row. Then place three buttons on that panel, as you see in Figure 12.8.

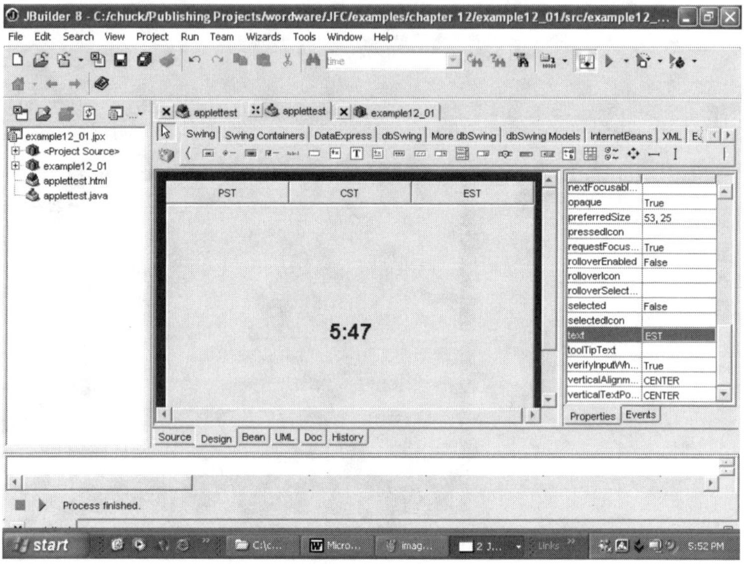

Figure 12.8 The time zone buttons

Step 5: Place the following code in the jbInit function. This code will initialize the clock so that it displays the current time, according to your system's clock.

```
Calendar curtime = Calendar.getInstance();
int h = curtime.get(10);    // 10 is the constant for hour
int m = curtime.get(12);    // 12 is the constant for minute
String time = h + ":" + m;
```

All we are doing is using the Calendar class to retrieve the current time.

Step 6: Now place the following code into the button labeled PST:

```
TimeZone t = TimeZone.getTimeZone("PST");
curtime.setTimeZone(t);
int h = curtime.get(10);// 10 is the constant for hour
int m = curtime.get(12);// 12 is the constant for minute
String time = h + ":" + m;
jLabel1.setText(time);
```

We will place almost identical code into the buttons labeled CST and EST, with the exception that the parameter passed to the TimeZone class will be the appropriate three-letter designation (i.e., matching the text property of that button).

What you have done at this point is create a sort of clock that will show you the current time in different time zones. When you run this application, you should see something much like what is shown in Figures 12.9 and 12.10.

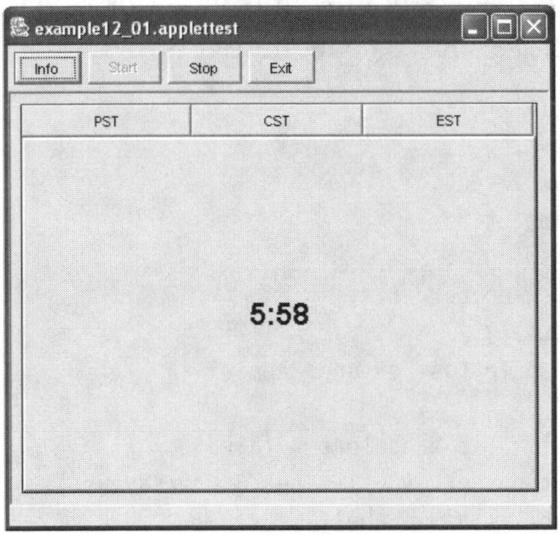

Figure 12.9 The clock applet part one

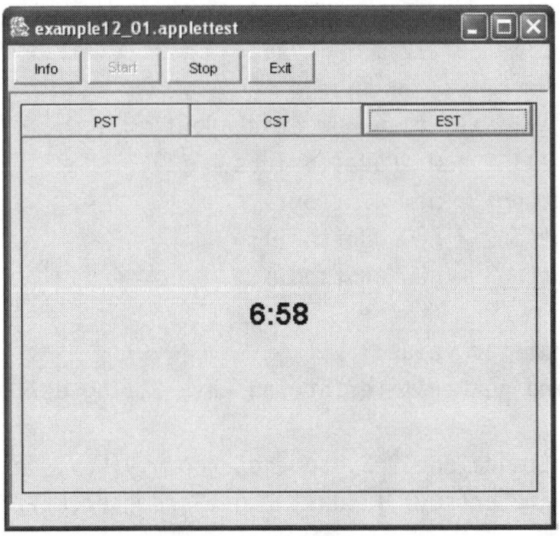

Figure 12.10 The clock applet part two

The purpose of this chapter is not to explore the intricacies of the Calendar or TimeZone classes. If you peruse the JBuilder help files, you will see a number of interesting methods associated with these classes. It would be a trivial matter to create a clock that tells you the current time in any part of the world. A bit of creativity could produce a clickable map that shows you the time in that part of the world.

For those readers not using JBuilder or who simply want to see the entire source code, here it is:

```
package example12_01;
import java.awt.*;
import java.awt.event.*;
import java.applet.*;
import javax.swing.*;
import javax.swing.border.*;
import java.util.*;
public class applettest extends Applet
{
  private boolean isStandalone = false;
  BorderLayout borderLayout1 = new BorderLayout();
  JLabel jLabel1 = new JLabel();
  Border border1;
  Calendar curtime = Calendar.getInstance();
  int h = curtime.get(10);    // 10 is the constant for hour
  int m = curtime.get(12);    // 12 is the constant for minute
  String time = h + ":" + m;
  GridLayout gridLayout1 = new GridLayout(1,3);
  JPanel jPanel1 = new JPanel(gridLayout1);
  JButton jButton1 = new JButton();
  JButton jButton2 = new JButton();
  JButton jButton3 = new JButton();

  //Get a parameter value
  public String getParameter(String key, String def)
  {
    return isStandalone ? System.getProperty(key, def) :
      (getParameter(key) != null ? getParameter(key) : def);
  }
  //Construct the applet
  public applettest()
  {
  }
```

```
//Initialize the applet
public void init()
{
  try
  {
    jbInit();
  }
  catch(Exception e)
  {
    e.printStackTrace();
  }
}
//Component initialization
private void jbInit() throws Exception
{
  border1 = BorderFactory.createCompoundBorder(BorderFactory
       .createBevelBorder(BevelBorder.RAISED, Color.white,
       Color.white, new Color(115, 114, 105), new Color(165,
       163, 151)), BorderFactory.createEmptyBorder
       (10,10,10,10));
  jLabel1.setFont(new java.awt.Font("Dialog", 1, 24));
  jLabel1.setForeground(new Color(0, 0, 201));
  jLabel1.setBorder(border1);
  jLabel1.setHorizontalAlignment(SwingConstants.CENTER);
  jLabel1.setText(time);
  this.setLayout(borderLayout1);
  jPanel1.setLayout(gridLayout1);
  jButton1.setText("PST");
  jButton2.setText("CST");
  jButton2.addActionListener(new applettest_jButton2_action
       Adapter(this));
  jButton3.setText("EST");
  jButton3.addActionListener(new applettest_jButton3_action
       Adapter(this));
  jPanel1.add(jButton1);
  jPanel1.add(jButton2, null);
  jPanel1.add(jButton3, null);
  this.add(jLabel1, BorderLayout.CENTER);
  this.add(jPanel1, BorderLayout.NORTH);
}
//Get Applet information
public String getAppletInfo()
{
  return "Applet Information";
}
```

```
  //Get parameter info
  public String[][] getParameterInfo()
  {
    return null;
  }
  void jButton1_actionPerformed(ActionEvent e)
  {
     TimeZone t = TimeZone.getTimeZone("PST");
     curtime.setTimeZone(t);
     int h = curtime.get(10);  // 10 is the constant for hour
     int m = curtime.get(12);  // 12 is the constant for minute
     String time = h + ":" + m;
     jLabel1.setText(time);
  }
  void jButton2_actionPerformed(ActionEvent e)
  {
    TimeZone t = TimeZone.getTimeZone("CST");
    curtime.setTimeZone(t);
    int h = curtime.get(10);  // 10 is the constant for hour
    int m = curtime.get(12);  // 12 is the constant for minute
    String time = h + ":" + m;
    jLabel1.setText(time);
  }
  void jButton3_actionPerformed(ActionEvent e)
  {
    TimeZone t = TimeZone.getTimeZone("EST");
    curtime.setTimeZone(t);
    int h = curtime.get(10);  // 10 is the constant for hour
    int m = curtime.get(12);  // 12 is the constant for minute
    String time = h + ":" + m;
    jLabel1.setText(time);
  }
}
class applettest_jButton2_actionAdapter implements java.awt
     .event.ActionListener {
  applettest adaptee;
  applettest_jButton2_actionAdapter(applettest adaptee) {
    this.adaptee = adaptee;
  }
  public void actionPerformed(ActionEvent e) {
    adaptee.jButton2_actionPerformed(e);
  }
}
class applettest_jButton3_actionAdapter implements
java.awt.event.ActionListener {
```

```
  applettest adaptee;
  applettest_jButton3_actionAdapter(applettest adaptee)
 {
    this.adaptee = adaptee;
  }
  public void actionPerformed(ActionEvent e)
{
    adaptee.jButton3_actionPerformed(e);
  }
}
```

This applet example should show you that creating an applet in Java is only slightly different from creating an application. It should also show you that JBuilder makes creating Swing-based applets very easy.

Creating Applets with Parameters

There are times when you might want your applet to have different behaviors in different web pages. You can have the HTML code pass certain parameters to your applet and then use those parameters to alter the behavior of your applet. When using JBuilder, the real difference is taken care of in Step 2 of the Applet Wizard. At this step you can add parameters to your applet. Let's look at an example that uses this.

Example 12.2

Step 1: Start a new project and add an Applet object.

Step 2: At the parameters screen of the wizard, add two Boolean parameters, seconds and militarytime. This should look much like what you see in Figure 12.11.

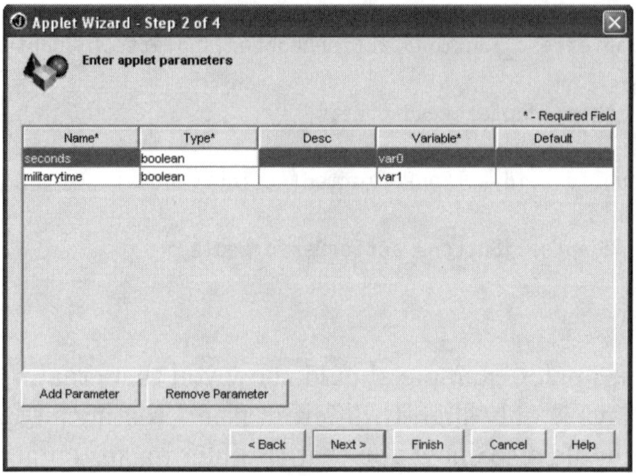

Figure 12.11 Adding parameters to the applet

For the rest of the wizard, you can just use default values.

Step 3: We are going to create something very much like our previous application. However, in this case the parameters will determine whether to display time with seconds and whether to use military time (i.e., 1300 is 1 P.M.). So in the beginning of your class, you will need to import java.util. In the jbInit function, you will have code very similar to what you used before with a few slight differences.

```
Calendar curtime = Calendar.getInstance();
int h = curtime.get(10);  // 10 is the constant for hour
int m = curtime.get(12);  // 12 is the constant for minute
int s = curtime.get(13);  // 13 is the constant for seconds
int mil = curtime.get(9); // 9 is the constant for AM/PM
if(mil ==1)  //a value of 1 would indicate that this is pm
  h = h + 12;
String time = h + ":" + m;
if(var0==true)
     time = time + ":" + s;
```

The changes are really pretty simple. The applet framework that JBuilder creates for us assigns the first parameter to the variable var0, the next to var1, and so on. So for our purposes, var0 tells us whether or not to display seconds, and var1 determines whether to display military time. For the rest of the code, we are simply going to repeat exactly what we did in Example 12.1. We will have three buttons at the top (PST, CST, and EST) and a label in the center. It should look much like what is shown in Figure 12.12.

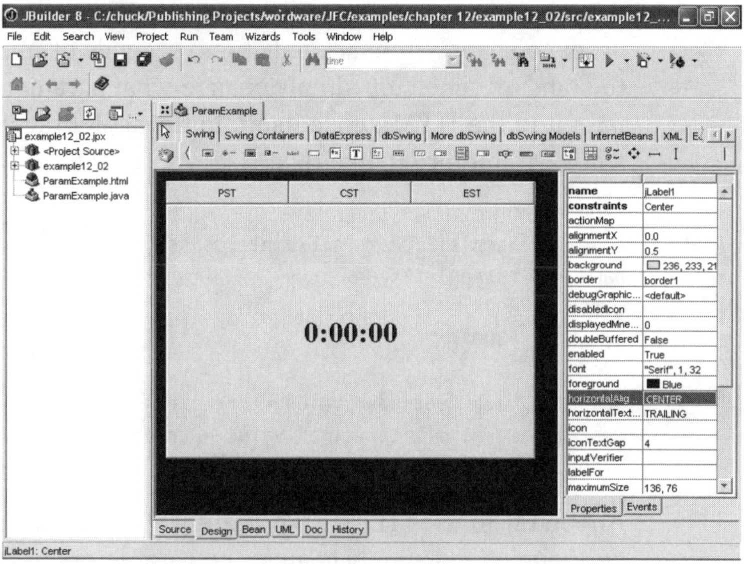

Figure 12.12 The layout for Example 12.2

You then place code in each of the action events for the buttons. That code will be much like the code you used in the previous example, with just a few changes to account for the display of seconds and military time.

```
TimeZone t = TimeZone.getTimeZone("PST");
Calendar curtime = Calendar.getInstance();
curtime.setTimeZone(t);
int h = curtime.get(10);  // 10 is the constant for hour
int m = curtime.get(12);  // 12 is the constant for minute
int s = curtime.get(13);  // 13 is the constant for seconds
int mil = curtime.get(9);
String time = h + ":" + m;
if(mil ==1)  // a value of 1 would indicate that this is pm
      h = h + 12;
if(var0==true)
     time = time + ":" + s;
jLabel1.setText(time);
```

You will put similar code in the other buttons, changing it so that it displays the appropriate time zone.

Step 4: This is where the *real* difference in this example happens. After you compile your applet, you need not recompile it in order to change from seconds to no seconds or military time to standard time. You simply change what parameters you pass it in the HTML code itself. In the applet tag you simply add a parameter tag like this:

```
<Applet
code = "example12_02.ParamExample.class"
name = "TestApplet"
width = "400"
height = "300"
>
<param name = "seconds" value = "true">
<param name = "militarytime" value = true>
</appplet>
```

Anyone who uses HTML to create web pages can now use your applet and simply change the parameters of the HTML applet tag in order to change the behavior of your applet. If you set both properties to true, you should see something much like what is shown in Figure 12.13.

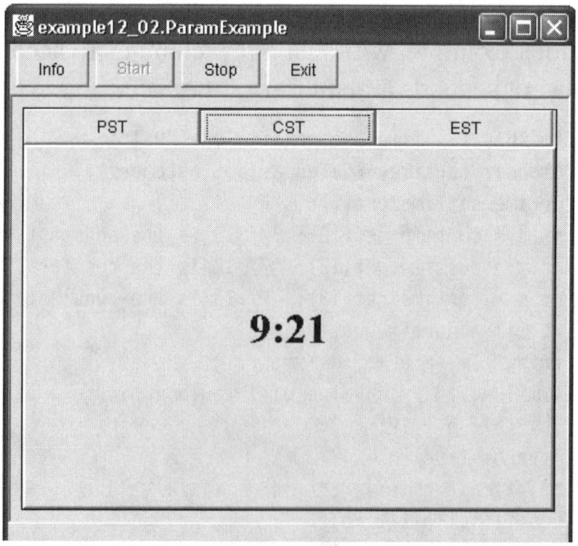

Figure 12.13 Running the applet

For those readers who are not using JBuilder or simply wish to see the complete code for the applet, it is provided here:

```
package example12_02;
import java.awt.*;
import java.awt.event.*;
import java.applet.*;
import java.util.*;
import javax.swing.*;
import javax.swing.border.*;
public class ParamExample extends Applet
{
  private boolean isStandalone = false;
  boolean var0;
  boolean var1;
  BorderLayout borderLayout1 = new BorderLayout();
  GridLayout gridLayout1 = new GridLayout(1,3);
  JLabel jLabel1 = new JLabel();
  Border border1;
  JPanel jPanel1 = new JPanel();
  JButton jButton1 = new JButton();
  JButton jButton2 = new JButton();
  JButton jButton3 = new JButton();
  BorderLayout borderLayout2 = new BorderLayout();
  //Get a parameter value
  public String getParameter(String key, String def)
  {
    return isStandalone ? System.getProperty(key, def) :
      (getParameter(key) != null ? getParameter(key) : def);
  }
  //Construct the applet
  public ParamExample()
  {
  }
  //Initialize the applet
  public void init()
  {
    try
    {
      var0 = Boolean.valueOf(this.getParameter("seconds",
           "false")).booleanValue();
    }
    catch(Exception e)
    {
      e.printStackTrace();
```

```
    }
    try
    {
      var1 = Boolean.valueOf(this.getParameter("militarytime",
           "false")).booleanValue();
    }
    catch(Exception e)
    {
      e.printStackTrace();
    }
    try
    {
      jbInit();
    }
    catch(Exception e)
    {
      e.printStackTrace();
    }
  }
  //Component initialization
  private void jbInit() throws Exception
  {
    Calendar curtime = Calendar.getInstance();
    int h = curtime.get(10);  // 10 is the constant for hour
    int m = curtime.get(12);  // 12 is the constant for minute
    int s = curtime.get(13);  // 13 is the constant for seconds
    int mil = curtime.get(9); // 9 is the constant for AM_PM
    String time ;
    if(mil ==1)  // a value of 1 would indicate that this is pm
      h = h + 12;
    time = h + ":" + m;
    if(var0==true)
         time = time + ":" + s;
    jLabel1.setText(time);
    border1 = BorderFactory.createCompoundBorder
         (BorderFactory.createBevelBorder(BevelBorder.RAISED,
         Color.white, Color.white, new Color(115, 114, 105),
         new Color(165, 163, 151)), BorderFactory.createEmpty
         Border(15,15,15,15));
    jLabel1.setFont(new java.awt.Font("Serif", 1, 32));
    jLabel1.setForeground(Color.blue);
    jLabel1.setBorder(border1);
    jLabel1.setHorizontalAlignment(SwingConstants.CENTER);
    jLabel1.setText("0:00:00");
    jPanel1.setLayout(gridLayout1);
```

```
  jButton1.setText("PST");
  jButton1.addActionListener(new ParamExample_jButton1_action
       Adapter(this));
  jButton2.setText("CST");
  jButton2.addActionListener(new ParamExample_jButton2_action
       Adapter(this));
  jButton3.setText("EST");
  jButton3.addActionListener(new ParamExample_jButton3_action
       Adapter(this));
  this.setLayout(borderLayout2);
  jPanel1.add(jButton1);
  jPanel1.add(jButton2);
  jPanel1.add(jButton3);
  this.add(jPanel1, BorderLayout.NORTH);
  this.add(jLabel1, BorderLayout.CENTER);
}
//Get Applet information
public String getAppletInfo()
{
  return "Applet Information";
}
//Get parameter info
public String[][] getParameterInfo()
{
  String[][] pinfo =
    {
    {"seconds", "boolean", ""},
    {"militarytime", "boolean", ""},
    };
  return pinfo;
}
void jButton1_actionPerformed(ActionEvent e)
{
  TimeZone t = TimeZone.getTimeZone("PST");
  Calendar curtime = Calendar.getInstance();
  curtime.setTimeZone(t);
  int h = curtime.get(10);  // 10 is the constant for hour
  int m = curtime.get(12);  // 12 is the constant for minute
  int s = curtime.get(13);  // 13 is the constant for seconds
  int mil = curtime.get(9);
  String time = h + ":" + m;
  if(mil ==1)  // a value of 1 would indicate that this is pm
        h = h + 12;
  if(var0==true)
       time = time + ":" + s;
```

```
    jLabel1.setText(time);
  }
  void jButton2_actionPerformed(ActionEvent e)
  {
    TimeZone t = TimeZone.getTimeZone("CST");
    Calendar curtime = Calendar.getInstance();
    curtime.setTimeZone(t);
    int h = curtime.get(10);  // 10 is the constant for hour
    int m = curtime.get(12);  // 12 is the constant for minute
    int s = curtime.get(13);  // 13 is the constant for seconds
    int mil = curtime.get(9);
    String time = h + ":" + m;
    if(mil ==1)  // a value of 1 would indicate that this is pm
          h = h + 12;
    if(var0==true)
         time = time + ":" + s;
    jLabel1.setText(time);
  }
  void jButton3_actionPerformed(ActionEvent e)
  {
    TimeZone t = TimeZone.getTimeZone("EST");
    Calendar curtime = Calendar.getInstance();
    curtime.setTimeZone(t);
    int h = curtime.get(10);  // 10 is the constant for hour
    int m = curtime.get(12);  // 12 is the constant for minute
    int s = curtime.get(13);  // 13 is the constant for seconds
    int mil = curtime.get(9);
    String time = h + ":" + m;
    if(mil ==1)  // a value of 1 would indicate that this is pm
          h = h + 12;
    if(var0==true)
         time = time + ":" + s;
    jLabel1.setText(time);
  }
}
class ParamExample_jButton1_actionAdapter implements
java.awt.event.ActionListener {
  ParamExample adaptee;
  ParamExample_jButton1_actionAdapter(ParamExample adaptee)
{
    this.adaptee = adaptee;
  }
  public void actionPerformed(ActionEvent e) {
    adaptee.jButton1_actionPerformed(e);
  }
```

```
}
class ParamExample_jButton2_actionAdapter implements java.awt
     .event.ActionListener {
  ParamExample adaptee;
  ParamExample_jButton2_actionAdapter(ParamExample adaptee)
{
    this.adaptee = adaptee;
  }
  public void actionPerformed(ActionEvent e)
{
    adaptee.jButton2_actionPerformed(e);
  }
}
class ParamExample_jButton3_actionAdapter implements java.awt
     .event.ActionListener {
  ParamExample adaptee;
  ParamExample_jButton3_actionAdapter(ParamExample adaptee)
{
    this.adaptee = adaptee;
  }
  public void actionPerformed(ActionEvent e)
{
    adaptee.jButton3_actionPerformed(e);
  }
}
```

You can see that adding parameters is not particularly difficult. It is, however, very useful. When you add parameters, you allow your applet to be customizable. If you intend to distribute your applet, you would do well to consider adding parameters to it. This way, end users (even those without any programming experience) can customize how the applet appears within their web pages.

Creating Dual-purpose Applets

The last item we have to cover is dual-purpose applets. If you think back to when you ran the Applet Wizard previously, you may recall that we left, for the most part, default values. However, on the very first screen, there is an option to check "Can run standalone." This is shown in Figure 12.14.

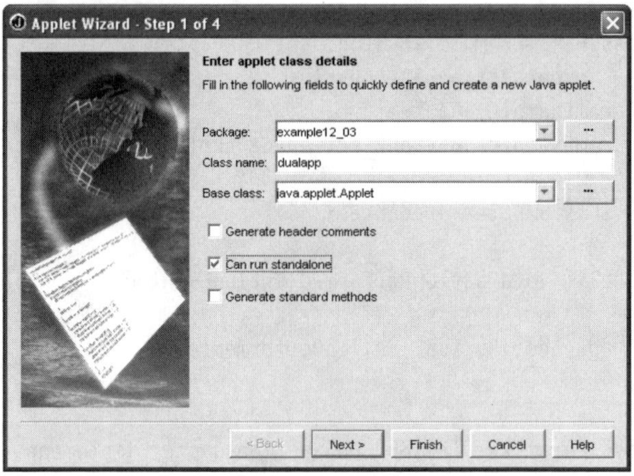

Figure 12.14 Choosing the standalone option

By standalone, it is meant that your applet can run as a standard Java application and need not be in the context of a browser. If you select this option, your applet can run either as an applet, within the context of a browser, or as a standalone application. This is really quite useful. It makes your applets all the more flexible. Let's take a look at a simple example that does this.

Example 12.3

Step 1: Create a new project with an applet. Be certain to select the standalone option.

Step 2: For our purposes here, we are only concerned with the standalone option, not the actual functionality of the applet. So in this case, unlike the preceding two examples, we use a very simple applet — simply a button with the caption "Click Me."

Step 3: In the action event of the button, change the button's text to read **Thanks**.

Your applet should look much like what is depicted in Figure 12.15

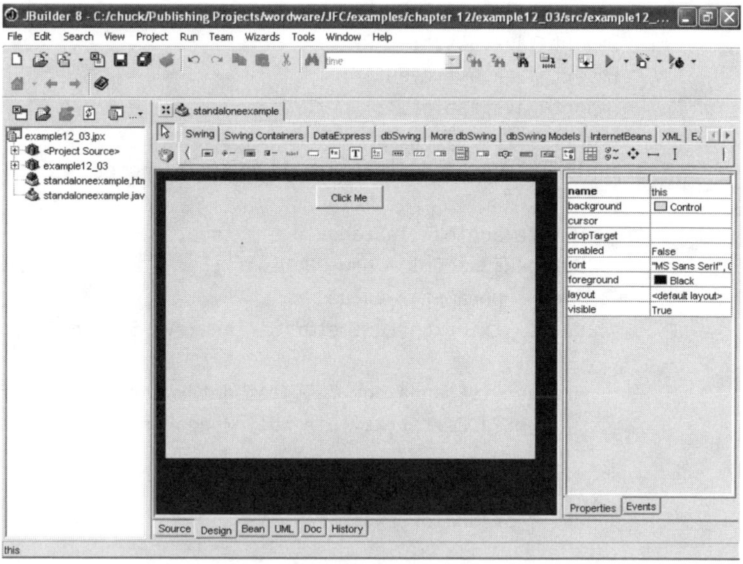

Figure 12.15 The standalone applet

When you run it, you will see what is shown in Figure 12.16.

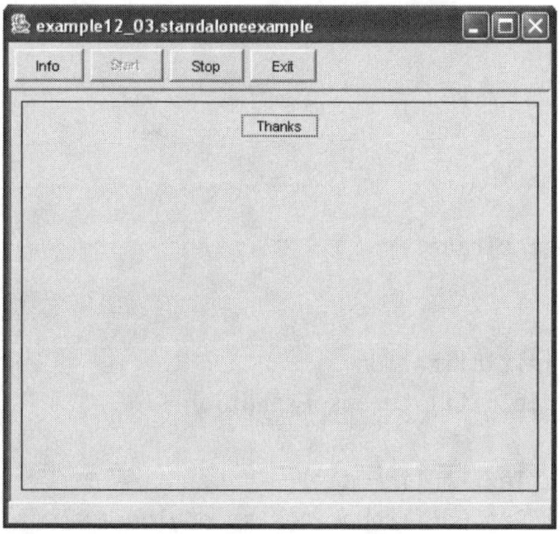

Figure 12.16 Running the applet

This applet is not particularly exciting. It is interesting though that you can run the applet as an applet or as a standalone application. The entire code is shown here with comments after:

```
package example12_03;
import java.awt.*;
import java.awt.event.*;
import java.applet.*;
import javax.swing.*;
public class standaloneexample extends Applet
{
  private boolean isStandalone = true;
  JButton jButton1 = new JButton();
  //Get a parameter value
  public String getParameter(String key, String def)
  {
    return isStandalone ? System.getProperty(key, def) :
      (getParameter(key) != null ? getParameter(key) : def);
  }
  //Construct the applet
  public standaloneexample()
  {
  }
  //Initialize the applet
  public void init()
  {
    try
    {
      jbInit();
    }
    catch(Exception e)
    {
      e.printStackTrace();
    }
  }
  //Component initialization
  private void jbInit() throws Exception
  {
    jButton1.setText("Click Me");
    jButton1.addActionListener(new standaloneexample_jButton1
         _actionAdapter(this));
    this.add(jButton1, null);
  }
  //Get Applet information
  public String getAppletInfo()
  {
    return "Applet Information";
  }
  //Get parameter info
```

```
  public String[][] getParameterInfo()
  {
    return null;
  }
  //Main method
  public static void main(String[] args)
  {
    standaloneexample applet = new standaloneexample();
    applet.isStandalone = true;
    Frame frame;
    frame = new Frame();
    frame.setTitle("Applet Frame");
    frame.add(applet, BorderLayout.CENTER);
    applet.init();
    applet.start();
    frame.setSize(400,320);
    Dimension d = Toolkit.getDefaultToolkit().getScreenSize();
    frame.setLocation((d.width - frame.getSize().width) / 2,
         (d.height - frame.getSize().height) / 2);
    frame.setVisible(true);
  }
  void jButton1_actionPerformed(ActionEvent e)
  {
     jButton1.setText("Thanks");
  }
}
class standaloneexample_jButton1_actionAdapter implements
      java.awt.event.ActionListener
{
  standaloneexample adaptee;

  standaloneexample_jButton1_actionAdapter(standaloneexample
       adaptee)
  {
    this.adaptee = adaptee;
  }
  public void actionPerformed(ActionEvent e)
  {
    adaptee.jButton1_actionPerformed(e);
  }
}
```

If you look closely at this code, you will see that the real trick is having the required functions for both applets and applications. There is a constructor and a main function, neither of which will ever be called if this is launched within a browser as an applet. Then you have the init functions that are used within the context of a browser. You now have an applet that can also run as a standalone application. Essentially, you create a standalone applet by adding in a main function and a constructor.

Summary

In this chapter we have explored using applets with Java Foundation Classes. I hope you have seen that there is really not much difficulty in using JFC within an applet. We have studied the structure of an applet, the required functions of an applet, and how to use these functions. We have also examined passing parameters to an applet and how to create an applet that can also run as a standalone application.

Applets are quite commonly encountered on web pages. If you incorporate JFC components in your applets, you will have a user-friendly applet. If you further utilize parameters and the standalone option, you will also have an extremely versatile applet that can be customized to fit end user needs.

Review Questions

1. What is an applet?
2. What are the four functions in all applets?
3. What must all applet classes extend?
4. What are parameters?
5. How do you pass parameters from HTML to your applet?
6. What is a standalone applet?
7. How do you create one?
8. Which applet function is least often overridden and used by applet programmers?

Chapter 13

Java 2D API

This chapter covers the following:

- Basics of the Java 2D API
- The Graphics2D class
- Coordinate spaces and the Graphics2D class
- The rendering process
- Images and the Java 2D API

Introduction

In Chapter 10 we briefly explored the Graphics class. Recall that the Graphics class existed in AWT but was expanded under Swing. Also recall that AWT is a part of the Java Foundation Classes. The Graphics class can be flexible and useful, and it is a significant part of Java graphics programming. But it is just a part and not the entirety. Java now includes an entire 2D graphics library referred to as the Java 2D API. The Java 2D API is a set of classes for advanced 2D graphics and imaging. These classes cover a number of different types of graphics, including line art, text, and image.

Basics of the Java 2D API

The Java 2D API is a greatly expanded and enhanced set of graphics tools. It goes far beyond the simple graphics produced by the Graphics class, which you saw in Chapter 10. The Java 2D API, first introduced in JDK 1.2, provides enhanced two-dimensional graphics, text, and imaging capabilities. You will quickly find that the Java 2D API is a rich set of graphics tools.

The Java 2D API provides the following functionality:

- A range of geometric primitives, such as rectangles, curves, and ellipses
- A mechanism for rendering virtually any geometric shape
- A uniform rendering model for display devices and printers
- Mechanisms for performing hit detection on shapes, text, and images
- Enhanced color support
- Support for printing complex documents

The basic rendering mechanism is the same as in previous versions of the JDK. The drawing system itself controls when and how programs can draw. When a component needs to be displayed, its paint or update method is automatically invoked with an appropriate graphics context. This should be familiar if you have used the Graphics class at all, which you should have done in Chapter 10 of this book!

The Graphics2D Class

The Java 2D API introduces a new type of Graphics object, namely the class java.awt.Graphics2D. Graphics2D is based on the old Graphics class and, in fact, extends the Graphics class to provide access to the enhanced graphics and rendering features of the Java 2D API. This means it can do anything the Graphics class can do and much more. The Graphics2D class extends the Graphics class in order to provide more sophisticated control over geometry, coordinate transformations, color management, and text layout. This class is now the fundamental class for rendering two-dimensional shapes, text, and images on the Java platform.

Using the Graphics2D class is only slightly more complex than using the standard Graphics class. If you recall, to use the standard Graphics class, you have a function, such as paint, that takes an instance of the Graphics class. You can also call the getGraphics function of a particular component. This will return an instance of the Graphics class. To use Java 2D API features, you cast the Graphics object passed into a component's rendering method to a Graphics2D object.

```
public void Paint (Graphics g)
{
    Graphics2D g2 = (Graphics2D) g;
}
```

The various state attributes associated with a Graphics2D object is referred to as the Graphics2D rendering context. To use any methods of this class, you must set up the Graphics2D rendering context and then call one of the Graphics2D rendering methods, such as one of the drawing methods. As you can probably guess, this class has a number of methods. The most important are summarized in Table 13.1.

Table 13.1 Graphics2D methods

Method	Purpose
void draw3DRect(int x, int y, int width, int height, boolean raised)	Draws a 3D highlighted outline of the specified rectangle.
abstract void drawImage (BufferedImage img, BufferedImageOp op, int x, int y)	Renders a BufferedImage that is filtered with a Buffered-ImageOp.
abstract void drawString(String str, int x, int y)	Renders the text of the specified string, using the current text attribute state in the Graphics2D context.
void fill3DRect(int x, int y, int width, int height, boolean raised)	Paints a 3D highlighted rectangle filled with the current color.
abstract void rotate(double theta)	Concatenates the current Graphics2D transform with a rotation transform.

Each of these methods, as well as others, provides a variety of ways to render two-dimensional graphics using the

Graphics2D class. Rather than simply list several of the methods in the Graphics2D class, why don't we take a look at an example that illustrates the use of many of these methods?

Example 13.1

Step 1: Start a new project with an Application object.

Step 2: On the design screen, leave the background frame with a border layout. Place a panel in the Center named **pnldisplay** and one in the West named **pnlwest**. The one in the Center should have a background color that is all white. The one in the West should have a vertical flow layout. You will then place three buttons on pnlwest. This should look much like what is shown in Figure 13.1.

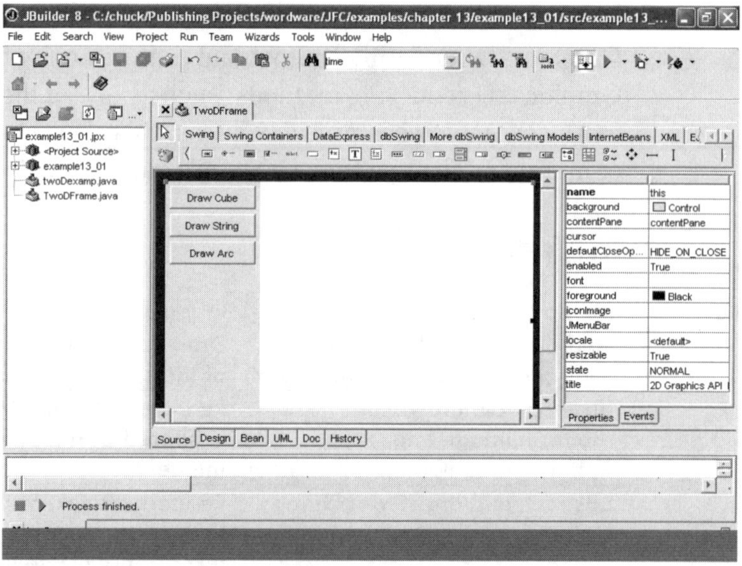

Figure 13.1 The example component layout

Step 3: Now for the good part — the code. In the Draw Cube button's action event, place this code:

```
g = pnldisplay.getGraphics();
g2 = (Graphics2D) g;
g2.draw3DRect(10,10,40,40,true);
Color c = new Color(200,0,0);
g2.setColor(c);
g2.fill3DRect(20,20,40,40,true);
g2.drawLine(10,10,20,20);
g2.drawLine(10,50,20,60);
g2.drawLine(50,10,60,20);
```

Note: You should pay attention to the first two lines, where we cast the existing graphics class as a Graphics2D class. This is what you must always do before using the Graphics2D class.

Now in the Draw String button, place this code:

```
g = pnldisplay.getGraphics();
g2 = (Graphics2D) g;
// note the value of 1 indicates bold.
Font f = new Font("Serif", 1, 24);
Color c = new Color(0,0,255);
g2.setFont(f);
g2.setColor(c);
g2.drawString("JBuilder is Cool",10,100);
```

Finally, in the Draw Arc button, place this code:

```
g = pnldisplay.getGraphics();
g2 = (Graphics2D) g;
Color c = new Color(255,0,0);
g2.setColor(c);
g2.drawArc(10,200,100,25,15,90);
```

Notice that in all three cases we had to first cast the existing Graphics class as a Graphics2D class. After that, using the Graphics2D class was not much different from using the old Graphics class. When you run your application, you should see something like what is shown in Figures 13.2, 13.3, and 13.4.

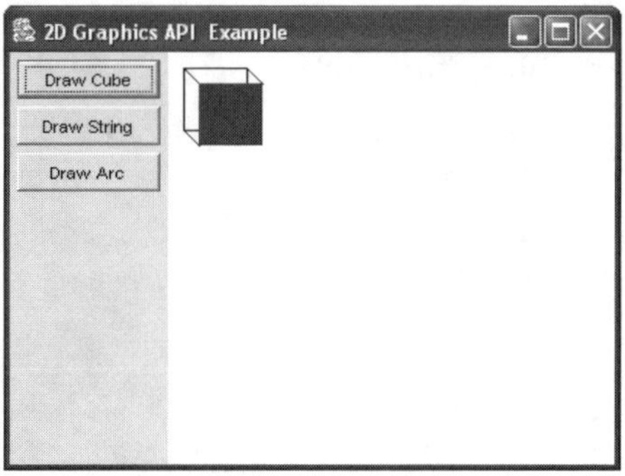

Figure 13.2 The Draw Cube button

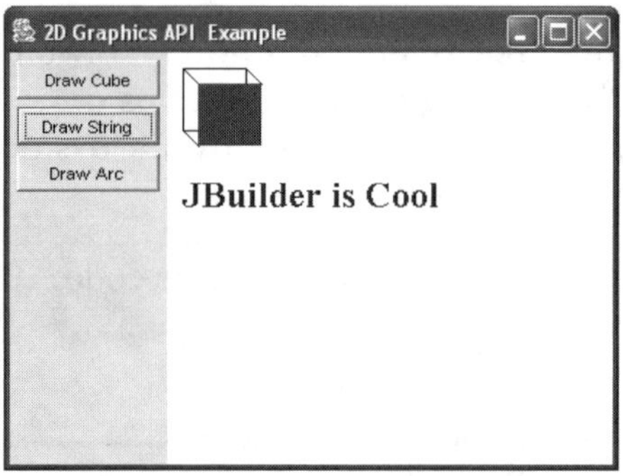

Figure 13.3 The Draw String button

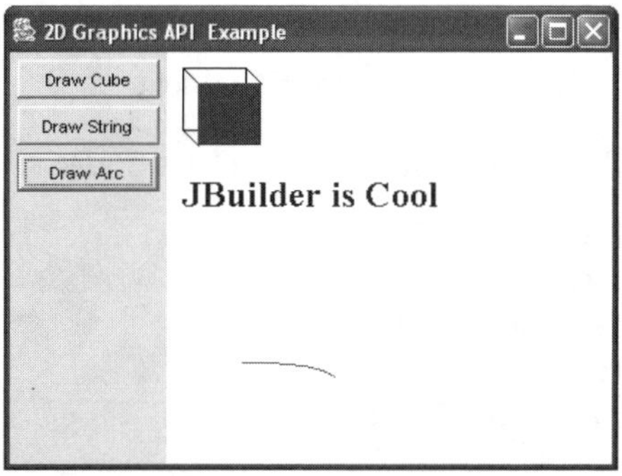

Figure 13.4 The Draw Arc button

For those readers not using JBuilder or who simply want to see the entire code, it is provided here:

```
package example13_01;
import java.awt.*;
import java.awt.event.*;
```

```
import javax.swing.*;
import com.borland.jbcl.layout.*;
public class TwoDFrame extends JFrame
{
  JPanel contentPane;
  BorderLayout borderLayout1 = new BorderLayout();
  JPanel pnldisplay = new JPanel();
  JPanel pnlwest = new JPanel();
  Graphics g;
  Graphics2D g2;
  JButton jButton1 = new JButton();
  VerticalFlowLayout verticalFlowLayout1 = new
       VerticalFlowLayout();
  JButton jButton2 = new JButton();
  JButton jButton3 = new JButton();
  //Construct the frame
  public TwoDFrame() {
    enableEvents(AWTEvent.WINDOW_EVENT_MASK);
    try
  {
      jbInit();
    }
    catch(Exception e)
{
      e.printStackTrace();
    }
  }
  //Component initialization
  private void jbInit() throws Exception
  {
    contentPane = (JPanel) this.getContentPane();
    contentPane.setLayout(borderLayout1);
    this.setSize(new Dimension(400, 300));
    this.setTitle("2D Graphics API  Example");
    pnldisplay.setBackground(Color.white);
    jButton1.setText("Draw Cube");
    jButton1.addActionListener(new TwoDFrame_jButton1_
         actionAdapter(this));
    pnlwest.setLayout(verticalFlowLayout1);
    jButton2.setText("Draw String");
    jButton2.addActionListener(new TwoDFrame_jButton2_
         actionAdapter(this));
    jButton3.setText("Draw Arc");
    jButton3.addActionListener(new TwoDFrame_jButton3_
         actionAdapter(this));
```

```
    contentPane.add(pnldisplay, BorderLayout.CENTER);
    contentPane.add(pnlwest, BorderLayout.WEST);
    pnlwest.add(jButton1, null);
    pnlwest.add(jButton2, null);
    pnlwest.add(jButton3, null);
  }
  //Overridden so we can exit when window is closed
  protected void processWindowEvent(WindowEvent e)
{
    super.processWindowEvent(e);
    if (e.getID() == WindowEvent.WINDOW_CLOSING)
{
      System.exit(0);
    }
  }
  void jButton1_actionPerformed(ActionEvent e)
  {
    g = pnldisplay.getGraphics();
    g2 = (Graphics2D) g;
    g2.draw3DRect(10,10,40,40,true);
    Color c = new Color(200,0,0);
    g2.setColor(c);
    g2.fill3DRect(20,20,40,40,true);
    g2.drawLine(10,10,20,20);
    g2.drawLine(10,50,20,60);
    g2.drawLine(50,10,60,20);
  }
  void jButton2_actionPerformed(ActionEvent e)
  {
    g = pnldisplay.getGraphics();
    g2 = (Graphics2D) g;
    // note the value of 1 indicates bold.
    Font f = new Font("Serif", 1, 24);
    Color c = new Color(0, 0, 255);
    g2.setFont(f);
    g2.setColor(c);
    g2.drawString("JBuilder is Cool", 10, 100);

  }
  void jButton3_actionPerformed(ActionEvent e)
  {
    g = pnldisplay.getGraphics();
    g2 = (Graphics2D) g;
    Color c = new Color(255,0,0);
    g2.setColor(c);
```

```
    g2.drawArc(10,200,100,25,15,90);
  }
}
class TwoDFrame_jButton1_actionAdapter implements java.awt
     .event.ActionListener
 {
  TwoDFrame adaptee;

  TwoDFrame_jButton1_actionAdapter(TwoDFrame adaptee)
  {
    this.adaptee = adaptee;
  }
  public void actionPerformed(ActionEvent e)
  {
    adaptee.jButton1_actionPerformed(e);
  }
}
class TwoDFrame_jButton2_actionAdapter implements java.awt
     .event.ActionListener
{
  TwoDFrame adaptee;
  TwoDFrame_jButton2_actionAdapter(TwoDFrame adaptee)
  {
    this.adaptee = adaptee;
  }
  public void actionPerformed(ActionEvent e)
  {
    adaptee.jButton2_actionPerformed(e);
  }
}
class TwoDFrame_jButton3_actionAdapter implements java.awt
     .event.ActionListener {
  TwoDFrame adaptee;
  TwoDFrame_jButton3_actionAdapter(TwoDFrame adaptee)
  {
    this.adaptee = adaptee;
  }
  public void actionPerformed(ActionEvent e)
  {
    adaptee.jButton3_actionPerformed(e);
  }
}
```

This example, while rather simple, should illustrate for you the essentials of using the Graphics2D class. It's not particularly complicated. In fact, it's not all that different from using the standard Graphics class. It does have some new methods and, in my opinion, renders a clearer and better image.

You may have noticed that in the preceding example, we made use of certain numeric constants. These numeric values were used to indicate specific values to certain classes, such as the Font class. Table 13.2 lists the most important constants for the Font class.

Table 13.2 The Font class constant values

Constant	Purpose
1	Bold
2	Italic
0	Plain

Keep in mind how this class handles attributes. Graphics2D holds references to its attribute objects. If you alter an attribute object that is part of the Graphics2D context, you need to call the appropriate set method to notify the context.

The preceding sections and the example should make you basically familiar with the Graphics2D class. In fact, this should provide you with enough information to appropriately utilize this class. However, for those readers who desire a more in-depth understanding of how and why this class works, the following two sections should provide that.

Coordinate Spaces and the Graphics2D Class

It should come as no surprise that any graphics technique must rely on some sort of coordinate system. In the methods we used in our previous example, we provided x and y starting coordinates and either ending coordinates or height and width. It is probably useful for you to understand how coordinates are handled with the Graphics2D class. All coordinates passed to a Graphics2D object are specified in a device-independent coordinate system called user space. It is important to note the "device-independent" part. That means coordinates are rendered the same, regardless of the device on which they are rendered. This is rather important, since it means that rendering to a printer will work basically the same way as rendering to your monitor. Obviously, at some point, some conversion must be made to the device-specific context that is being used to render the graphics. The Graphics2D object contains an AffineTransform object as part of its rendering state. It is this object that defines how to convert coordinates from user space to device-dependent coordinates in device space.

There is a good reason to have an intermediate object handle the conversion from user space to the device-specific context. When you are referring to coordinates in device space, that usually means individual device pixels. Some Graphics2D objects can be used to capture rendering operations for storage into a graphics metafile for playback on a device of unknown physical resolution at a later time. Since the resolution may not be known at the time the rendering operations are captured, the Graphics2D Transform object is used to transform user coordinates to a virtual device space that approximates the expected resolution of the target device. Further transformations might need to be applied at playback time if the estimate is incorrect.

All Graphics2D objects are associated with a target that defines where rendering takes place. In the example you saw earlier in this chapter, the target was a panel that was rendered on the screen of your monitor (as opposed to being rendered on a printer). There, a GraphicsConfiguration object is used to define the characteristics of the rendering target, such as pixel format and resolution. The same rendering target is used throughout the life of a Graphics2D object.

When you create a Graphics2D object, the Graphics-Configuration specifies the default transform for the target of the Graphics2D. This target could be a component or an image. In our example earlier in this chapter, the target was a component (specifically, a panel). This default Transform object maps the user space coordinate system to screen and printer device coordinates (if it is being printed) in such a manner that the origin maps to the upper left-hand corner of the target region of the device with x coordinates extending from the left-most side to the right and y coordinates extending from the top downward. In many cases you will be able to use the Graphics2D object without any concern for the coordinate system used (beyond, of course, knowing where the x and y coordinates begin). However, if you encounter any significant issues with your graphics display, knowledge of this coordinate system may be invaluable in ascertaining the cause and taking corrective action.

The Rendering Process

When you run your application or applet, it may seem that the graphics are rendered in one fell swoop. This, however, is not the case. The rendering process can actually be broken down into four phases. Each of these phases is controlled by the Graphics2D rendering attributes. The renderer can optimize many of these steps. The most common way to optimize the process is by caching the results for future use. This means that if the same graphics procedure is called again, the rendering process has been cached and need not be redone.

The steps in the rendering process are:

1. Determine what to render.
2. Determine what colors to render.
3. Constrain the rendering operation to the current clip.
4. Apply the colors.

The first step is relatively easy to comprehend. The appropriate graphics object to render must be determined. Are you rendering a 3D rectangle, an arc, an image, or some other object? Determining what colors to render should also be relatively simple to grasp. The appropriate colors must be determined in order to have an accurate rendering.

Constraining the rendering operation to the current clip may sound a bit odd. The clip is specified by a shape in user space and controlled by the program using the clip manipulation methods of Graphics and Graphics2D. It is this stage at which any transformation from user space to device-dependent space must occur. This user clip is transformed into device space by the current Transform object and combined with the device clip. The combination of the user clip and device clip defines the composite clip, which determines the final clipping region.

Just as there are stages in the rendering process, there are different types of rendering operations. There are, in fact, three types of rendering operations:

- Shape operations
- Text operations
- Image operations

Shape operations are any operations that utilize the drawShape method, either directly or indirectly. The current paint in the Graphics2D context is queried for a PaintContext, which specifies the colors to render in device space.

Text operations are any operations that will render text. The obvious method that should spring immediately to mind is drawString. If the argument is a string, the currently selected font is asked to convert the Unicode characters in the string into a set of glyphs for presentation.

If the argument is an AttributedCharacterIterator, the iterator is asked to convert itself to a TextLayout using its embedded font attributes. This is done because TextLayout implements more sophisticated glyph layout algorithms.

If the argument is a GlyphVector, no intermediary object is required. This is because the GlyphVector object already contains the appropriate font-specific glyph codes with explicit coordinates for the position of each glyph.

The final type of operation is the image operation. The region of the image is defined by the bounding box of the source image. This bounding box is specified in image space, which is the image object's local coordinate system. That image space will need to be converted to user space for rendering purposes.

If an AffineTransform is passed to drawImage(Image, AffineTransform, ImageObserver), the AffineTransform will be used to transform the bounding box from image space to user space. If no AffineTransform is supplied, the bounding box is treated as if it is already in user space.

Images and the Java 2D API

The Java 2D API implements a new imaging model. This model supports the manipulation of fixed-resolution images stored in memory. A new Image class in the java.awt.image package, BufferedImage, can be used to hold and manipulate image data retrieved from a file or URL. For example, a BufferedImage can be used to implement a process known as double buffering. In double buffering, the graphic elements are rendered off-screen to the BufferedImage and are then copied to the screen through a call to Graphics2D drawImage. The classes BufferedImage and BufferedImage-Op also enable you to perform a variety of image-filtering operations, such as blur and sharpen. This ability to filter the image is one of the many new features in the Java 2D API.

Working with images in the Java 2D API may sound complex, and it can be. If you wish to use all the various options available to you, it would take an entire book just to explore those. However, the essentials are very much like they were with the old Graphics object. Let's take a look at an example.

Example 13.2

Step 1: Create a new project with an Application object.

Step 2: Leave the background layout as border. Place a white panel named **pnlDisplay** in the Center area and another panel named **pnlwest** on the West area. Put one button on the

West panel. It should look much like what is shown in Figure 13.5.

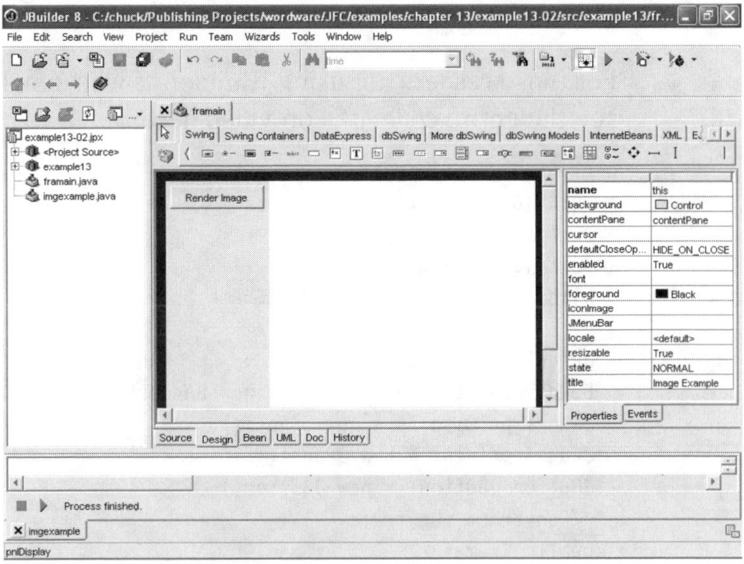

Figure 13.5 The layout for Example 13.2

Step 3: In that button's action event, place the following code:

```
Image img1 = Toolkit.getDefaultToolkit().getImage("java.gif");
Graphics g = pnlDisplay.getGraphics();
Graphics2D g2 = (Graphics2D) g;
g2.drawImage(img1,10,10,this);
g2.finalize();
```

Now when you run your application and press the button, an image will be displayed, as shown in Figure 13.6.

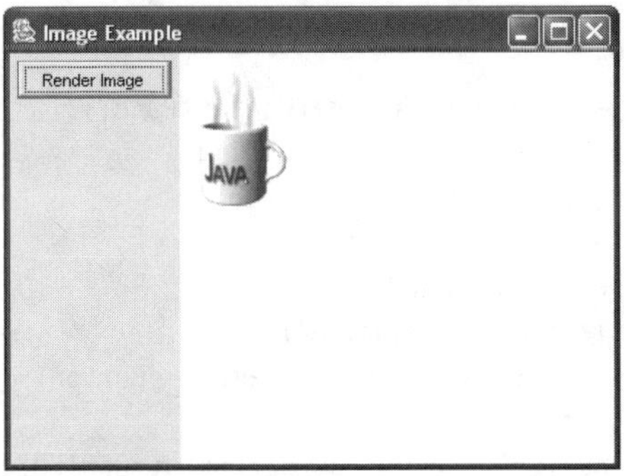

Figure 13.6 Displaying an image

Note: The image used in this code is included in the source code for this book. You can use any image you like.

For those readers not using JBuilder or who simply wish to see the entire code, it is provided here:

```
package example13;
import java.awt.*;
import java.awt.event.*;
import javax.swing.*;
public class framain extends JFrame
{
  JPanel contentPane;
  BorderLayout borderLayout1 = new BorderLayout();
  JPanel pnlDisplay = new JPanel();
  JPanel pnlwest = new JPanel();
  JButton jButton1 = new JButton();
  //Construct the frame
  public framain()
  {
    enableEvents(AWTEvent.WINDOW_EVENT_MASK);
    try
    {
      jbInit();
    }
    catch(Exception e)
    {
      e.printStackTrace();
    }
  }
  //Component initialization
  private void jbInit() throws Exception
  {
    contentPane = (JPanel) this.getContentPane();
    contentPane.setLayout(borderLayout1);
    this.setSize(new Dimension(400, 300));
    this.setTitle("Image Example");
    pnlDisplay.setBackground(Color.white);
    jButton1.setText("Render Image");
    jButton1.addActionListener(new framain_jButton1_
         actionAdapter(this));
    contentPane.add(pnlDisplay, BorderLayout.CENTER);
    contentPane.add(pnlwest, BorderLayout.WEST);
```

```
    pnlwest.add(jButton1, null);
  }
  //Overridden so we can exit when window is closed
  protected void processWindowEvent(WindowEvent e)
  {
    super.processWindowEvent(e);
    if (e.getID() == WindowEvent.WINDOW_CLOSING)
    {
      System.exit(0);
    }
  }
  void jButton1_actionPerformed(ActionEvent e)
  {
        Image img1 = Toolkit.getDefaultToolkit().getImage
             ("java.gif");
        Graphics g = pnlDisplay.getGraphics();
        Graphics2D g2 = (Graphics2D) g;
        g2.drawImage(img1, 10, 10, this);
        g2.finalize();
  }
}
class framain_jButton1_actionAdapter implements java.awt
     .event.ActionListener
{
  framain adaptee;

  framain_jButton1_actionAdapter(framain adaptee)
  {
    this.adaptee = adaptee;
  }
  public void actionPerformed(ActionEvent e)
  {
    adaptee.jButton1_actionPerformed(e);
  }
}
```

As you can see, the essentials of displaying an image with the Graphics2D class are not much different than displaying them with the old Graphics class. There are simply many more options available to you now.

Summary

This chapter introduced you to the Java 2D API. You were shown how to use the new Graphics2D class, how the rendering process works, and how to work with images in the Java 2D API.

Review Questions

1. What package is the Graphics2D class found in?
2. What must you do with the Graphics2D class before you can use it?
3. What are the steps in the rendering process?
4. What types of rendering operations are there?
5. What value passed to the Font class will cause the font to be bold?
6. Name at least one thing that the Java 2D API handles.
7. What determines the region of an image during a rendering operation?
8. What is double buffering?

Chapter 14

Threads and Swing

This chapter covers the following:

- Thread basics
- The single-thread rule
- Using threads in Java
- Thread-safe applications in JBuilder

Introduction

We have saved one particularly important topic until the end of the book. That topic is how to handle threads when working with Swing. The first question might be, why was this topic put on hold? The answer is simple: All the examples that we created so far could be done without worrying at all about threads. The second question you may have is, what is a thread?

To answer that question, we need to consider how an operating system handles various applications. Each application (or applet) is running in its own memory space, which is often referred to as a process. That means there is a particular range of memory addresses (a chunk of memory, if you will) that is allocated for that application. Because each is running in a separate process, the failure of one application does not crash other applications that are running.

Sometimes within a given application, you need several different activities to take place. Consider a word processor. You want it to process input from the keyboard as its primary task. However, you may also want your word processor to perform some type of background spell checking and perhaps even periodic automatic saves. How does a computer handle this? The answer is threads. You can think of a thread as a subprocess. It is an individual action taking place within the context of a process or memory space. Many applications are single threaded; they only have one thread. However, the word processor would be multithreaded. It would have one thread to handle the input from the keyboard, another to perform spell checking, and yet another to deal with the periodic save.

Threads all occur within the same process or memory space. For this reason, it is important that threads are handled correctly. If one thread changes the value of a variable, other threads that access that variable will get the changed value, rather than the original value. It is also important to note that, since they are in the same memory space, if one thread crashes, the entire application (i.e., all of its threads) crashes.

Some people find the following analogy helpful. Think of a process as a lane of a highway in which cars are running smoothly. If cars in one of the other lanes crash, that will not impede this lane. Now think of threads as individual cars in a lane. If one car crashes, the entire lane will be blocked.

Thread Basics

Now that you have a basic understanding of what a thread is, it's time to consider threads in the context of Java. Different programming languages provide different methodologies for handling threads. If your program creates and refers to its GUI components in the proper way, you may not need to worry about threads. What, you may ask, is the proper way? If your program is an applet, the proper way is to construct its GUI in the init method. This seems relatively simple and obvious. However, I have seen code that attempted to do this in the start method, with potentially disastrous results. If your program is an application, rather than an applet, you would do well to consider the following generic example for how to properly construct the interface:

```
public class MyApp
{
    public static void main(String[] args)
  {
        JFrame f = new JFrame(...);
        ...//Add components to the frame here...
        f.setVisible(true);
    }
}
```

You see that the elements of the GUI are created at the beginning of the class, and methods of the GUI components are handled in event handler functions. If you follow this format, you will have a thread-safe application. However, there are two important cases where this standard template might not be sufficient to guarantee a thread-safe application. One case would be if your program creates threads to perform tasks that affect the GUI. The second situation would be if it manipulates GUI components that are already visible in response to anything but a standard event. We discuss how to handle these situations in the following sections.

The Single-Thread Rule

Threads in Swing are really not that complicated. It all comes down to a simple rule called the single-thread rule. That rule simply states that Swing components can be accessed by only one thread at a time. Usually, that thread will be the event-dispatching thread. So never write code that would have more than one thread access the GUI at a time. A more formal version of the single-thread rule would be:

> Once a Swing component has been realized, all code that might affect or depend on the state of that component should be executed in the event-dispatching thread.

Of course, this may lead you to ask: What does it mean to say a component has been "realized"? *Realized* simply means that the component has been painted on-screen or that it is ready to be painted. A Swing component that's a top-level window is realized by having one of these methods. Once a window is realized, all the components that it contains are realized. Another way to realize a component is to add it to a container that's already realized. In other words, if a panel is already displayed and you add a button to that panel, the button is realized.

As with most rules, this one has a few exceptions. There are situations when you can ignore the single-thread rule and still have thread-safe code.

Note: If you need access to the UI from outside event-handling or painting code, you can use the SwingUtilities class invokeLater or invokeAndWait methods. These methods are discussed in more detail later in this chapter.

Note: In the Swing API documentation, thread-safe methods are marked with the text: "This method is thread safe." Don't expect to see this often, as most Swing methods are not thread safe.

There are actually four exceptions to the single-thread rule. Each is explained in detail in the following paragraphs, but here is a list of them:

- Using the main thread
- Using init
- Using repaint and revalidate
- Using listener threads

The first exception involves using the main thread to manipulate GUI components. As long as no components (Swing or otherwise) have been realized in the current run-time environment, it's perfectly acceptable to construct and show a GUI in the main thread of an application.

Another exception involves using applets. An applet's GUI can be constructed and shown in the init method. In fact, it should be. Existing browsers don't paint an applet until after its init and start methods have been called. Thus, constructing the GUI in the applet's init method is safe, as long as you never call show() or setVisible(true) on the actual applet object.

A third exception involves two methods that are always thread safe. There are, in fact, two JComponent methods that are safe to call from any thread. These methods are repaint and revalidate. The reason that these methods are safe lies in the manner in which they execute. Both of these methods queue requests to be executed on the event-dispatching thread.

The last exception involves listener threads. It's always safe to call the addListenerTypeListener and removeListenerTypeListener methods from any thread. These methods' add and remove operations do not affect an event dispatch that's underway.

These exceptions might sound a bit complex; don't worry. To be perfectly frank, you have been able to complete 13 chapters of this book without worrying at all about threads. Proper handling of threads could constitute an entire book. All we are trying to accomplish in this chapter is giving you a basic understanding of threads and how they work in conjunction with Swing applications.

Once the GUI has been initialized, most of the work occurs in the event-dispatching thread. The event-dispatching thread is simply the primary thread of the application. It is, therefore, the event responsible for dispatching various events, hence the name. Once the GUI is visible, most Java programs are driven by events. Recall that events are simply actions — often those taken by the user, such as button actions or mouse clicks.

Though most programs work in the way just described, some programs need to perform non-event-driven GUI work after the GUI is visible. That is why we have had this discussion regarding the use of threads, the single-thread rule, and exceptions to that rule. You might wonder what types of applications we are talking about, since all the applications you have seen so far have been single threaded. Here are two examples:

- Those applications or applets that must perform a lengthy initialization operation before they can be used. Due to the lengthy initialization, this type of application will need to display some GUI while the initialization is occurring. For this reason, initialization should not occur in the event-dispatching thread. If it did, you could encounter a situation where repainting and event dispatch would stop. However, once initialization is complete, the GUI update/change should occur in the event-dispatching thread.
- Those applications and applets in which the GUI must be updated as the result of nonstandard events. Consider a server application that receives requests from other applications running on different machines. These requests can come at any time, and they result in one of the server's methods being invoked in some possibly unknown thread. That method can update the GUI by executing the GUI-update code in the event-dispatching thread.

Fortunately, Java provides you with some methods that can assist you in running code within the event-dispatching thread. These methods are found in the SwingUtilities class. The SwingUtilities class provides two such methods to help you run code in the event-dispatching thread:

- invokeLater
- invokeAndWait

The invokeLater method requests that some code be executed in the event-dispatching thread. This method returns immediately, without waiting for the code to execute. The invokeAndWait method acts much like invokeLater, except this method waits for the code to execute.

Using Threads in Java

This chapter has discussed, at some length, the intricacies of thread use as it relates to Java. All of that would probably be more comprehensible to you if we took a brief tour of thread use in Java in general. Though the concept of threads may be new to you, threads are actually a part of every Java program. Recall that a thread is merely a single sequential flow of control within a program. This means that every program has at least one thread. The applications and applets that you worked with in the first 13 chapters of this book were single threaded. When your program is single threaded you don't need to set up a thread explicitly; the Java Virtual Machine handles this for you. However, one of the most powerful aspects of the Java language is that you can easily program multiple threads of execution to run concurrently within the same program, and you can do it rather easily. This is refreshing for readers who have worked with multithreaded applications in languages such as C++, where multithreading can be a tricky process.

You actually encounter multithreaded applications all the time. Recall the word processor example mentioned earlier. It seems to be handling keyboard input, spell checking, and auto saving simultaneously. In actuality, these actions are not occurring simultaneously. Each is being handled by a different thread, and each thread takes turns operating. It is possible to set the priority of a given thread so that, if need be, it can usurp processor attention from a thread with a lower priority.

When you create a class that will use threads, it will automatically have a few functions that you can use to cause the thread to execute, suspend execution, or halt. The methods you have available to you are summarized in Table 14.1.

Table 14.1 Thread methods

Method	Usage
void run()	This method causes the thread to execute.
void start()	This method also causes the thread to execute.
void destroy()	This method destroys the thread without any cleanup.
void interrupt()	This method interrupts execution of the thread.
void resume()	This method is deprecated. This method exists solely for use with suspend().
void suspend()	This method temporarily halts execution of the thread. It is essentially a "pause" method.
static void sleep(long millis)	This method causes the currently executing thread to temporarily cease execution for the specified number of milliseconds.
static void yield()	This method causes the currently executing thread object to temporarily pause and allow other threads to execute.

If you wish to use threads in your application, you can use one of two techniques to implement the run() method for a thread:

- Subclass the java.lang.Thread class
- Implement the java.lang.Runnable interface

If you are creating a new class whose objects you want to execute in separate threads, you will probably want to subclass the java.lang.Thread class. The Thread class's default run() method does not do anything, so your class will need to override that with your own run method. The run() method is the first thing that executes when a thread is started. As an example, the following class, ThreadExample1, subclasses the Thread class and overrides its run() method. In this example, the run() method merely identifies a thread and prints its name to the screen. The for loop simply counts integers from the start value to the finish value and prints each count to the screen. Then, before the loop finishes execution, the method prints a message that indicates that the thread has finished executing.

```
public class ThreadExample1 extends Thread
{
```

```
   private int start;
   private int finish;
   public CountThread(int from, int to)
{
     this.start = from;
     this.finish = to;
   }
   public void run()
{
      System.out.println("this.getName() + "begun
           executing...");
         for (int i = start; i <= finish; i++)
         {
            System.out.print (i + " ");
         }
   System.out.println(this.getName() + " finished executing.");
   }
}
```


To test the ThreadExample1 class, you can create a test application, much like the one shown here:

```
public class ThreadTester
{
   static public void main(String[] args)
   {
      ThreadExample1 thread1 = new ThreadExample1 (1, 5);
      ThreadExample1 thread2 = new ThreadExample1 (10, 15);
      thread1.start();
      thread2.start();
   }
}
```

The main() method of the test application creates two instances of theThreadExample1 class. Both threads are then started by calling their start() methods. The output from this test application could look like this:

```
Thread-0 started executing...
1 2 3 4 5
Thread-0 finished executing.
Thread-1 started executing...
10 11 12 13 14 15
Thread-1 finished executing.
```

Notice that we used this.getName to display a name for the thread. You should also notice that the first thread was called Thread-0 and the next one Thread-1. Unless you specifically assign a name to a thread, Java will automatically give it a name in the form Thread-*n*, where *n* is some number starting with 0. You could choose to assign a name to a thread in the class constructor or with the setName(String) method.

It is important that you keep one fact in mind: Threads in Java are not guaranteed to execute in any particular sequence. In fact, each time you execute ThreadTester, you could possibly get a different output. The process of scheduling threads is controlled by the Java thread scheduler. You do not have direct programmatic control over that.

The preceding example was fine if you want the class you are using to extend the Thread class. As you already know, in Java you can only inherit from a single class; there is no multiple inheritance. So what do you do if you want to use threads with a class that is already inheriting from some other class? Fortunately, Java provides an interface that you can implement. That interface is the java.lang.Runnable interface, which provides threading support for classes that do not inherit from the Thread class. It provides only one method, the run() method, which you have to implement for your class. Let's take a look at a modification of our previous example, this one implementing the Runnable interface:

```
public class ThreadExample2 implements Runnable
{
   private int start;
   private int finish;
   public ThreadExample2 (int from, int to)
   {
      this.start = from;
      this.finish = to;
   }
   public void run()
   {
      System.out.println(Thread.currentThread() + " started
           executing...");
      for (int i=start; i <= finish; i++)
      {
```

```
            System.out.print (i + " ");
        }
    System.out.println(Thread.currentThread() + " finished
        executing.");
    }
}
```

Just as you need to change the Thread class itself, you will need to slightly modify the test application:


```
public class ThreadTester
{
    static public void main(String[] args)
   {
        CountThreadRun thread1 = new CountThreadRun(1, 5);
        new Thread(thread1).start();
        CountThreadRun thread2 = new CountThreadRun(10, 15);
        new Thread(thread2).start();
   }
}
```

As you can see, using threads is not particularly difficult. In fact, it is rather straightforward.

Thread-Safe Applications in JBuilder

We have spent several pages wading through the intricacies of thread use. It is now time to create a JBuilder application that uses threads.

Example 14.1

Step 1: Create a new project with an Application object.

Step 2: Leave the border layout for the frame and add two panels: one in the Center and one in the West. The one in the West should have a vertical flow layout. The panel in the Center should use a flow layout. Place two buttons on the West panel and one label on the Center panel. It should look much like what is depicted in Figure 14.1.

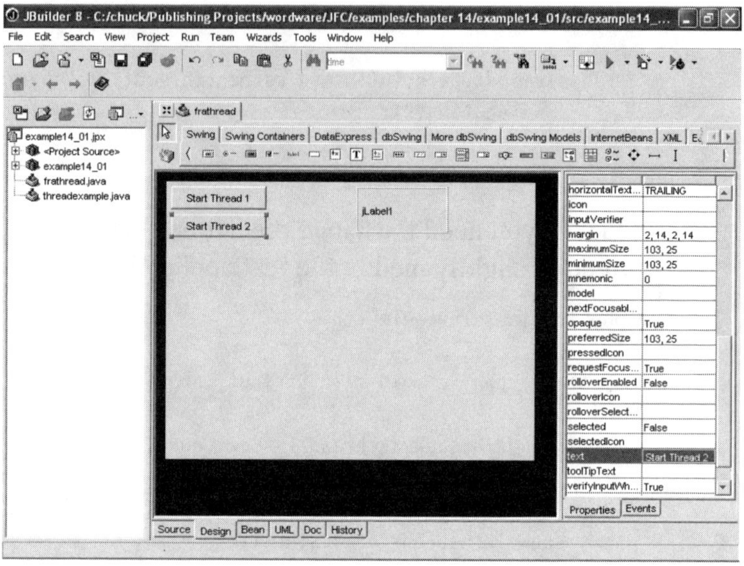

Figure 14.1 The component layout

Step 3: After the final bracket of the main class that JBuilder created for you, you will add a new class. This is very similar to our previous example.

```
class ThreadExample1 extends Thread
{
   public String name;
   public ThreadExample1(String threadname)
   {
     name = threadname;
   }
   public void run()
   {
      name = name + " Has begun!";
   }
}
```

Step 4: In the action event of the button labeled Start Thread 1, place the following code:

```
ThreadExample1 mythread = new ThreadExample1("Thread A");
mythread.run();
String txt = jLabel1.getText();
txt = txt + mythread.name;
jLabel1.setText(txt);
```

You will place almost identical code in the action event of the other button — the only difference being that it should read Thread B. When you run this application, you should see something much like what is depicted in Figures 14.2 and 14.3.

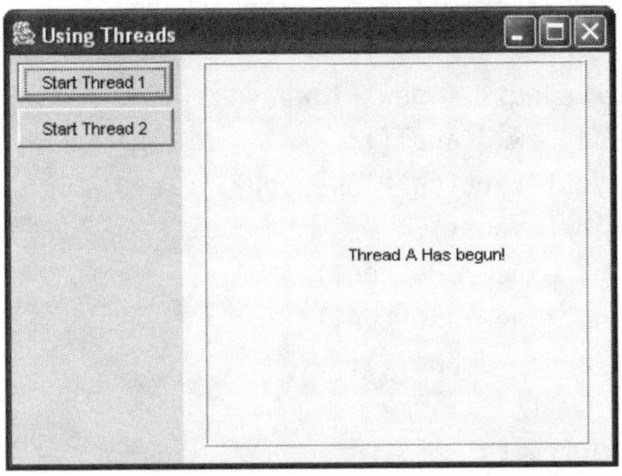

Figure 14.2 Running the JBuilder thread example

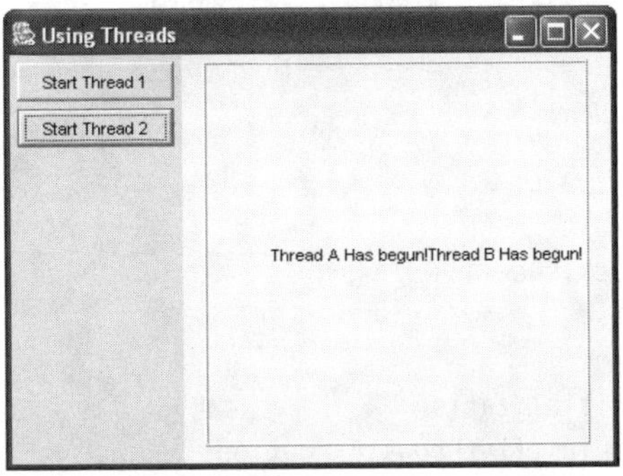

Figure 14.3 The JBuilder thread example continued

Note: Each time you press one of the buttons, a new thread will be started. If you continue to click the buttons continuously, you might eventually (but after a long period of time) cause some problems for your machine.

For those readers who are not using JBuilder or wish to see the entire code, it is provided here:

```
package example14_01;
import java.awt.*;
import java.awt.event.*;
```

```
import javax.swing.*;
import com.borland.jbcl.layout.*;
import javax.swing.border.*;
public class frathread extends JFrame
{
  JPanel contentPane;
  BorderLayout borderLayout1 = new BorderLayout();
  JPanel jPanel1 = new JPanel();
  FlowLayout flowLayout1 = new FlowLayout();
  JPanel jPanel2 = new JPanel();
  VerticalFlowLayout verticalFlowLayout1 = new
       VerticalFlowLayout();
  JButton jButton1 = new JButton();
  JButton jButton2 = new JButton();
  JLabel jLabel1 = new JLabel();
  Border border1;
  //Construct the frame
  public frathread()
  {
    enableEvents(AWTEvent.WINDOW_EVENT_MASK);
    try {
      jbInit();
    }
    catch(Exception e)
    {
      e.printStackTrace();
    }
  }
  //Component initialization
  private void jbInit() throws Exception
  {
    contentPane = (JPanel) this.getContentPane();
    border1 = BorderFactory.createCompoundBorder(new
         EtchedBorder(EtchedBorder.RAISED, Color.white,
         new Color(178, 178, 178)), BorderFactory
         .createEmptyBorder(5, 5, 5, 5));
    contentPane.setLayout(borderLayout1);
    this.setSize(new Dimension(400, 300));
    this.setTitle("Using Threads");
    jPanel1.setLayout(flowLayout1);
    jPanel2.setLayout(verticalFlowLayout1);
    jButton1.setText("Start Thread 1");
    jButton1.addActionListener(new frathread_jButton1
         _actionAdapter(this));
    jButton2.setText("Start Thread 2");
```

```
    jButton2.addActionListener(new frathread_jButton2
         _actionAdapter(this));
    jLabel1.setBackground(Color.white);
    jLabel1.setBorder(border1);
    jLabel1.setMaximumSize(new Dimension(100, 50));
    jLabel1.setMinimumSize(new Dimension(100, 50));
    jLabel1.setPreferredSize(new Dimension(100, 50));
    jLabel1.setText("jLabel1");
    contentPane.add(jPanel1, BorderLayout.CENTER);
    jPanel1.add(jLabel1, null);
    contentPane.add(jPanel2, BorderLayout.WEST);
    jPanel2.add(jButton1);
    jPanel2.add(jButton2, null);
  }
  //Overridden so we can exit when window is closed
  protected void processWindowEvent(WindowEvent e)
  {
    super.processWindowEvent(e);
    if (e.getID() == WindowEvent.WINDOW_CLOSING)
    {
      System.exit(0);
    }
  }
  void jButton1_actionPerformed(ActionEvent e)
  {
    ThreadExample1 mythread = new ThreadExample1("Thread A");
    mythread.run();
    String txt = jLabel1.getText();
    txt = txt + mythread.name;
    jLabel1.setText(txt);
  }
  void jButton2_actionPerformed(ActionEvent e)
  {
    ThreadExample1 mythread = new ThreadExample1("Thread B");
    mythread.run();
    String txt = jLabel1.getText();
    txt = txt + mythread.name;
    jLabel1.setText(txt);
  }
}
class ThreadExample1 extends Thread
{
  public String name;
  public ThreadExample1(String threadname)
  {
```

14 Chapter

```
    name = threadname;
  }
  public void run()
  {
    name = name + " Has begun!";
  }
}
class frathread_jButton1_actionAdapter implements java.awt
     .event.ActionListener
{
  frathread adaptee;

  frathread_jButton1_actionAdapter(frathread adaptee)
  {
    this.adaptee = adaptee;
  }
  public void actionPerformed(ActionEvent e)
  {
    adaptee.jButton1_actionPerformed(e);
  }
}
class frathread_jButton2_actionAdapter implements java.awt
     .event.ActionListener
{
  frathread adaptee;
  frathread_jButton2_actionAdapter(frathread adaptee)
  {
    this.adaptee = adaptee;
  }
  public void actionPerformed(ActionEvent e)
  {
    adaptee.jButton2_actionPerformed(e);
  }
}
```

As you can see, using threads in JBuilder is really no different than using them in Java. For much of your programming career, you may not need multithreaded applications. Hopefully, after reading this chapter, you have enough of a basic grasp to get started with threads.

Summary

In this chapter you were introduced to threads in the context of Java Swing-based applets and applications. You were given the basic rules for such applications, exceptions to those rules, and some general guidelines for writing thread-safe Swing applications. You have also seen specifics on how to use threads in the context of Java, and you have seen an example of a multithreaded application designed in JBuilder.

Review Questions

1. What is a thread?
2. What are the four exceptions to the single-thread rule?
3. What is the single-thread rule?
4. What are the two methods that the SwingUtilities class provides to help you with thread safety?
5. What are two problems that can arise from unsafe thread handling?
6. What is another term for "process"?
7. What does it mean to say a component has been realized?
8. What are the two ways that you can implement threads in your class?

Appendix A

Other Resources

This appendix is provided to allow you to further your studies of any of the items presented in this book. Obviously, one book cannot cover it all, so these resources are meant to help you. Each of the resources provided is an excellent place to advance your knowledge in a given area. This list is not as large as it could be because I have purposely only listed those resources that I would personally recommend to a student or colleague.

Products

Borland JBuilder
 http://www.inprise.com/jbuilder/

JBuilder downloads
 http://www.borland.com/jbuilder/offers/

Sun Microsystems' JFC page
 http://java.sun.com/products/jfc/

Sun Java SDK
 http://java.sun.com/products/jdk/1.1/index.html

Online Java Tutorials

Sun Microsystems GUI Construction with JFC
 http://suned.sun.com/US/catalog/courses/SL-320.html

JFC tutorial
 http://www.acm.org/sigchi/chi99/cp/?show=tut_15

Dev Central Java tutorials
http://devcentral.iftech.com/articles/Java/default.php

Java Cabana
http://www.javacabana.com/

JFC/Swing tutorial
http://www.olabs.com/training/courses/ol319.html

AWT tutorial
http://www.javaworld.com/javaworld/jw-07-1996/jw-07-awt.html

Another JFC/Swing tutorial
http://www.javaworld.com/jw-03-1998/jw-03-swinggui.html

JGuru.com
http://www.jguru.com/

Free Java help
http://www.freejavahelp.com/

Java developers list
http://www.jfind.com/

Java AWT package
http://java.sun.com/products/jdk/1.2/docs/api/java/awt/package-summary.html

Java Magazines

Java Developer's Journal
http://www.javadevelopersjournal.com/java/

Java Report Online
http://www.adtmag.com/java/index.asp

Java Pro
http://www.fawcette.com/javapro/

Java World
http://www.javaworld.com/

Other Online Tutorials and Guides

Sun Microsystems's Java Applet Page
http://java.sun.com/applets/

Java Boutique Applet Repository
http://javaboutique.internet.com/

Java on the Brain
http://www.javaonthebrain.com/

Books on Java, JBuilder, and Related Topics

Charlie Calvert's Learn JBuilder
Charlie and Margie Calvert, Wordware Publishing, Inc.
http://www.wordware.com

JBuilder 7.0 EJB Programming
Chuck Easttom, Wordware Publishing, Inc.
http://www.wordware.com

Appendix B

JFC/Swing Glossary

API: Application programming interface — a set of functions in one object that are exposed to the external environment and that a programmer can utilize

AWT: Abstract Windowing Toolkit

AWTEventClass: The parent class for all of the specific AWT event classes. There are several AWT event classes to handle specific AWT events.

event object: An object that represents an event and is used as an argument for event listeners

exception: An unexpected interruption in the normal flow of your program's execution

GUI: Graphical user interface

helper class: A class that is used to provide some needed functionality to the main class

inner class: A class that is defined within another class

JDK: Java Development Kit — Sun Microsystems' free Java development tool. It is command-line based.

JNI: Java Native Interface — a method for allowing Java to communicate with COM objects

JVM: Java Virtual Machine — the actual Java environment that any Java component must run in

ListenerInterface: An interface that, when implemented, allows a class to be a listener for a specific type of event

local variable: Any variable declared within a function is considered a local variable, and its scope is limited to that function.

member variable: A member variable is declared at the beginning of a class, outside of any functions. Its scope extends throughout the class.

RAD tool: Rapid application development tool — any tool used to ease software development by providing a graphical interface within which to program

run-time error: An unexpected error that occurs at run time

Swing: This is a whole host of new classes, many of which are enhanced versions of classes that you find in AWT.

syntax error: An error in the implementation of the programming language that you are using

Answers to Review Questions

Chapter 1

1. What is AWT?

   Abstract Windowing Tookit — a set of graphical interface components that have been superceded by Swing but are still widely used

2. What is Swing?

   A set of graphical interface components that replace the AWT components and, in fact, add in some entirely new components

3. What is JFC?

   Java Foundation Classes — a rather large set of classes that are part of Java 2. Among other things, the JFC adds new graphical classes.

4. What are the four major groups of JFC classes?

   User interface components, Java 2D, accessibility features, drag-and-drop support

5. What is the purpose of the JFC Accessibility features?

   The term accessibility simply refers to making your application accessible to people with disabilities.

6. List any four key JFC classes.

   JButton, JPanel, JMenu, JPopupMenu, JLabel, JRadioButton, JProgressBar, JScrollBar (see Table 1.1)

7. What is the purpose of using Swing instead of AWT?

   The entire point of the JFC/Swing GUI classes is to provide a set of classes that will allow you to create windowing components that are platform independent.

8. What is the purpose of the BorderFactory class?

   It is used to create borders to place around components.

9. What version of the Sun JDK first shipped with JFC/Swing?

   If you have the Sun JDK version 1.3.0 or greater or you have JBuilder version 5.0 or later, then you have access to JFC and Swing.

10. What is a pluggable look and feel?

    The term pluggable simply refers to the fact that you can update the look and feel of an application on the fly.

Chapter 2

1. What are the five layout managers?

   Grid, Gridbag, Flow, Card, Border

2. What two components are actually subclasses of the Window class?

   Dialog and Frame

3. Which component must be associated with a frame?

   Dialog

4. What are the zones of a border layout manager?

   North, South, East, West, Center

5. What is the top-level component of an applet?

   The browser itself

6. List the nine noncontainer AWT components.

   TextField, TextArea, Label, Button, Canvas, Choice, Checkbox, List, Scrollbar

7. What is the default layout manager for the Frame class?

   The BorderLayout manager

8. What event is called when a user clicks on a button?

   The Action event

9. The Applet is a subtype of what class?

   The Panel class

10. What is the default layout manager for the Applet class?

    The FlowLayout manager

Chapter 3

1. What two classes listed in this chapter do *not* allow multiline display?

   JTextField and JLabel

2. What class would you use to display HTML?

   JEditorPane

3. What class would you use if you did not want the actual keystrokes to be shown on the screen?

   JPasswordField

4. List two methods of the JTextField component.

   setText() and getText() (see Table 3.2)

5. List two methods of the JPasswordField component.

   getEchoChar and setEchoChar (see Table 3.4)

6. What it the primary difference between JTextField and JTextArea?

   JTextArea allows for multiline display.

7. What is the EditorKit?

   A helper class used by several of the input components

8. How would you add text at the end of a JTextArea?

   With the append method

9. Name one difference between the AWT TextArea and the JFC JTextArea.

   The AWT version inherently handles scrolling, while the JFC version does not.

10. What is the primary difference between JTextPane and JTextArea?

    JTextPane allows more formatting options.

Chapter 4

1. What are the three options for look and feel?

   CDE/Motif, Metallic, Windows

2. How many layout mangers are there in AWT?

   Five

3. How many layout mangers are there in JFC?

   Ten

4. Which layout manager would be most appropriate if you wished to display one component or container at a time?

   The CardLayout manager

5. What is the difference between the Grid and the Gridbag?

   With the Grid, each row must have the same number of fields. With the Gridbag, each row can have a different number of fields.

6. Which layout managers simply place the components one after the other until the edge of the container is reached?

   FlowLayout and VerticalFlowLayout

7. Which layout manager is used to place components in an exact coordinate position?

   The XYLayout manager

8. Which layout manager has zones such as East and North?

   The BorderLayout manager

9. Which layout manager sizes the components in relation to the size of the other components on the container?

   The PaneLayout manager

10. List five of the layout managers found in JFC.

    BorderLayout, BoxLayout2, CardLayout, FlowLayout, GridLayout, GridbagLayout, OverlayLayout, PaneLayout, VerticalFlowLayout, XYLayout

Chapter 5

1. Name the Swing containers.

   JPanel, JScrollPane, JTabbedPane, JSplitPane, JBox

2. Which container is used most often?

   JPanel

3. What property would you set to make sure your scroll bar pane always displays a vertical scroll bar?

   setHorizontalScrollBarPolicy or *setScrollBarVerticalPolicy*

   Example:

   jScrollPane1.setHorizontalScrollBarPolicy(JScroll-Pane.HORIZONTAL_SCROLLBAR_ALWAYS);

4. Can you change the size of the divider in a split pane?

   Yes, using the Divider_size property

5. Which container would be used to create placeholders and connections between components?

   Box

6. How many versions of the Box container does JBuilder have?

   Two: vertical and horizontal

7. What method would you use to move the scroll bar?

   setValue(int);

Chapter 6

1. From a user's perspective, what is an event?

   Any action the user can take: clicking a button, moving a mouse, etc.

2. What is an event handler?

   A function that responds to an event

3. What is the parent class of all event classes?

   AWTEvent

4. List four common event classes.

   ActionEvent, ComponentEvent, AdjustmentEvent, TextEvent, ItemEvent (see Table 6.1)

5. What is a listener?

   A special class designed to respond to a given event

6. What are three advantages to using inner class adapters?

   - *The code is generated inline, thereby simplifying the code.*
   - *No separate class is generated.*
   - *The inner class has access to all variables in scope where it is declared, unlike the standard event adapters that have only public and package level access.*

7. How many constructors are there for the AWTEvent class?

   Two

Chapter 7

1. What component does the JComboBox inherit from?

   JComponent

2. Which components in this chapter allow the user to select multiple options?

   JCheckBox and JList

3. What method do you use with a combo box to insert an item at a specific place in the combo box?

   insertItemAt

4. When is a slider the ideal component?

   When you need the user to select from a range of numeric values

5. In what situation is a toggle button the appropriate component?

   When you need the user to select one of two mutually exclusive choices

6. What is the primary difference between a check box and a radio button?

   The check box allows the selection of multiple options; the radio button only allows the user to select a single option.

7. What is the main advantage of a list over a combo box?

   The combo box only allows the user to select a single item, while the list allows multiple choices to be selected.

8. What method do you use to retrieve multiple selections from a list?

   getSelectedValues()

9. What does that method return?

   An array

Chapter 8

1. What classes are needed to create a complete drop-down menu?

   JMenuBar, JMenu, JMenuItem

2. What is the purpose of the JMenuBar class?

   To provide a base, or anchor point, for JMenu class instances to be associated with

3. How would you add a line separating menu items?

   Call the addSeparator method

4. How would you clear a menu?

   Call the removeAll method

5. Can JToolBars be made floatable?

   Yes, by using the setFloatable method

6. How would you make a toolbar initially display as vertical rather than horizontal?

   Either call the constructor that will allow you to set the orientation, or call the setOrientation method

7. Can you simulate a user clicking a menu item?

   Yes, with the doClick method

8. Must new menu items be added at the end of the current list of menu items?

   No, you can use the JMenuItem insert(JMenuItem mi, int pos) function to insert a menu item at any position you wish.

Chapter 9

1. By default, are dialogs modal or modeless?

   Modeless

2. What does it mean to say that a given dialog is modal?

   It means that dialog must be addressed before any other part of the application can be utilized.

3. What does the “this” argument in showDialog represent?

   It is a reference to the parent class of the dialog.

4. What are three ways that you can choose colors in JColorChooser?

   Swatch, HSB, RGB

5. What method will get you the name of the file that you have selected with JFileChooser?

   getName()

6. In JFileChooser, what method is called if the user selects the Cancel button?

   cancelSelection()

7. What methods would you use to change the intensity of a color that you had selected with the JColorChooser?

   brighter() and darker()

Chapter 10

1. How do you create an instance of the Graphics class?

   You must use the getGraphics method of the container on which you wish to display the graphics.

2. List any four methods of the Graphics class.

   drawLine, drawArc, drawOval, drawRect, setColor, draw3DRect, drawRoundRect (see Table 10.1)

3. What class does the Graphics class inherit from?

   Object

4. How would you fill a rectangle that you have drawn with the Graphics class?

   By using the fillRect method

5. What do the numbers passed to graphics methods represent?

   The beginning and ending coordinates for the object being drawn

6. How would you clear all the drawing done by an instance of the Graphics class?

   By calling the dispose method

7. What does the point 0,0 represent in the Graphics class coordinate system?

   The point of origin, the upper left-hand corner

8. How would you change the color that the instance of the Graphics class is using?

   By calling the setColor method

Chapter 11

1. What is a resultset?

   The set of records returned after an SQL statement has been executed

2. What is dbSwing?

   A set of data-aware classes that are subclasses of various Swing components

3. What is the purpose of the Connection class?

   To represent an actual connection to an underlying data source

4. Why must you use the next method of the ResultSet class when you first connect to the data source?

   Because the result set is initially pointing to an indeterminate location

5. What is the purpose of the execute method of the Statement class?

   To execute any valid SQL statement on the underlying data source

6. List any three methods of the ResultSet class.

   deleterow, close, next, previous, first, last, insertrow, getrow, getarray (see Table 11.1)

7. Can you use the classes from java.sql without specific error handling?

   No, those classes must be contained within their own try/catch blocks.

8. What package do you import in order to use classes such as Connection, ResultSet, and Statement?

   import java.sql.;*

Chapter 12

1. What is an applet?

   A Java application that can run in the context of a web browser

2. What are the four functions in all applets?

   init, start, stop, and destroy

3. What must all applet classes extend?

   Applet

4. What are parameters?

   Variables that are passed to your applet from the HTML page containing the applet

5. How do you pass parameters from HTML to your applet?

   Using the param tag — <param name = "something" value = "somevalue">

6. What is a standalone applet?

   An applet that can also run as an application

7. How do you create one?

   By adding in a constructor and a main function

8. Which applet function is least often overridden and used by applet programmers?

   Destroy

Chapter 13

1. What package is the Graphics2D class found in?

   Java.awt

2. What must you do with the Graphics2D class before you can use it?

   Cast a standard Graphics object

   Example:

   Graphics2D g2 = (Graphics2D) g;

3. What are the steps in the rendering process?
   1. *Determine what to render.*
   2. *Determine what colors to render.*
   3. *Constrain the rendering operation to the current clip.*
   4. *Apply the colors.*

4. What types of rendering operations are there?
   - *Shape operations*
   - *Text operations*
   - *Image operations*

5. What value passed to the Font class will cause the font to be bold?

   The value of 1

6. Name at least one thing the Java 2D API handles.
   - *A range of geometric primitives, such as rectangles, curves, and ellipses*
   - *A mechanism for rendering virtually any geometric shape*
   - *A uniform rendering model for display devices and printers*

- *Mechanisms for performing hit detection on shapes, text, and images*
- *Enhanced color support*
- *Support for printing complex documents*

7. What determines the region of an image during a rendering operation?

   The region of the image is defined by the bounding box of the source image.

8. What is double buffering?

   In double buffering, the graphic elements are rendered off-screen to the BufferedImage and then copied to the screen through a call to Graphics2D drawImage.

Chapter 14

1. What is a thread?

   A subprocess within an application's memory space

2. What are the four exceptions to the single-thread rule?

   - *Using the main thread*
   - *Using init*
   - *Using repaint and revalidate*
   - *Using listener threads*

3. What is the single-thread rule?

   Once a Swing component has been realized, all code that might affect or depend on the state of that component should be executed in the event-dispatching thread.

4. What are the two methods that the SwingUtilities class provides to help you with thread safety?

   - *invokeLater*
   - *invokeAndWait*

5. What are two problems that can arise from unsafe thread handling?

   If one thread changes the value of a variable, other threads that access that variable will get the changed value, rather than the original value. It is also important to note that since they are in the same memory space, if one thread crashes, the entire application (i.e., all of its threads) crashes.

6. What is another term for "process"?

   Memory space

7. What does it mean to say a component has been realized?

   Realized simply means that the component has been painted on-screen or that it is ready to be painted.

8. What are the two ways that you can implement threads in your own class?

   - *Subclass the java.lang.Thread class*
   - *Implement the java.lang.Runnable interface*

Appendix D

Introduction to Database Programming

Chapter 11 of this book deals with database programming using JFC. Most readers are probably quite familiar with basic database concepts. However, for those readers who may not be familiar with these concepts or require a refresher, this appendix is provided.

Most business programming is, at some level, database programming. What is an employee control program but a database program? What is a point of sale or inventory control program but a database program? It is highly unlikely that you will get far in any career as a professional programmer without being required to perform some sort of database programming.

Introduction to Databases

This section is designed to give you a very brief introduction to creating tables using Microsoft Access. Access is one of the most popular relational database systems on the market today (at least for small- to medium-sized databases). But first let me define some database terms:

Field: This is a particular piece of data like Last Name, Address, Phone, etc. In SQL Server or Oracle, this is referred to as a column.

Record: This is all the fields for a particular entry. For example, all the fields that make up a single employee's file are a record.

Table: These are related records stored together. For example, all the records of all the employees might be stored in an Employee table.

Database: These are related tables stored together. For example, the Employee table, Inventory table, and Finance table might be stored together in a common small business database.

Relational Database Management System: RDMS refers to data that is related. Let's say you have a database that includes employee data. For each employee, you would want a job description. What if you have 20 people with the same job description (20 Java programmers, for example)? Do you really want to rewrite the job description 20 times? In the relational database model, you simply have a table of job descriptions and each employee's record in the Employee table is related or linked to his or her job description. This drastically reduces the amount of overhead that a database requires. It also makes for a very logical layout to your database.

This method of storing data is different from the previously used flat file. A flat file simply stores information, one record after another. A text document is an example of a flat file. There is no relationship between records or fields. This makes for an inordinately large data file and one that has a lot of duplication. It is also quite difficult to perform searches.

Creating a Database/Table

To do this in Access, first start with a new, blank database by selecting Blank Access Database, as shown in Figure D.1.

Figure D.1 Getting started with MS Access

Note: You can have the wizard create the entire database for you, but that would not allow you to learn much about database structures.

You will then be asked where to create that database and what to name it. After making these choices, you should see a dialog box much like the one depicted in Figure D.2.

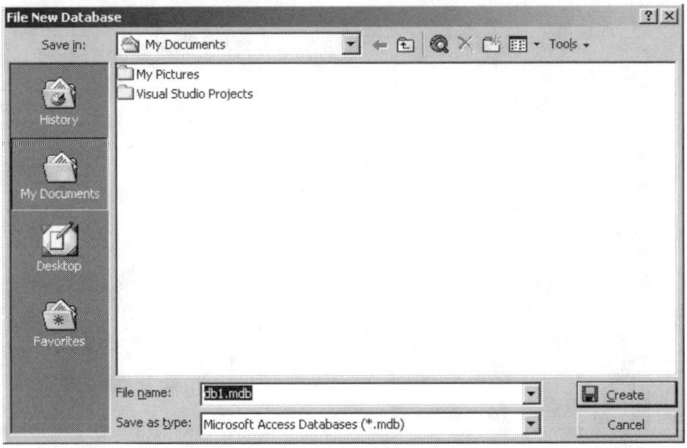

Figure D.2 The dialog box for saving a new database

Click **Create**. To create a new table, select **Tables**, **New**, and then choose **Create table in Design view**. This is shown in Figure D.3.

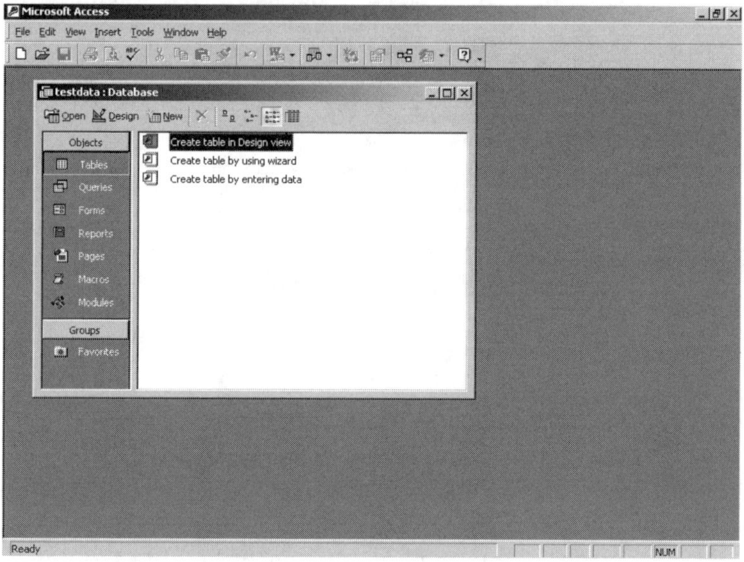

Figure D.3 The Design view

You are now looking at a grid for designing a database table. This is shown in Figure D.4.

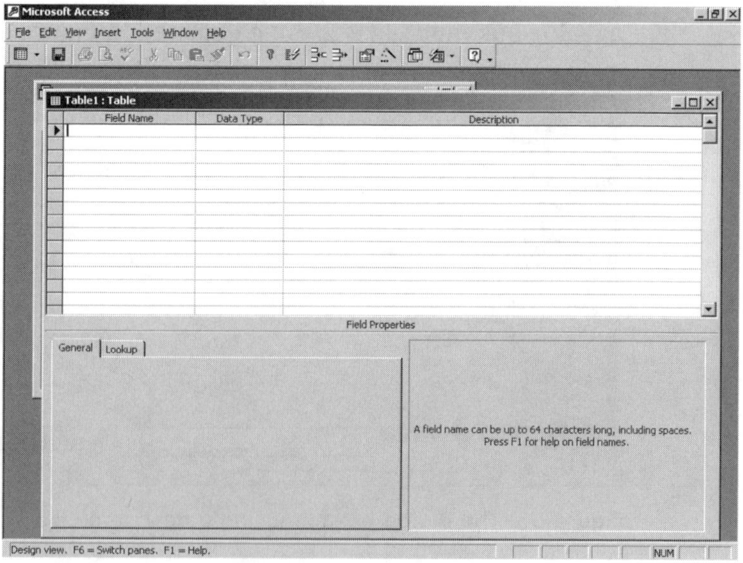

Figure D.4 The design grid

Continuing with the table that we began in the previous paragraphs, let's create fields for Last Name, First Name, Street Address, City, State, Zip Code, Phone Number, and Email. You can also either add a field here such as "Entry Key" and then right-click on it and select Primary Key, or you can wait until you close the Design view and you will be prompted to let Access create a primary key for you. A primary key is a field used to uniquely identify each record in the database. Your table should look something like the image depicted in Figure D.5.

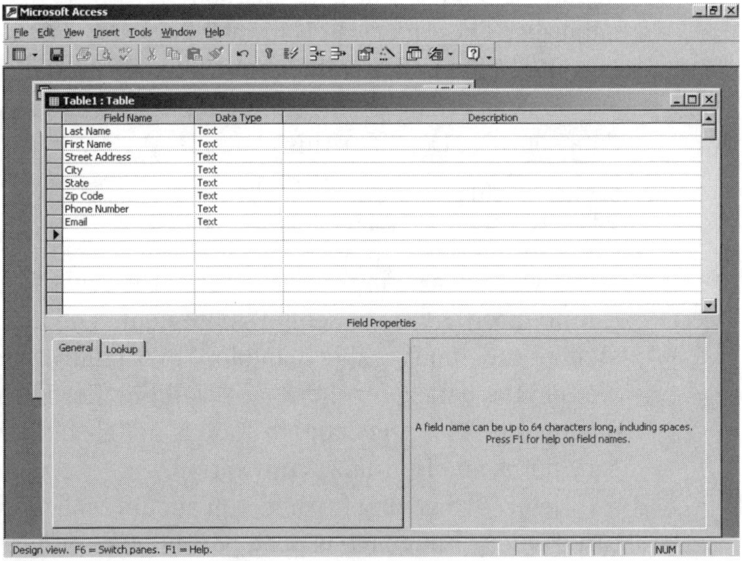

Figure D.5 The completed table

When you close the design window, you will be asked to give your table a name. Call your table Contacts. After you have saved it, double-click on the table to open it and add one or more sample records.

SQL

Now that you have seen how to create a simple database and table in MS Access, it is time to introduce you to SQL, or Structured Query Language. SQL is the language used to talk to relational databases. The Relational Database model for database design was invented by Dr. E.F. Cobb in 1969 and published in *Computer World* in 1985.

SQL was first implemented in 1974 at IBM in the San Jose Research Laboratory. SQL is essentially a nonprocedural language that uses English-like words to talk to a database. The American National Standards Institute (ANSI) is continually updating its versions of SQL standards.

You can create SQL statements in Java and pass them to data sources. Consider this example:

```
String sz_sql;
sz_sql = "SELECT * FROM mytable ";
```

Here we took a string variable and set it equal to an SQL (pronounced S-Q-L or sequel) statement. The asterisk (*) symbol is computer shorthand for "everything." So basically we told the data control to give us all the files in the table named mytable. The capitalization is not absolutely necessary but is an often-used convention.

Before we go any further, you should realize that Structured Query Language is *not* a part of Java (or any other programming language for that matter); that's why we have to put SQL statements in a string. It is the language used by relational databases. Most relational databases utilize Structured Query Language, including MS Access, MS SQL Server, Oracle, MS Access, and Sybase SQL Anywhere.

Frequently you will have a more complex SQL statement with clauses like:

```
"...WHERE [state] =California"
```

The basic format is:

```
"SELECT [field1],[field2],.... FROM [sometable] WHERE
[somefield] = SomeCriteria"
```

The WHERE clause denotes some condition. Basically, you are saying that you want all the specified fields if a certain criteria is met.

The ORDER BY statement simply orders the records based on a particular field you wish to order by. Here is an example:

```
strSQL = strSQL & "ORDER BY[Publishers.State]"
```

This statement says to sort the records returned by our SQL query by the state of the publisher. Programmers frequently use this statement to arrange data in a particular manner. For example, one might add this statement to an employee database:

```
strSQL = strSQL + "ORDER BY [Employee ID]
```

This way, all the records are now in order by Employee ID number. I use this statement a lot, since it is the quickest and easiest way to sort records. In some cases, I will create a drop-down menu or command buttons that sort by a different criteria. Using the ORDER BY statement in this way, I let my users sort their data in any fashion that they wish.

What if you want to search more than one table for the publishers' records? Have no fear — SQL offers the INNER JOIN statement:

```
SELECT Publishers.[company Name] FROM Publishers
INNER JOIN Titles ON Publishers.PubID = Titles.PubID
```

This statement just says to get all the company names of publishers from either the Publishers table or the Titles table if the publishers' IDs match.

What about duplicate records? Especially in the above examples, the same record may be duplicated many times. One way around this is to simply add the DISTINCT statement to your SELECT, such as:

```
strSQL = "SELECT DISTINCT..."
```

We have just covered the SELECT, INNER JOIN, and DISTINCT statements. While there is certainly a great deal more to SQL, this will give you a start. You will probably use the SELECT statement on a regular basis. Consider the ORDER BY statement as a good way to sort the records in your data control in any way that you wish.

Tip: Always double-check the spelling of your SQL statements. A single misspelling, and it will *not* work.

This is just a brief working introduction to Structured Query Language. It should get you up and running so that you can use SQL in your programs. I strongly suggest that you make a point of learning more about SQL early on in your programming career.

Appendix E

HTML Primer

This appendix is provided as a rather brief tutorial on HTML. HTML is the language of the web and essential for any web-based project. Chapter 12 of this book covers applets, which happen to run inside of web pages. Many readers are probably already familiar with HTML and can completely skip this appendix. It is merely provided for those readers who either lack any background in HTML or require a brief refresher.

HTML, or Hypertext Markup Language, is a relatively simple markup language that web browsers can use to display web pages. You can write HTML code in any text editor; I personally use Windows Notepad. When you save the file, just remember to save it as a .htm or .html file. The browser recognizes files with the .htm and .html extensions and will look in them for valid HTML code. HTML has a long history and has gone through a number of revisions. Each successive revision adds more functionality to HTML, and with the current version (as of this book's publication) of HTML (Version 4.0), it is a very powerful language that can take some time to learn. Fortunately, most work on web pages can be done with just the essentials of HTML, and that is what this appendix teaches you.

Note: Many tags in HTML *must* be closed. For example, the <B> tag must be closed with </B>. However, some tags such as <TD> and <TR> do not have to be closed. Some HTML programmers prefer to close them anyway. I do not.

The first question is, how do we get the web browser to know that our document has HTML code for it to read? HTML code is composed of *tags* that let the browser know what is to be done with certain text. At the beginning of your document, you place the command <HTML>, and at the end you put </HTML>. The web browser then knows that the code between the two tags is supposed to be HTML:

```
<HTML>
  put HTML code here
</HTML>
```

You have to admit that this is pretty simple. But this web page won't do much. So how about we do the obligatory "Hello World" sample that every programming book starts off with. It will show you how to create a simple web page with some basic HTML formatting.

```
<HTML>
<HEAD>
   <TITLE>My First HTML Page</TITLE>
</HEAD>
<BODY>
<P><CENTER>
   <B><FONT SIZE="+2">Hello World</FONT></B>
</CENTER>
</BODY>
</HTML>
```

Believe it or not, this brief example shows you most of what you need to know about HTML. To begin with, note that everything is contained between the <HTML> and </HTML> tags. These two commands define the beginning and the end of the HTML document. The web browser will ignore any items outside these commands. Next, we have a section that is contained between the <HEAD> and </HEAD> commands. This is the header portion of your HTML document. The <TITLE> and </TITLE> commands contain the title that will actually appear in the title bar of your browser.

Then we have the <BODY> and </BODY> commands. As you might have guessed, this is the body of your HTML document. This is where most of your web page's code is going to go. Now inside the body section, we have some text and some additional code that define how the text appears in the browser. The <P> command defines the beginning and the end of a paragraph. The <B> and </B> commands tell the browser to make whatever text is between them bold. The <FONT SIZE="+2"> command tells the browser how big the text should be (there are a variety of methods for doing this, as we shall see). The </FONT> command ends the font section of the HTML code. If you entered the HTML code correctly, you should be able to view your web page in any browser and see an image much like that in Figure E.1.

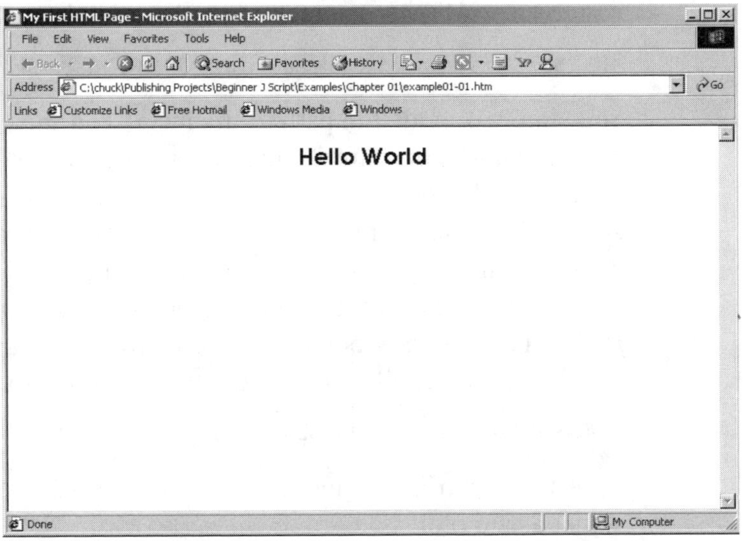

Figure E.1 A basic HTML document

By now, I hope that you have noticed a pattern. All the commands have an opening command and a closing command. Well, this is true for all but a few HTML commands. Just remember this rule: You close the commands in the opposite order of how you opened them. Notice in the above sample code that I opened the commands before the text, like this: <P><CENTER><B><FONT SIZE="+2">. Then I closed them like this: </FONT></B></CENTER>. (Note that <P> does not have to be closed.) This is important to remember. You can think of this as "backing out" of your commands.

Images and Hyperlinks

What we have so far gives you a very simple web page that displays one phrase in bold text. Admittedly, this is not very impressive, but if you understand the concepts involved with using these HTML commands, then you basically understand HTML. Now let's expand your knowledge of HTML. Usually web pages contain more than simply a title and some text. Other items you might put in a web page include images and links to other web pages. Placing an image on an HTML document is rather simple:

```
<IMG SRC="imagepath\imagename" WIDTH=52 HEIGHT=88 ALIGN=bottom>
```

You simply provide the path to the image and the name of the image, including its file extension (such as .gif, .bmp, .jpg, etc.). The other properties in this command allow you to alter the placement and size of the image. You can alter its width and height as well as its alignment.

Also note that when you first place an image on an HTML page, it has a border around it. You can get rid of this by adding "BORDER=0" into the tag, as in this example:

```
<IMG SRC="somepic.gif" BORDER=0>
```

Putting a hyperlink to another web site or an email address is just as simple:

```
<A HREF="http://www.wordware.com">
```

This link will connect to the URL (Uniform Resource Locator) contained inside the quotation marks. In order to use this methodology to create an email link, simply use the following:

```
<A HREF="mailto:sombody@somemail.com">
```

You simply have to change the http:// portion to mailto:. Notice that all three of the preceding methods have one thing in common: They do not close the command in the typical manner of other HTML commands. Now let's examine the source code for a simple but complete HTML document:

```
<HTML>
<HEAD>
 <TITLE>Using Images And Links in HTML</TITLE>
</HEAD>
<BODY BGCOLOR=white>
<P>
<CENTER><B><FONT SIZE="+2">My First Web Page with Links!
</FONT></B></CENTER>
<P>I am learning HTML !. I <B><I>LOVE</I></B> HTML!
<P><CENTER><IMG SRC="java.gif"></CENTER>
<P>
<P><CENTER>You can email me at</CENTER>
<P>
<CENTER><A HREF="mailto:chuckeasttom@yahoo.com">Email ME</A>
</CENTER>
<P><CENTER>Or go to this publisher's Web Site </CENTER>
<P><CENTER><A HREF="http://www.wordware.com">Wordware
Publishing</A></CENTER>
</BODY>
</HTML>
```

First, here are a few clarifications. You should note a new command at the beginning:

```
<BODY BGCOLOR=white>
```

You can change the background color of your page using this command and any standard color. You can also set a background image for your HTML document with a similar command:

```
<BODY background="mypicture.gif">
```

You can use any image that you wish in place of the java.gif image. If you entered the code properly and used the image included with the companion files, then your web page should look something like Figure E.2.

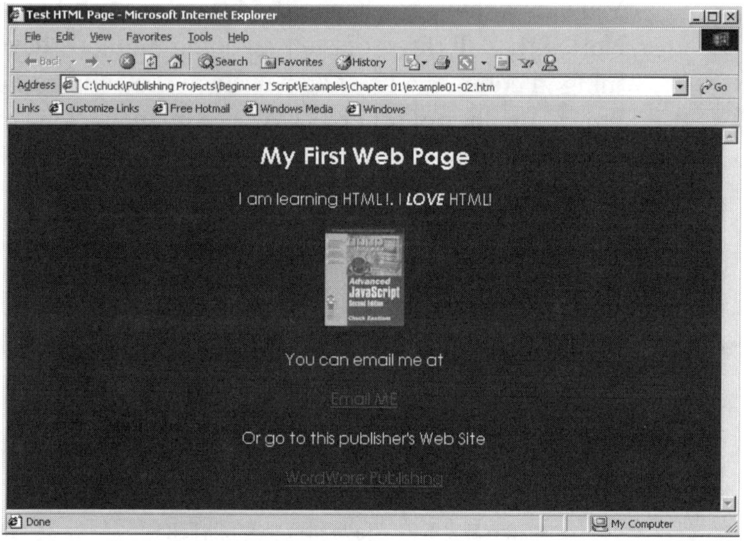

Figure E.2 Using images and hyperlinks

Now I will be the first to admit that this sample web page is very trivial. But it does contain the basics of HTML. With the material we have covered so far, you can display images, texts, links, email links, background colors, and background images. Not too bad for just a few short pages.

Colors and Backgrounds

Let's examine a few other simple items that we can add to our HTML documents. The first is altering text color. You can set the default text color for the entire document, and you can alter the color of specific text. You alter the default text color for the entire document using a technique very similar to the one used to alter the background color of the document:

```
<BODY TEXT="blue">
```

This text simply tells the browser that unless otherwise specified, all text in this document should be blue. In addition to changing the default color of all text in a document, you may wish to simply change the color of a specific section of text. This is fairly easy to do as well. Instead of using the BODY TEXT command, we use the FONT command:

```
<FONT COLOR="red">This is red text</FONT>
```

This, like the other color commands, can be used with any standard color.

There are a wide variety of tags that you can use to alter the appearance and behavior of text and images. Just a few others for you to consider would be the <BLINK> </BLINK> tag, which, as the name implies, causes the text to blink (this is only supported by Netscape and will not work in Internet Explorer). Another example is the <STRIKE></STRIKE> tag that causes the text to appear with a line through it, a strikethrough. The tags we have covered so far are enough to allow you to accomplish much of what you need in HTML.

Tables

The next HTML command we examine is the table. You frequently see tables on web pages, and they are a very good way to organize data. You can use the tables with or without a border, and I explain the various reasons to use one method or the other.

First, here is how you create a table with a border:

```
<TABLE BORDER=1>
 <TR>
   <TD>
     <P>This
     <P>Is a
 <TR>
   <TD>
     <P>Table
   <TD>
     <P>With a border
</TABLE>
```

By now you should be able to recognize that the <TABLE> and </TABLE> tags actually contain the table. Each <TR> tag designates another row in the table. In fact, TR is short for table row. The <TD> tag creates a cell within that row (TD refers to table data). Using those three tags, you can create a table with any number of rows or columns that you wish. Notice that the BORDER property is set to 1 in the first line of this code. This means that the border has a width and is therefore visible.

In some instances you may not want the border to show. Tables can be used to simply hold images and text in relative positions. In cases such as this, you may not wish the border to show. Here is an example of a table whose borders will not show:

```
<P><TABLE BORDER=0 CELLSPACING=0 CELLPADDING=0>
  <TR>
     <TD>
        <P>This
     <TD>
        <P>is a
   <TR>
     <TD>
        <P>Table
     <TD>
        <P>With no borders or padding
</TABLE>
```

Notice that the BORDER, CELLPADDING, and CELL-SPACING are all set to 0. This causes the table itself to not be displayed. However, the contents of the table will display. You should also notice that in both examples I have placed text in each cell.

Lists

It is common to present data in lists. With HTML, you have access to a variety of types of lists. The first we discuss is the unordered list.

```
<UL>
    <LI> First Item
    <LI> Second Item
</UL>
```

The <UL> and </UL> tags define the code that lies between them as being part of an unordered list. The <LI> tags identify list items. An unordered list item will simply appear as a bullet.

An ordered list is not much different. The <LI> list item stays the same. But the <UL> is going to change somewhat.

```
<OL type = I>
     <LI> First Item
     <LI> Second Item
</OL>
```

The type = portion of the tag tells the browser what type of list this is. We used a capital I in our example, and that will give you capital Roman numerals for your list items.

Table E.1 contains all the types of ordered lists and how they appear in your browser.

Table E.1 List types

List Type	Appearance in Browser
Type = I	I. First Item II. Second Item
Type = i	i. First Item ii. Second Item
Type = 1	1. First Item 2. Second Item
Type = a	a. First Item b. Second Item
Type = A	A. First Item B. Second Item

Marquee

A fascinating item that you can add to your web page is the marquee. A scrolling marquee takes a message or an image and scrolls it across the screen. The basic format is this:

```
<MARQUEE LOOP = INFINITE> Hey this is really cool </MARQUEE>
```

In addition to text, you can place an image in the marquee that you can scroll across the screen.

```
<MARQUEE LOOP = INFINITE> <IMG SRC = "mypic.gif"></MARQUEE>
```

You can also change the direction in which the marquee moves. The DIRECTION tag will tell the marquee which direction to scroll to, not from.

```
<MARQUEE LOOP = INFINITE DIRECTION = RIGHT>Hey this is a cool
marquee </MARQUEE>
```

You can choose from the following directions: left, right, up, and down. Marquees provide an interesting and relatively easy way to display eye-catching information on your web page.

Applets

The entire point of this appendix is to teach you enough HTML that you can use Java applets in your HTML code. It would, therefore, seem prudent to cover the topic of applets. Applets can be inserted into your code quite simply.

```
<applet
    code = "thejavaclass.class">
</applet>
```

These HTML tags will insert the applet at that particular location. The "thejavaclass.class" file is the actual class file for your compiled applet. It is assumed that the class file is in the same directory as the HTML document. Also, should that class file require other class files, they will also need to be placed inside that same directory.

You can do quite a bit more with this applet tag. You can, for example, set the height and width of your applet's display. You can also place the applet tags inside of other tags. You could use other HTML tags to put the applet in a center location, in a table, or even as part of a scrolling marquee. The following HTML sample page illustrates this:

```
<HTML>
<HEAD>
     <TITLE>Applet Stuff</TITLE>
</HEAD>
<BODY BGCOLOR = white>
```

```
    <CENTER>Applet stuff
        <HR>
    <MARQUEE LOOP = INFINITE>
    <APPLET
        CODE ="myapplet.class"
        HEIGHT = "120"
        WIDTH = "200"
        HSPACE = "20"
        VSPACE = "20">
        </APPLET>
    </MARQUEE>
    </CENTER>
</BODY>
</HTML>
```

As you can see, the code is really quite simple. It's just a matter of using a few new tags to place your applet inside of an HTML page. In this instance, our applet is centered and inside a marquee! This means that our applet will be constantly scrolling across the center of the HTML page.

Note: Some people spend a lot of money for web development software. Personally, I think that a thorough knowledge of HTML, Java applets, and some scripting language like JavaScript is more than enough to create any web effect you like. Just use these free tools, along with a little creativity, and you won't need expensive web development software packages!

Index

About the Companion Files

The companion files can be downloaded from the following web site:

www.wordware.com/files/jbuilder

These files contain all the examples discussed in the book, and are organized into folders named for each chapter. Simply copy the files to your hard drive to work with them.